THE CONSTRUCTION OF
CHILDREN'S CHARACTER

THE CONSTRUCTION OF
CHILDREN'S CHARACTER

Ninety-sixth Yearbook of the
National Society for the Study of Education

Part II

Edited by

ALEX MOLNAR

Editor for the Society

KENNETH J. REHAGE

Distributed by THE UNIVERSITY OF CHICAGO PRESS • CHICAGO, ILLINOIS

The National Society for the Study of Education

Founded in 1901 as successor to the National Herbart Society, the National Society for the Study of Education has provided a means by which the results of serious study of educational issues could become a basis for informed discussion of those issues. The Society's two-volume Yearbooks, now in their ninety-sixth year of publication, reflect the thoughtful attention given to a wide range of educational problems during those years. Each year the Society's publications contain contributions to the literature of education from scholars and practitioners who are doing significant work in their respective fields.

An elected Board of Directors reviews proposals for Yearbooks, selects the proposals that seem suitable for a Yearbook, and appoints an editor, or editors, to oversee the preparation of manuscripts for the projected volume.

The Society's publications are distributed each year without charge to members in the United States, Canada, and elsewhere throughout the world. The Society welcomes as members all individuals who desire to receive its publications. Information about current dues and a listing of its publications that are still in print may be found in the back pages of this volume.

This volume, *The Construction of Children's Character,* is Part II of the Ninety-sixth Yearbook of the Society. Part I, published at the same time, is entitled *Service Learning.*

Library of Congress Catalog Number: 95-072097
ISSN: 0077-5762

Published 1997 by
THE NATIONAL SOCIETY FOR THE STUDY OF EDUCATION

5835 Kimbark Avenue, Chicago, Illinois 60637
© 1997 by the National Society for the Study of Education

Contributors to the Yearbook

ALEX MOLNAR, Editor, University of Wisconsin at Milwaukee

VICTOR BATTISTICH, Developmental Studies Center, Oakland, California
JACQUES A. BENNINGA, California State University, Fresno
BEVERLY CROSS, University of Wisconsin, Milwaukee
GENEVA GAY, University of Washington, Seattle
ALFIE KOHN, Belmont, Massachusetts
JAMES S. LEMING, Southern Illinois University
THOMAS LICKONA, State University of New York, Cortland
ALAN L. LOCKWOOD, University of Wisconsin, Madison
NEL NODDINGS, Stanford University
DAVID E. PURPEL, University of North Carolina, Greensboro
ERIC SCHAPS, Developmental Studies Center, Oakland, California
WILLIAM H. SCHUBERT, University of Illinois at Chicago
HUGH SOCKETT, George Mason University, Fairfax, Virginia
DANIEL SOLOMON, Developmental Studies Center, Oakland, California
EDWARD A. WYNNE, University of Illinois at Chicago

v

Acknowledgment

The National Society for the Study of Education is indebted to all who have had a part in producing this volume. We are especially grateful to Professor Alex Molnar who developed the plan for the book and invited contributions from authors who have thought deeply about character education. Their work makes it possible for readers to understand the nature and dimensions of the controversies that surround this very complex subject.

Professor Margaret Early of the University of Florida at Gainesville has again read every manuscript submitted for this Yearbook with great care. Her comments and suggestions reflect the enormous amounts of time and thought that she has given to this work.

Jenny Volpe, assistant in the NSSE office, has prepared the name index with her customary meticulous attention to detail.

KENNETH J. REHAGE
Editor for the Society

Editor's Preface

The Construction of Children's Character presents a comprehensive and critical assessment of contemporary character education theory and practice from a variety of perspectives: historical, cultural, philosophical, psychological, empirical, political, and ethical.

Over the past decade the widespread belief that the United States is in a period of moral decline has led to numerous proposals to address the perceived crisis through programs of character education in schools. The most popular approaches to children's moral development in the 1960s and 1970s grew out of the work of Raths, Harmin, and Simon on "values clarification" and the work of Kohlberg on the development of moral reasoning in children.

The values clarification approach to moral education is, in essence, a rational decision-making model that has, over time, demonstrated few proven effects. Kohlberg's theory of moral development, despite revisions to his original thinking and some evidence that it can be used with success in classrooms, has other problems. For example, the idea that a complex process such as moral development can be fruitfully understood as a more or less linear progression from one stage to the next assumes a relationship between moral categories that is at least questionable.

Current school-based efforts to promote the development of good character in children are more likely to attempt to teach "core" ethical values and are usually tied to a conception of civic renewal. The currently popular approaches to character education are not without problems. For example, the meaning of "character" remains elusive. Contemporary approaches to character education seem to assume that there is an idealized essence of human beings called "character." However, this view of character appears to have paradoxical qualities. Sometimes character is described as if it is innate and other times as if it is learned. Not surprisingly, character is therefore often talked about in character education literature as if it were both an individual quality and an individual responsibility.

Although there is the occasional bow to the need for people of good character to act collectively, our collective social character and our common social responsibilities are generally of less interest in character education programs than reinforcing "good" individual behaviors and censoring "bad" ones.

Regardless of approach, the·idea that character education should be an important element in the curriculum and instructional program of public schools is controversial. Some critics reject the idea that schools should be involved in teaching values, while others contend that current character education efforts are little more than an attempt to promote conservative social ideology. Proponents of character education disagree among themselves. Some detail proper values which students are to be taught directly while others argue that character development must be part of a larger process of constructing an ethical community in the schools—a community that is connected to the concerns, and reflective of the diversity, of society outside the classroom. The debate over the impact of character education is also robust with hotly contested claims of empirical support for the efficacy of character education programs.

The widespread interest in and controversy surrounding character education among the general public, school practitioners, and educational researchers make it important to subject contemporary character education efforts to careful scrutiny from a number of standpoints. For this reason, contributors to this volume have been selected to insure that a breadth of perspective, experience, and approach are brought to bear on the problem of assessing character education.

The Construction of Children's Character is organized into five sections intended to help the reader form a well-grounded understanding of the complex nature of character education in the United States. Section One establishes the philosophical, educational, and historical contexts important to an understanding of the movement for character education. The authors of the essays in Section Two are well-known advocates of traditional views of character and character education. The essays in Section Three have been prepared by authors who have what I have called an "expansive view" of character education, that is, their views illustrate how concerns about the development of children's character are also seen in other aspects of the child's experience in schools. Section Four contains chapters by authors who are among the critics of character education in the schools. Finally, in Section Five the author contends that there is a great need for a precise definition of character education. He draws upon the work of authors of previous chapters (as well as others) as he formulates and proposes a definition to answer the question "What Is Character Education?"

ALEX MOLNAR
Milwaukee, March, 1997

Table of Contents

Section One
The Philosophical/Educational/Research Context

Section Two
Traditionalist Views of Character and Character Education

Section Three
Expansive Views of Character and Character Education

Section Four
Critics of Character Education

Section Five
Character Education: Searching for a Definition

Section One
THE PHILOSOPHICAL/EDUCATIONAL/ RESEARCH CONTEXT

CHAPTER I

Character Education and Community

NEL NODDINGS

In the last decade, there has been a considerable increase of interest both in the idea of community and in character education. Indeed, many scholars and policymakers believe that character education must be a function of well-ordered communities. From this perspective, it is insufficient (and perhaps even impossible) for education to produce the disinterested, rational mind long cherished by the liberal tradition. To educate adequately for *character*, a community must stand for something, and it must transmit its values effectively to the young.

The Foundation of Character in Community

Character education as a specific approach to moral education traces its roots to Aristotle.[1] In contrast to views that emphasize reasoning, problem solving, and critical thinking, character education concentrates on the development of virtues. Aristotle devoted most of his *Nicomachean Ethics* to an analysis of the good life and the virtues that it requires and nurtures.[2] Because the individual is from the start part of a tradition, character education is inextricably joined to community. A strong community defines and exhibits what is meant by the good life; it produces exemplars whose virtues should be emulated.

In contemporary philosophy, Alasdair MacIntyre extols the Aristotelian approach. Each of us, MacIntyre says, is "whether (one) recognize(s) it or not, one of the bearers of a tradition."[3] From this perspective,

---

Nel Noddings is Lee L. Jacks Professor of Child Education in the School of Education at Stanford University.

each of us is part of a story; we have a role to fill, and certain obligations, rewards, expectations, and virtues accompany that role. Not only are we inevitably part of a story, but we must hear stories to become articulate members of the traditions into which we are born. MacIntyre writes:

It is through hearing stories about wicked stepmothers, lost children, good but misguided kings, wolves that suckle twin boys, youngest sons who receive no inheritance but must make their own way in the world and eldest sons who waste their inheritance on riotous living and go into exile to live with the swine, that children learn or mislearn both what a child and what a parent is, what the cast of characters may be in the drama into which they have been born and what the ways of the world are. Deprive children of stories and you leave them unscripted, anxious stutterers in their actions as in their words. Hence, there is no way to give us an understanding of any society, including our own, except through the stock of stories which constitute its initial dramatic resources.[4]

By starting with "wicked stepmothers" and "lost children," MacIntyre violates the recommendations of at least some prominent child psychologists,[5] but his point about the centrality of stories is accepted by virtually all character educators and many who do not locate themselves specifically in this school.[6] As social beings, we are products of, as well as contributors to, traditions of behavior. We are not first disengaged, rational mechanisms and *then* participants in a society; rather, whatever rationality we eventually exhibit is itself a product of the tradition in which we are raised and educated.[7]

Stories—biographies, myths, historical accounts, epics, parables—play a central role in establishing identity and in both moral and political education. Michael Oakeshott writes:

And if the understanding of politics I have recommended [a tradition of behavior that includes continuities of conflicts] is not a misunderstanding, there is little doubt about the kind of knowledge and the sort of education which belongs to it. It is knowledge, as profound as we can make it, of our tradition of political behavior. Other knowledge, certainly, is desirable in addition; but this is the knowledge without which we cannot make use of whatever else we may have learned.[8]

Oakeshott puts knowledge about the community and its political traditions first among all forms of knowledge. To convey this knowledge adequately, a community must be concerned not only with the intellectual development of its children but also with their development as moral persons and citizens.

Character education, with its emphasis on stories and tradition, dominated moral education in schools in the United States until around the middle of this century. Early in the twentieth century, for example, the Character Education League produced a curriculum designed for use in both homes and schools.[9] Its stated intention was to teach about and develop in children thirty-one virtues that, it declared, should culminate in a thirty-second integral virtue—character. Particular virtues were assigned to specific grades in school, and teachers were given considerable advice on how to teach each virtue.

This way of approaching moral education was not new with the Character Education League. It was represented earlier in the McGuffey readers, and, of course, it has long been the dominant mode in religious education. The connection with religion underscores the strong association between character education and community. To be effective, character education must be conducted in a group or society that exhibits widespread agreement on basic values.

The eclipse of character education by cognitive developmentalism in the latter half of this century was caused, at least in part, by a growing sensitivity to the heterogeneity of American society. Many of us began to be aware that Jewish children were uncomfortable with daily recitation of the Lord's Prayer, that nonbelievers might have a sustainable objection to both prayer and Bible-reading in public schools, that, indeed, the population of the United States did not form one community but many. Whatever one's final judgment on this heterogeneity might be—whether one celebrates the recognition or deplores the "disuniting of America"[10]—it must be acknowledged that many earlier abuses and much of the Anglo-Protestant arrogance toward immigrant groups and nonwhite races were called into question.

In such a climate—one in which a multiplicity of values is acknowledged—cognitive approaches to moral education seem safer and more generous than an approach that requires community homogeneity. Further, cognitive methods are more clearly compatible with the liberal tradition. Instead of attempting to inculcate specific values, advocates of cognitive methods concentrate on the development of moral reasoning. They, too, use stories, but the stories are philosophical fictions designed to trigger critical thinking. If they illustrate a tradition, it is the Enlightenment tradition of Descartes and Kant—one that extols the power of mind and reason. Besides their compatibility with liberal ideology, cognitive methods seem more congruent with the growing emphasis on science and mathematics.

But the shift to cognitive methods has raised a host of questions. First, the methods of Kohlberg and his associates[11] (the most prominent program emphasizing moral *reasoning*) seem to many to be more suited to research than to teaching. When they are designed for the classroom, teachers need special preparation to use them.[12] The long-accepted expectation that *all* teachers were to be teachers of morals was shaken. Second, the emphasis on reasoning and critical thinking offended many parents and policymakers who prefer a more Aristotelian emphasis on the inculcation of traditional values. Third, the abstract and theoretical nature of cognitive programs (their "content-emptiness") seemed to aggravate a growing sense of alienation in American society. These programs seemed to many to endorse the "purposive-rational action" described by Max Weber as characteristic of modernity.[13] Such action concentrates on means-ends connections and neglects deliberation and appreciation of ends. The sacred and eternal disappear in a welter of methods and procedures.

These concerns have played a part in reviving interest in community and in traditional values. Conservative philosophers, sociologists, and theologians have been deploring the loss of community throughout the twentieth century. For example, in the 1950s, Robert Nisbet wrote:

Surely the outstanding characteristic of contemporary thought on man and society is the preoccupation with personal alienation and cultural disintegration. . . . The widening concern with insecurity and disintegration is accompanied by a profound regard for the values of status, membership, and community.[14]

More recently, Robert Bellah and his colleagues have raised concern about the loss of biblical and republican traditions. Community spirit, they contend, has been too often sacrificed to individualism and the pursuit of secular and ephemeral forms of self-actualization. Further, real communities are not purposive-rational, loosely linked groups seeking to solve their individual problems. Rather,

A *community* is a group of people who are socially interdependent, who participate together in discussion and decision making, and who share certain *practices* that both define the community and are nurtured by it. Such a community is not quickly formed. It almost always has a history and so is also a *community of memory*, defined in part by its past and its memory of its past.[15]

Strong communities cherish their traditions and see to it that the young are thoroughly acquainted with these traditions. The dependence is two-way. A strong community, according to writers such as

MacIntyre, Oakeshott, Bellah, and Nisbet, depends on shared practices, and it is necessary for the production of worthy and acceptable citizens. Moral education—character education—is therefore a central task for a strong community.

The revival of interest in communities has been accompanied by strong philosophical attacks on liberalism. A growing body of critical thought charges that liberalism has overemphasized the autonomy of individuals, perpetuated a myth of the presocial individual, promoted an arrogant universalism (everyone is "just like" us), neglected the role of community, and contributed to the society predicted by Weber—one dominated by a bureaucratic and therapeutic mentality.[16]

Whereas liberals favor a society in which procedural fairness ensures that everyone will be able to pursue his or her own legitimate goods,[17] traditionalists and communitarians see such a society as chaotic, even nihilistic. A true *society*, from this latter perspective, must stand for something; it must establish and discuss the goods it seeks. In this conflict of ideologies, we see a fundamental problem for teachers of morals: How are we to discuss moral issues in productive depth if we do not belong to the same community? How are we to inculcate commonly accepted values in the young if we do not trust one another's motives for doing so? Richard Bernstein, in a sympathetic discussion of Jacques Derrida's ethical position, writes:

There can be no dialogue, no communication unless beliefs, values, commitments, and even emotions and passions are shared in common. Furthermore, I agree with Gadamer and MacIntyre that dialogic communication presupposes moral virtues—a certain "good will"—at least in the willingness to really listen, to seek to understand what is genuinely other, different, alien, and the courage to risk one's more cherished prejudgments. But too frequently this commonality is not really shared, it is *violently* imposed. A false "we" is projected.[18]

Can the required moral virtues be inculcated without projecting a false "we"? How much commonality is required to do the work of character education?

The Two Sides of Community

Human beings are social animals. We seek not only love and companionship but civic association. The longing for community arises from a deep need to feel a part of something larger than ourselves. The goods we seek in community are captured in a quotation from

John Winthrop's "A Model of Christian Charity": "We must delight in each other, make others conditions our own, rejoyce together, mourn together, labor and suffer together, always having before our eyes our community as members of the same body."[19]

However, looking at the same community, James Haught saw a picture at odds with Christian charity:

They created a religious police state where doctrinal deviation could lead to flogging, pillorying, banishment, hanging—or cutting off ears, or boring through the tongue with a hot iron. Preaching Quaker beliefs was a capital offense. Four Stubborn Quakers defied this law and were hanged. In the 1690s, fear of witches seized the colony. Twenty alleged witches were killed and 150 imprisoned.[20]

Thus we see in one example the bright side and the dark side of community. In most normal, happy people the longing to belong is balanced by a longing to be free. The theologian Paul Tillich discussed this balance in some depth and warned against both extremes— the selfishness, alienation, and meaninglessness that result from extreme individualism and the loss of self and fanaticism that arise in totalitarian communities.[21]

Interestingly, both liberals and traditionalists have accused each other of paving the road to totalitarianism. According to the "vacuum" theory expressed by Robert Nisbet (among others), liberalism produces a vacuum of values that, because of the very nature of human beings, must be filled.[22] Totalitarian ideologies rush in to fill the vacuum and satisfy the desire to belong. Other conservative critics have seen the form of liberalism that stresses equality (instead of freedom) as the precursor of communism. A third charge, to which we will return because of its present importance, is that liberalism has contributed to the destruction of intermediate groups—families, neighborhoods, religious groups, small charitable organizations, local schools—and thus has undermined the basic units of moral education.[23] In its zeal for equality, critics argue, liberalism has placed too much power in the State which, by its very nature, cannot do the work of civil society.

The charges against liberalism are, however, indirect. In contrast, liberals can point to direct connections between some forms of traditionalism and fascism. For example, despite his plea "for an attitude of piety toward nature, other human beings, and the past,"[24] Richard Weaver's widely read work used language reminiscent of philosophical idealism and fascism. His insistence on distinction, hierarchy, structure, self-discipline, orderliness, and an integrated world picture echoed a message frequently heard in fascist literature.[25]

The sharing and collective orientation advocated by traditionalists can easily be taken to extremes. If it were not for the word "Aryan" in the following and the fact that Adolf Hitler is its author, we might give enthusiastic assent to its basic message:

This will to sacrifice in staking his personal labor and, if necessary, his own life for others, is most powerfully developed in the Aryan. He is greatest, not in his mental capacity *per se*, but in the extent to which he is ready to put all his abilities at the service of the community. With him the instinct of self-preservation has reached the most noble form, because he willingly subjects his own ego to the life of the community and, if the hour should require it, he also sacrifices it.[26]

Thus Tillich was certainly right in warning against the extremes of both individualism and communitarianism. Emphasis on strong communities—the communities of memory praised by Bellah et al.—can lead to the psychological violence feared by Derrida. Ann Russell Mayeaux points to the inadequacy of both communities of memory and communities of terror:

The community of memory engages in self-deception by glamorizing its own past over against the reality of the Other whose speech it pre-empts. The community of terror expunges the past through violence. . . . Thus, it too eradicates the Other's existence.[27]

Mayeaux rejects both the traditionalism of Bellah et al. and the universalism of rules and principles characteristic of liberalism. Instead, she says that we must take personal responsibility for the Other. Edith Wyschogrod, too, warns against solutions that are backward-looking:

If liberal theories . . . fail to persuade, it will not do to return nostalgically and uncritically to an older ethos. Nostalgia is amnesia, a wiping out of both the sea changes brought about by recent history and the sins of older communities such as slavery in ancient Greece and the persecution of Jews, Moslems, and heretics by medieval Christianity. This backward thrust is an example of . . . the myth of the tabula rasa and leads to impossible dreams such as Alasdair MacIntyre's hope for the restoration of a monastic ethic or a return to an Aristotelian version of the good life as one governed by the classical virtues.[28]

The postmodern themes suggested by Derrida, Mayeaux, and Wyschogrod prefigure forms of community based on the primacy of the Other. We are called upon to listen, to respond to others according to their needs, not according to their membership in a symbolic community nor according to "universal" rules that they themselves may reject. It may be that, in such communities, the virtues to be prized will be relational rather than personal. Relational attributes such as trust, good cheer, equality, peace, and compatibility may be more important in such communities than personal virtues such as courage, honesty, and industry.[29]

However, wherever community is emphasized, character education will be important. As Philip Selznick puts it, "we look to virtue and character as the foundations of morality."[30] Both the actions of individuals and the policies of communities are judged in large part by their consequences for character. Selznick writes: "This is a guide to making rules, and to applying them as well. The question is: What kind of person, institution, or community will result from following a particular course of conduct or from adopting a given rule or policy?"[31]

The difficulty with this sensible position is that someone needs to decide what sort of character we will promote. All responsible parents make such decisions in raising their children,[32] and healthy societies also describe and extol the characters they seek to promote. But the enterprise hovers always on the edge of coercion. When we have an ideal in mind, it becomes easy to suppose that people who fail to meet it are, as Isaiah Berlin wrote, "blind or ignorant or corrupt. This renders it easy for me to conceive of myself as coercing others for their own sake, in their, not my, interest."[33]

Selznick would avoid the pitfalls of righteous coercion by embracing a view he calls "communitarian liberalism."[34] Other sensitive writers also recognize (and would avoid) the dark side of community. John W. Gardner, for example, lists "wholeness incorporating diversity" as the first ingredient of today's ideal community."[35] He recognizes how difficult it is to establish this condition—"to prevent the wholeness from smothering diversity—[and] to prevent the diversity from destroying the wholeness."[36] It is especially difficult given that a community by its very nature must have "some core of shared values." Indeed, Gardner says, "of all the ingredients of community this is possibly the most important." And, again, the connection to moral education is explicit:

The community teaches. If it is healthy it will impart a coherent value system. If it is chaotic or degenerate, lessons will be taught anyway—but not lessons that heal and strengthen. We treasure images of values education in which an older mentor quietly instructs a child in the rules of behavior, but that is a small part of a larger and more turbulent scene. The child absorbs values, good and bad, on the playground, through the media, on the street—everywhere. It is the community and culture that hold the individual in a framework of values.[37]

The difficulties in establishing communities that honor diversity and yet share values (beyond that of diversity) are illustrated in current events. At the level of national politics, where a reasonable example might be set, public figures rarely acknowledge the rightness or wrongness of particular recommendations. Instead, sides are chosen and defended by symbolic identification. Distrust is obvious and pervasive; indeed, it is almost obligatory since lack of it breeds a new form of suspicion, and people are expected to embrace party lines.

In schools, attempts to launch programs of moral education are criticized as much with respect to who suggests them as they are with regard to content. The struggles of the Heartwood curriculum provide a troubling example.[38] This curriculum is in the character education tradition; it sets out to illustrate and encourage seven significant virtues, and its stories are collected from a variety of cultures. Thus, in addition to shared values (the seven virtues) it honors cultural diversity. But members of the Christian right have attacked the curriculum because it does not trace the virtues to God as their source. The idea that virtues could arise and be regularly displayed in a secular community is, for these critics, a repugnant one. What can be done in such cases? Even if the schools were to acknowledge (as they are usually willing to do) that *some* people believe that the virtues are derived only from God, many of these critics would not be satisfied, because they believe that their view is true and thus binding on everyone.

Consider also the continuing arguments over whether and how children should be protected against the media onslaught of sex, profanity, crime, and violence. Many people—perhaps the majority—feel that children should be so protected, but a considerable number argue that this protection should be provided by parents and not by public regulation. In this argument, the liberal emphasis on the freedom of parents to raise their children according to their own conceptions of the good takes top priority. But what is to become of the children whose parents cannot or will not provide such protection? Has the *community* no responsibility for them?

Many other examples could be given to illustrate the complexity in trying to establish a communitarian liberalism or a liberal communitarianism. Theoretically, the two words—communitarian and liberal—point to traditions that may be incompatible. One emphasizes communal good; the other, individual goods. In practice, however, if some of the philosophical distinctions are ignored or passed over in favor of listening to and caring for one another, it may be possible to build communities that cherish a core of individual freedom. But the possibility presents enormous problems for schooling. In theory, we can support open dialogue on a nearly full range of topics and opinions, but notice that I have to say "nearly full" because most of us would balk at a "fair hearing" for Nazism or sadism. To complicate matters further, there are groups who are explicitly opposed to the sort of dialogue that seems essential in establishing a community that can care for radically different others and respect ideological diversity. The task will not be an easy one.

A Reasonable Position for Educators

Educators today are especially keen on community building.[39] In part, this great interest is a result of the deterioration of traditional communities. Many educators believe that schools must supply what parents and geographical neighborhoods seem unable to provide—a sense of belonging, of caring for one another, of sharing in a coherent tradition. One of the functions of a community, as we have seen, is to engage in moral education. What role should teachers play in this?

A fundamental premise of traditional education has been that *every* teacher is a teacher of morals.[40] This premise can be construed in two ways: first, that every teacher *should be* a teacher of morals and, second, that every teacher *is*—willingly or not—a teacher of morals. It seems to me that both construals are correct. Teachers—even when they deny that they do so—transmit something of moral values[41] and, since this transmission is inevitable, they should seek to do a responsible job of it.

Is it necessary, then, to choose a program of moral education as one might a mathematics or reading curriculum? Must a teacher decide, for example, between character education and cognitive developmentalism? I want to argue in this last section that wise teachers can use important ideas from both traditions, and enhance cultural literacy at the same time. For example, stories, judiciously chosen and discussed, can inspire (as character educators claim), set the stage for critical thinking (as cognitivists recommend), and enlarge students' catalog of cultural knowledge.

From this perspective, teachers should not neglect affect and inspiration in favor of detached critical thinking. As early as 1955, C. S. Lewis criticized such attempts strongly, warning that setting aside the

emotions would neither provide protection from dogmatism nor satisfy the innate longing most students have for matters that seize the
heart. Lewis wrote:

By starving the sensibility of our pupils we only make them easier prey to the
propagandist when he comes. For famished nature will be avenged and a hard
heart is not infallible protection against a soft head.[42]

Lewis uses as an example the story of the Roman father who taught
his son that it is "sweet and seemly" to die for one's country, and he
notes that certain advocates of critical thinking have only two choices
in their treatment of this story: to debunk it thoroughly or, if they ap-
prove of the basic message in the story, to substitute some reasoned
argument for young men to submit to military service. Lewis deplores
both approaches, for they tend to produce "men without chests"—men
who operate with head or guts but no authentic spirit.

However, there is a third choice. One can present a powerful emotional alternative and invite discussion. Thus, the story of the Roman
father might be followed by this poem of Wilfred Owen's:

> If in some smothering dreams you too could pace
> Behind the wagon that we flung him in,
> And watch the white eyes writhing in his face,
> His hanging face, like a devil's sick of sin:
> If you could hear, at every jolt, the blood
> Come gargling from the froth corrupted lungs,
> Obscene as cancer, bitter as the cud
> Of vile, incurable sores on innocent tongues—
> My friend, you would not tell with such high zest
> To children ardent for some desperate glory
> The old lie: Dulce et decorum est
> Pro patria mori.[43]

Further, poetry—that of Rupert Brooke, for example—can be used
to support the message of the Roman father. In such an approach, students encounter the deep passion of opposing positions, and they may
come to see that reasonable, decent people often differ dramatically.
Besides inspiring and setting the stage for critical discussion, such
encounters expand cultural literacy. Students may be encouraged to
read Lewis's *The Chronicles of Narnia*. They may be attracted to the
powerful poetry and fiction that emerged from World War I: the
poems of Siegfried Sassoon, Charles Sorley, Joyce Kilmer, and Alan

Seeger as well as those by Owen and Brooke; Remarque's *All Quiet on the Western Front*; Hemingway's *A Farewell to Arms*. They may learn something of Rome and how this particular story later affected generations of British school boys. They may even learn a bit of Latin. Finally, struggling with contradictory ideas thought to be noble and right by opposing sides, they may acquire a tragic sense of life—a sense that even the best critical thinking cannot resolve some of the deepest human dilemmas.

Teachers in all subject areas can use stories effectively, and it is not necessary that the stories always illustrate opposing positions. Sometimes stories can make students aware of continuing social and political problems and assure them that their teachers share the social conscience of a thoughtful community. Mathematics teachers, for example, might use the delightful science fiction story *Flatland* to further both mathematical and moral interests.[44] *Flatland*, the story of a two-dimensional society, introduces important concepts of dimensionality and relativity, but it is also filled with illustrations of sexism, classism, and religious mysticism. Indeed, mathematics teachers sometimes reject it *because* of its sexism (even though the sexism is satirical). However, from the perspective taken here, *Flatland*'s sexism, classism, and mysticism give us excellent reasons for discussing such matters in mathematics classes. Imagine a society in which all males are polygons, and class status depends on the number of one's sides. Isosceles triangles are the working poor, so to speak, and those polygons with so many sides that they are almost indistinguishable from circles are the priests at the top of the social hierarchy. Every father in Flatland hopes that his sons will have more sides than he has. What of women? In this highly classed society, women are, through all generations, mere line segments! They are, no matter the status of their husbands, essentially nonpersons.

In addition to classism and sexism, *Flatland* introduces a good bit of mysticism. The narrator of the story, an upstanding square, is visited by a three-dimensional entity. Of course, no one believes him, and he finishes his tale in prison. He is regarded as either mad or subversive but definitely dangerous to his community. In the mystical tradition, he longs for another visitation, something to affirm what he knows really happened. But how can one explain a third dimension to people living in two-dimensional space? How would we describe a four-dimensional entity to our peers?

Stories like *Flatland* not only help to build community through shared ideas and conversation, but they provide an opportunity to criticize community and develop some of the cautionary ideas discussed earlier. Communities often fail to accept dissenting or unusual ideas. They demand conformity and punish dissent. They may also establish rigid rules for belonging and use the rules to exclude people whose symbolic affiliations preclude their acceptance of the rules. Discussion of such issues is vital if we are to avoid the dark side of community.

Biographical stories can also provide inspiration and induce critical thinking. The story of James Sylvester, a great mathematician, is instructive.[45] Although Sylvester did his undergraduate work at Cambridge, the university would not grant him a degree because, as a Jew, he could not give the expected responses to the Thirty-Nine Articles required by the Church of England. He received his degree from Trinity College in Dublin. Years later, as a famous mathematician, he received an honorary degree from Cambridge. His story gives mathematics teachers another opportunity to discuss racial and religious prejudice.

Sylvester's story also is a powerful example of one form of the "good life." He loved music and literature, and even his mathematical papers are sprinkled with Latin quotations and references to the classics. He was enormously energetic and enthusiastic and accepted a new position at Oxford when he was seventy-one. The following quotation from Sylvester captures his love of both life and mathematics:

There is no study in the world which brings into more harmonious action all the faculties of the mind. . . . The mathematician lives long and lives young; the wings of the soul do not early drop off, nor do its pores become clogged with the earthy particles blown from the dusty highways of vulgar life.[46]

Teachers prepared with a repertoire of inspiring stories probably also have an advantage in keeping their students' attention. By acknowledging a wide variety of legitimate interests in their students, such teachers are demonstrating their own commitment to a way of educating that is moral in its procedures as well as its content.

Stories are not the only feature of moral education that is compatible with both character education and cognitive approaches. We could talk about the role of conversation in all its forms—from philosophical argumentation to everyday conversation.[47] We could profitably discuss practice—how to demonstrate moral behavior in our teaching and how to provide students with opportunities to care for one another. Many ideas from each school of thought might be examined carefully to see whether they can be taken up or honestly adapted by the other. I have concentrated here on stories because their use seems so obviously acceptable to both groups.

I'll finish with a question for further investigation. Why are teachers so poorly prepared to draw on stories in their disciplinary instruction? There may be a wide and dangerous gap between the narrow expertise characteristic of today's liberal studies and the equally narrow expertise of professional schools. Too often there is little of the truly liberal in the content of liberal studies[48] and not much content in professional studies. Disciplines traditionally included in the liberal arts have become, for the most part, highly specialized centers of expertise. Few professors in these disciplines address the questions that were once thought to be central to liberal studies: How should I live? What kind of life is worth living? How do I find meaning in life?[49] Education schools and departments also fail to address these questions and concentrate on pedagogy, classroom management, school structure, and related topics. The sort of knowledge that relates subject matter and teaching itself to the great questions of life seems to have fallen into a chasm. If such a gap does in fact exist, we need to fill it in so that teachers are prepared to do the work of moral education.

NOTES

1. See the discussion in Betty A. Sichel, *Moral Education* (Philadelphia: Temple University Press, 1988).

2. See Aristotle, *Nicomachean Ethics*, trans. Terence Irwin (Indianapolis: Hackett, 1985).

3. Alasdair MacIntyre, *After Virtue* (Notre Dame: Notre Dame University Press, 1981), p. 221.

4. Ibid., p. 216.

5. See the warning against telling children stories about ogres and wicked stepmothers in Bruno Bettelheim, *The Uses of Enchantment: The Meaning and Importance of Fairy Tales* (New York: Alfred A. Knopf, 1976).

6. See, for example, Robert Coles, *The Call of Stories: Teaching and the Moral Imagination* (Boston: Houghton Mifflin, 1989).

7. On this, see Alasdair MacIntyre, *Whose Justice? Which Rationality?* (Notre Dame: Notre Dame University Press, 1988); also Charles Taylor, *Sources of the Self* (Cambridge: Harvard University Press, 1989).

8. Michael Oakeshott, "Political Education," in *Liberalism and its Critics*, ed. Michael Sandel (New York: New York University Press, 1984), p. 232.

9. See James Terry White, *Character Lessons in American Biography* (New York: Character Development League, 1909).

10. See Arthur Schlesinger, Jr., *The Disuniting of America: Reflections on a Multicultural Society* (New York: W. W. Norton, 1992).

11. See Lawrence Kohlberg, *The Philosophy of Moral Development* (San Francisco: Harper & Row, 1981).

12. One example of a program that concentrates on reasoning is Philosophy for Children. See any issue of *Thinking* (Montclair, N.J.: Montclair State University).

13. See Richard J. Bernstein, *The New Constellation* (Cambridge: MIT Press, 1992), p. 54.

14. Robert A. Nisbet, *The Quest for Community* (New York: Oxford University Press, 1953), p. 3.

15. Robert N. Bellah, Richard Madsen, William M. Sullivan, Ann Swidler, and Steven M. Tipton, *Habits of the Heart* (Berkeley: University of California Press, 1985), p. 323.

16. Besides the MacIntyre and Taylor references, see Max Weber, *The Protestant Ethic and the Spirit of Capitalism*, trans. Talcott Parsons (New York: Scribner's, 1958).

17. See John Rawls, *A Theory of Justice* (Cambridge: Harvard University Press, 1971).

18. Bernstein, *The New Constellation*, p. 51.

19. Winthrop is quoted in Bellah et al., *Habits of the Heart*, p. 28.

20. James A. Haught, *Holy Horrors* (Buffalo, N.Y.: Prometheus Press, 1990), pp. 123-124.

21. See Paul Tillich, *The Courage to Be* (New Haven: Yale University Press, 1952).

22. See the discussion in George H. Nash, *The Conservative Movement in America* (New York: Basic Books, 1979).

23. On the deterioration of intermediate groups, see Francis Fukuyama, *Trust: The Social Virtues and the Creation of Prosperity* (New York: Free Press, 1995); also Mary Ann Glendon, *Rights Talk* (New York: Free Press, 1991).

24. See the discussion of Richard Weaver's *Ideas Have Consequences* (Chicago: University of Chicago Press, 1948) in Nash, *The Conservative Movement in America*.

25. Compare the language in *Ideas Have Consequences* with that in Giovanni Gentile, *Genesis and Structure of Society*, trans. H. S. Harris (Urbana, Ill.: University of Illinois Press, 1960).

26. Adolf Hitler, *Mein Kampf* (New York: Reynal & Hitchcock, 1939/1925), p. 408.

27. Anne Russell Mayeaux, "Towards the Fifth Centenary: Dominicans, the 'Other' and the Unavowable Community," *Providence* 1, no. 3 (1993): 265.

28. Edith Wyschogrod, *Saints and Postmodernism: Revisioning Moral Philosophy* (Chicago: University of Chicago Press, 1990).

29. One sees such a shift of emphasis in some existing communities, e.g., the Quaker community. See Kim Hays, *Practicing Virtues: Moral Traditions at Quaker and Military Boarding Schools* (Berkeley: University of California Press, 1994).

30. Philip Selznick, *The Moral Commonwealth* (Berkeley: University of California Press, 1992), p. 34.

31. Ibid., p. 35.

32. Ruddick, for example, says that one of the great demands of maternal thinking is "to shape an acceptable child." See Sara Ruddick, "Maternal Thinking," *Feminist Studies* 6, no. 2 (1980): 342-367.

33. Isaiah Berlin, "Two Concepts of Liberty," in *Liberalism and its Critics*, ed. Michael Sandel, p. 24.

34. Selznick, *The Moral Commonwealth*, p. xi.

35. John W. Gardner, *Building Community* (Washington, D.C.: Independent Sector, 1991), p. 15.

36. Ibid., p. 16. Amitai Etzioni also makes this point in his *The Spirit of Community* (New York: Touchstone, 1993).

37. Gardner, *Building Community*, p. 17.

38. See the account of Heartwood's struggle in "A Textbook of Virtues," Education Life, *The New York Times*, January 8, 1995.

39. See, for example, Thomas J. Sergiovanni, *Building Community in Schools* (San Francisco: Jossey-Bass, 1994).

40. See David E. Purpel, *The Moral and Spiritual Crisis in Education* (New York: Bergin & Garvey, 1989).

41. See Philip W. Jackson, Robert E. Boostrom, and David T. Hansen, *The Moral Life of Schools* (San Francisco: Jossey-Bass, 1993).

42. C. S. Lewis, *The Abolition of Man: How Education Develops Man's Sense of Morality* (New York: Collier Books, 1955).

43. Wilfred Owen, "Dulce et Decorum Est," in Wilfred Owen, *Collected Poems of Wilfred Owen* © 1963 by Chatto and Windus, Ltd. Reprinted with permission of New Directions Publishing Corp., New York.

44. Edwin A. Abbott, *Flatland* (New York: Dover, 1952).

45. See the account in E. T. Bell, *Men of Mathematics* (New York: Simon and Schuster, 1965/1937).

46. James Sylvester, as quoted in Bell, *Men of Mathematics*, p. 405.

47. See Nel Noddings, "Conversation as Moral Education," *Journal of Moral Education* 23, no. 2 (1994): 107-118. See also idem, "Learning to Engage in Moral Dialogue," *Holistic Education Review* 7, no. 2 (1994): 1-9.

48. See Bruce Wilshire, *The Moral Collapse of the University* (Albany: SUNY Press, 1990).

49. See Thomas H. Naylor, William H. Willimon, and Magdalena R. Naylor, *The Search for Meaning* (Nashville: Abingdon Press, 1994).

CHAPTER II

Character Education from Four Perspectives on Curriculum

WILLIAM H. SCHUBERT

Every curriculum shapes character. Therefore, an inescapable curriculum issue centers on whether a separate curriculum for character education should be attempted or whether all curricula should be developed carefully to enhance the construction of character. Granted, some curricula are explicitly established to influence the character of students; nevertheless, every learning experience in some way modifies traits that distinguish who a person is and what he or she represents. In fact, every experience alters perspectives about what is worth being and doing. When intentionality is invoked and educators consciously try to influence the character of students and help them develop meaning and purpose to guide their lives, such influence could be said to be a "curriculum" of character education. This, however, occurs in all curricula, whether labeled *character education* or not. Moreover, literature on *hidden curriculum* indicates that even without overt intentionality, many messages are conveyed by the structures and processes of institutions and by informal learning experiences outside institutions. Such messages can be moral or political and they shape character accordingly.[1]

For purposes of this chapter, I assume that a *curriculum* (i.e., a set of social relationships and experiences that constitutes an educational event) enables all participants in that event (students, teachers, parents, others) to construct or refine their *character* (i.e., the configuration of mental, moral, and emotional traits that make up the essence of who they are). I often think of a person's character as the basic beliefs or moral values that guide decision and action. As an elementary school teacher for eight years, I was convinced that what I offered to students, the opportunities to learn and grow that I provided, *and* the way I conducted myself as their teacher constituted a curriculum that

William H. Schubert is Professor of Education at the University of Illinois at Chicago.

shaped their character. Today, having taught other teachers for over twenty years, I am convinced that the same is the case with them. Thus, I restate my initial message—all curricula teach character and thereby play a major role in the character that is socially constructed in students' lives. Anyone who is deeply concerned about the construction of character should focus not merely on a particular course but on the whole curriculum.

In this chapter, I want to sketch how four quite different curricular perspectives have an impact on character. To do so, I shall create a spokesperson for each point of view, introducing them as a *social behaviorist*, an *intellectual traditionalist*, an *experientialist*, and a *critical reconstructionist*. These characterizations grow out of my studies of the literature of the curriculum field from the late nineteenth century to the present, including the history of curriculum.[2] Their recurrence in the literature reminds me of positions advocated for the practical reform of schools over the years.[3] As in a symposium, I am inviting these four guests to address here the way in which they see curriculum influencing character. I have asked each speaker to focus briefly on three questions: (1) What is most worth knowing and experiencing? (2) How is the answer to this question a basis for constructing the character of children and youth? (3) How can educators' reflections on curriculum and instruction enhance the construction of character?

While different positions on a curriculum for character education could be sketched here (and some will be noted), it is the students' overall experience in school that continuously and most pervasively influences the construction of their character. I am therefore convinced that it is more valuable to ferret out the *character* of character education implicit in general curriculum orientations than it is to compare and contrast different approaches directly designed to influence character education. It is more valuable to focus on dimensions of character which are taught subtly by overarching curriculum orientations applying to all subject areas precisely because that is a greatly neglected emphasis. (This is not to minimize the importance of analyzing different approaches that are designed specifically for character education. That is done elsewhere in this volume.)

What I hope readers of this chapter will do is to question the assumptions that lie behind general orientations to curriculum, looking for messages that influence students' construction of character. For instance, when the social behaviorist asks educators to design curriculum through a study of what *successful* persons do (and what they need to know in order to do it), the principles of moral behavior saturate any image of success that is set forth. From this perspective character becomes merely contingent on whatever image of success dominates. The intellectual traditionalist, on the other hand, holds that the best development of character occurs only when students are exposed to the liberal arts traditions of great works and disciplines of knowledge.

The social behaviorist and intellectual traditionalist positions dominate school practice. Although different on many counts, these two positions have at least one similarity that is challenged by the experientialist and critical reconstructionist, namely their locus of authority. Both the intellectual traditionalist and the social behaviorist see authority as residing in external forces. The intellectual traditionalist's authority lies in a set of experts who create or analyze and interpret the great works; it is also lodged in the logic of the disciplines of knowledge. The social behaviorist's authority resides in the prevailing images of social success and in the empirical research methodology of social and behavioral sciences and the resulting knowledge. In contrast, the experientialist and critical reconstructionist hold that the best solutions to the pressing problems of society and everyday life are created by those who experience those problems. So, when the experientialist speaker advocates developing curriculum from the interests and concerns of students, there is an implicit assumption that learning best emerges from students who are enabled to ask: What is worthwhile for me (and us) to know and experience? This question is not answered for students by experts and then bestowed upon them. Curriculum is only deemed appropriate *for* students if it is also *of* and *by* them. When students carefully address what is worth knowing and experiencing, they must deal with what kind of a person they want to become, what moral principles and beliefs they want to live by—in short, their character. The critical reconstructionist shares this experientialist hope for curriculum, but sees it suppressed by those who dominate society. Thus, the critical reconstructionist argues that students, educators, and parents should resist and contest this oppression. The obvious implication for character education from the critical reconstructionist stance is that character is best formed through participation in projects that expose injustice and attempt to overcome it.

These four perspectives merely illustrate the complexity of the character education that occurs in the everyday experience of curriculum. The challenge is to look deeply for the multitude of messages that shape character in the daily experience of education as one listens to the advice of contending parties in debates about curriculum and character education.

The Social Behaviorist Speaks

I am an advocate of precise, systematic, strategic planning. Whenever possible curriculum and instruction should be based on evidence provided in research literature. There is, indeed, a vast array of untapped educational research that could inform the policy and practice of curriculum and teaching. What I mean is that we should have evidence to support what we advocate—not just stories and anecdotal reports, but rigorous scientific evidence. Nevertheless, I am the first to admit that not all important educational questions can be answered by research studies. For instance, our basic assumptions about the question of worthwhile knowledge usually are not subject to scientific proof. (I'll return to this in a moment.)

There is, however, a great deal of scientific evidence about how to achieve purposes once they are delineated. Here I want to talk about the four basic questions asked by Ralph W. Tyler in his landmark book, *Basic Principles of Curriculum and Instruction* (1949).[4] That small book has been a kind of bible of curriculum construction for almost half a century. His first question is about determining purposes, a question more mired in philosophical dispute than are the other three questions. The second deals with how to determine learning experiences (though I prefer the term "activities" as did one of my heroes, Franklin Bobbitt, in the 1920s). To determine learning activities can be an analytic and empirical process of aligning purposes with what teachers have students do. Tyler's third question deals with how to organize the curriculum, which in turn invokes issues of scope, sequence, environment, and instruction. Without belaboring these matters, let me say that scope involves selecting from the range of possible content areas whatever best facilitates the purposes. Sequence refers to the order in which the learning activities proceed and naturally relates to the issue of prerequisite knowledge. Environment deals with the physical, psychosocial, institutional, and interpersonal dimensions of school and classroom life, as well as with how curricular materials are arranged for use there. Finally, Tyler's fourth question deals with evaluation, essentially asking how to determine the extent to which purposes have been achieved. Suffice it to say that there is much more scientific evidence available for designing consistent policy and practice than is usually employed. Sadly, major summary statements in noted handbooks and encyclopedias of education, curriculum, teaching, and evaluation are often ignored by leaders of educational practice.

One could use the model I just summarized to implement any program of character education. It is essentially an amoral model for curriculum development, except that the moral content of character education is embodied in the nature and quality of curriculum purposes. Embedded in any statement of purposes is a set of values. Whenever we advocate that anything be learned, we in effect argue that the values inherent in it constitute part of the character we see as worthwhile. Sometimes this is not made clear, and in such cases implied values rule by default. Not favoring rule by default (who would?), I say we should be as clear, concise, and exact as possible in refining purposes by expressing them as behavioral objectives, which state desired outcomes in terms of manageable, observable, and hopefully measurable behaviors. I suppose that is why I am labeled by Schubert as a social *behaviorist*.

If that is the "behaviorist" part, where is the "social?" To clarify, I return to Franklin Bobbitt.[5] We often are admonished to begin the curriculum-making process by doing a needs assessment. However, it is impossible to do a needs assessment defensibly without systematically determining what *should be*. That's where the "social" manifests itself. In following Bobbitt's work in the first quarter of the century, I recommend that educators revive the process of "activity analysis." An activity analysis is an empirical process of determining by observation and report what successful members of society spend their time doing. The key to determining purposes for the curriculum, then, is to discover what successful members of society *need to know* in order to do what they spend their time doing. Only when this is done can a needs assessment be valuable, for at that point students' knowledge can be compared with the knowledge of successful members of society. The rest of curriculum design can then be based on educational research that provides evidence about how activities, organizational patterns, and evaluation can be orchestrated to enable students to acquire knowledge that will help them become successful members of society. The point for character education should be obvious. Activity analysis should be done to determine what character traits, such as guiding values or practices of virtues, are common to successful persons. These are then integrated into the curricular content.

The only flaw in the process is the ambiguity of what constitutes a successful person. What image of success is embodied, for example, in major achievement tests that too often drive the curriculum? By "drive the curriculum" I mean that test construction agencies (via mandated tests aligned with goals or outcomes in each of the several states) are the tail that wags the dog of curricular purposes. Careful debate at the local, state, regional, and national levels needs to be carried out by representative groups to determine what is meant by "successful." Such debate is the essence of democratic deliberation (and some criticize me for being elitist).

Thus, the key question for educators is, What should we deem success in our society? In other words, Who are successful persons? What are their main traits and abilities? While these broad questions pertain to curriculum as a whole, the specific concern for the construction of character would be, What is a successful person, morally speaking? Who are moral people? A worthwhile activity for educators would be to enumerate characteristics likely to be found in a person of admirable moral character, i.e., one whose behavior is morally defensible. To address this carefully means that we cannot blindly accept conventional or popular notions of success without looking to the contributions these behaviors make to society. Such contributions constitute the character that schools should teach. If that is done in each generation of school children, society will become incrementally more successful generation after generation. What more could we want than to adopt the character of the morally most successful members of our society?

The Intellectual Traditionalist Speaks

I certainly can tell you what more we could want. We could want all of our young persons to have access to the best that human beings have created throughout history. What is the best? It is embodied in the "great works." The classics of literature, music, art, theatre, philosophical and social treatises, mathematics, sciences, and social sciences need to be recognized as the essence of human imagination and reason that constitute the best education for all. Why? Not just because they have stood the test of time, but because these works embody essential insights about the great ideas—ideas that transcend cultures, historical eras, geographical areas, and differences of race, class, gender, and age. These are the great ideas of truth, beauty, goodness, liberty, equality, and justice, as Mortimer Adler is wont to say.[6] Or if you prefer a more existential rendition, Robert Ulich refers to "the great events and mysteries of life: birth, death, love, tradition, society and the crowd, success and failure, salvation, and anxiety."[7]

The essence of the great works lies in their penetrating insight into these perennial mysteries. This is the case, of course, only when they are taught well. They must be taught by teachers who deeply know and appreciate the classics or disciplines that they teach. This probing intellectual, this inspiring sage, this questioning explorer of the many dimensions of human experience, this great teacher and lifelong learner—steeped in the great works of diverse cultures and of eras—*is* the paragon of character, an exemplar of *what* we should encourage children to emulate.

Admittedly, among my intellectual traditionalist friends, there are staunch advocates of particular value positions, some of whom would promote didactic character education. One such advocate is William Bennett. In his *The Book of Virtues*[8] he encourages readers to focus on the virtuous messages from literature. Another example of one who favors didactic advocacy of basic traditional values is Edward Wynne, as can be seen in his many writings and in his chapter in this volume. Another exemplar among intellectual traditionalists is E. D. Hirsch, who gained great popular attention with his book entitled *Cultural Literacy* and who now has expanded his compendia of what should be taught and learned in a set of books entitled *What Every (insert grade level) Grader Should Know.*[9] Although he is criticized for pushing the Western canon, Hirsch's grade level books include a greater variety of races, geographical regions, and historical eras than many would expect.

In the final analysis, I agree with both Hirsch and Adler, who do not advocate a particular set of character traits but argue instead that the best development of character derives from an in-depth study of the world's great intellectual traditions. To know the best of human creations in art, music and dance, literature, philosophy, history and social thought, natural and social science, and mathematics puts a person in the best position to build and refine his or her character. In fact, that should be the purpose of education. At the risk of sounding too Western again, I would say (with Goethe, Schiller, and others[10]) that education is the building of psychological, moral, and spiritual character by selecting from the best intellectual traditions available to us.

The big policy issue is how to find enough teachers to inspire all of the students when we take on the great project of universal schooling, rather than merely tutoring those who are privileged. We need teachers who understand with Gilbert Highet that the art of teaching consists of knowing and loving your subject and your students. He recommends that the best way to learn about teaching is to study the masters (Jesus, Socrates, Matthew Arnold, Leo Tolstoy, Gandhi, Mark Hopkins, and so forth).[11] And a basic approach to encourage teachers to reflect on their teaching from an intellectual traditionalist angle is to ask such questions as: What great works or disciplines of knowledge have made a powerful impact on your life? What essential beliefs, ideas, or principles, derived from your studies, are the pillars of conduct for your life? What conditions contributed to or inspired the development of those central ideas, and how might similar conditions be employed to shape the character and intellectual interests of your students?

The Experientialist Speaks

My notions of curriculum and character education are virtually inseparable. Curriculum, whatever students experience, shapes character; conversely, whatever shapes character (whether experienced in or out of school) is a viable form of curriculum. To convey these points I usually ask audiences to reflect on the most important things they have learned. To differentiate a bit among kinds of things learned, I often ask them to jot down three: first, a *skill* that enhances their life by coming in handy time and again; second, a *body of knowledge* that they frequently draw upon; and third, a *value* that guides their life. The last of these is probably most indicative of character education; nevertheless, I submit that each of the three answers for anyone's life would constitute a significant portion of the character of that person. So I ask teachers (or anyone engaged in this activity) to reflect carefully on the experiences that brought them to the skill, the knowledge, and the value that they identified.

Take values, for instance. I ask educators to think of a principle or a belief or a tenet of their personal value system. Then I ask them to reconstruct their pathway to the present state of that guiding force for them. I ask them to engage others in the same kind of consideration and then to compare journeys by exchanging stories about them. The stories reveal qualities of influence that made profound differences in the lives of those engaged in sharing, giving them increased meaning and direction. Here enters John Dewey, the exemplar of the experientialist curriculum, in my view. Dewey declares, "Education is that reconstruction or reorganization of experience which adds to the meaning of experience, and which increases ability to direct the course of subsequent experience."[12]

To drive this point home in another way, I sometimes ask educators to think of the most important decisions they have made in their lives. I suggest decisions about who to marry or live with, whether to have children, how to raise children, what career path to tread, where to live, what life style to adopt, and so on. Then I ask about their basis for making these decisions: "Did you say, 'Hmmm, I wonder who to spend my life with—so I guess I'll consult a research report (social behaviorist), or hmmm, I wonder how I should raise my children—which classic should I consult?'" Participants are quick to realize that they have a great faith, a Deweyan *common faith*[13] in themselves and their loved ones when it comes to their most important decisions. They trust their own experiences and those of their closest relatives and friends. I suggest that they should devote the same seriousness to decisions about education as they do to decisions about their own life.

The character education that my position reveals is one that encourages learners to continuously face life with a desire to learn and grow. It begins with what John Dewey called the *psychological* (or interests and concerns in the life of the learner) and moves back and forth on a continuum between the psychological and the *logical* (fund of knowledge already created by human beings from their everyday experience or that which is created by experts and resides in the disciplines).[14] Students do have deep concerns and interests that grow out of their everyday lives. They should not deposit their concerns and interests at the doorstep of school (after which they are expected to enter and to learn other things); rather, student interests and concerns should be the hub around which the curricular wheel turns and finds its path. Students should be able to fashion meaningful projects that help them refine a sense of purpose or direction. Teachers, aware of the funds of knowledge that exist, should add meaning to these projects by showing how social studies, the arts, sciences, mathematics, language arts, and all the rest can deepen and broaden whatever interest or concern is the basis for a project or inquiry. This is the natural way of learning in an interdisciplinary fashion, integrated around the emerging life interests of learners and their concerns about who they are becoming.[15]

When students have opportunity to share their genuine concerns, they are astounded at the compatibility between their interests and those of others.

At this one point (but few others) I feel a rather close kinship with the intellectual traditionalist. What all humans share is a fundamental interest in life's great mysteries and concerns. Experientialist teachers, therefore, do not have to worry about needing to create a separate curriculum for each student. Naturally shared interests (common concerns about love, birth, tradition, death, salvation, justice, freedom, goodness, and the like) enable small groups of students to realize the value of pursuing shared interests together. Experientialist teachers also do not need to create a separate curriculum for each student because students are curriculum developers along with their teachers.

The essence of an experientialist curriculum is that its organizing center is the continuous asking of the basic curriculum questions: What is worth experiencing, knowing, being, and sharing? This is a question for teachers and students alike. It is a never-ending question, one which should always be reconceptualized, reconstructed, and refined to enable more worthwhile educational experiences to ensue. To fully engage in this question is, in fact, the ongoing story of character education at its best. It can be stimulated by the multicultural and diverse images of character inspired by literature, such as that presented in a 1995 publication, *A Call to Character*, edited by Colin Greer and Herbert Kohl.[16] However, even such an excellent text only supports the process of directly and consciously refining one's own character.

The Critical Reconstructionist Speaks

I agree to a large extent with the experientialist; however, I cannot abide his essential naïveté. I speak of a political or ideological naïveté that assumes it is possible to engage in genuine, open, and honest discussion or deliberation with others who are embedded in a network of social and economic hierarchies that give unequal privilege and opportunity. Anyone who thinks for a moment about his or her own workplace knows that, given the hierarchies and reward structures, it is impossible to engage in genuine, open, and honest communication between supervisors and those supervised at all levels. Such unequal opportunity to communicate (and thus unequal opportunity to grow) is symptomatic of societal attribution of privilege according to such factors as race, class, gender, ability, health, age, nationality, place, language and culture, marital status, sexual orientation, connections to others in power, certification, ethnicity, appearance. To illustrate this I often ask educators to make a chart with these factors down the side and along the top such categories as "self," "significant others," and "your students." I ask them to tell stories of opportunity or special privilege being granted or denied on the basis of such categories in their own life, in the life of significant other(s), and in the lives of their students.

To illustrate from the educational research literature, I often point to Joel Spring's provocative book, *The Sorting Machine*,[17] and ask them to think of how entry to hierarchies can be eased or impeded by certification or finances or knowing individuals in power positions. I may tell them about Jean Anyon's critical study of the alternative images of success conveyed through the hidden curriculum (or structure of school experience) in four different social class environments.[18] Students in lower socioeconomic school contexts were taught that the route to success is to follow the rules (i.e., you are taught by the way school is set up to get ahead by learning the rules and then by following them). Middle-class students, in contrast, learn that success derives from "giving the right answers" (discovering what authorities want and then giving it to them—learning to nod, whether listening or not; appearing attentive; looking beneath the surface to discover what is really wanted in an assignment that is too large to complete in the time given). Students from professional-class environments learn that the route to success is to "be creative" (often meaning to stay busy discovering new modes of thought or expression, while not making any waves or rocking any boats of the ruling class). Students of the executive or ruling class are, in contrast to all the others, enabled and encouraged to manipulate the system. They learn, for instance, if a rule is broken, that it may be easier to change it than to abide by it. This picture is one of hegemony at work, i.e., a recapitulation by means of schooling of the social hierarchies in the larger society in a way that perpetuates the power of the dominant social class.

Anyon's research raises serious questions about the extent to which character and character education are class-based, questions that educators should strive to analyze relative to their own situation. For instance, should teachers be content to enable students to adopt the character traits that may lead to jobs in their respective settings (e.g., teaching to lower-class students the value of following rules; to middle-class students, the value of giving *right* answers and impressing the authority figure; to professional-class students, the value of developing creative responsiveness to problems; and to ruling-class students, the value of manipulating the system)? Of course, they should not. It is obvious that each of these orientations bespeaks character traits that cut to the quick of morality: bowing unquestioningly to the rules devised by superiors; or nodding reluctantly to authority figures even when they contradict one's conviction; or remaining busy in creative activity to escape the need to oppose unjust exercise of power. Every student ought to be taught to manipulate the system. But what would happen to lower, working, or middle-class students who tried this? Some suggest that the system would crush them. To what extent must teachers fit students to the conventional or dominant character traits of the socioeconomic class in which the students currently live? What might teachers and students do to transcend the walls of social class and define *acceptable* character?

My obvious message from this example is that character education differs from school to school on the basis of social class. It also differs according to other factors previously mentioned such as race, gender, health, age, and culture. The only antidote to the hegemony of these factors is to make students aware of the inequities that exist in their lives, and to enable them to engage in projects such as those suggested by the experientialist. However, the projects should be politically oriented to the injustices faced by the students. The solution, certainly, is not so simple as telling students in each social class to manipulate the system, for that would only result in children and youth who are crushed by the dominating system. Teachers cannot be justified in promoting a "children's crusade"! Nevertheless, educators must be activists who strive for the reduction of what Jonathan Kozol aptly labels "savage inequalities."[19] As citizens concerned with education they need to do this. Further, in classrooms with young persons, they dare not ignore George Counts's classic radical question, "Dare the school build a new social order?"[20] They need, also, to heed the admonition of a great African-American educator of the same era, Carter G. Woodson, who starkly reminded us of what racism can do to courage when he said, "When you control a man's thinking you do not have to worry about his actions. You do not have to tell him not to stand here or go yonder. He will find his *proper place* and will stay in it. You do not need to send him to the back door. He will go without being told. In fact, if there is no back door, he will cut one for his special benefit. His education makes it necessary."[21]

The problem-posing pedagogy of Paulo Freire[22] has great potential to develop a literacy of context for the many who are oppressed. Such a pedagogy starts with artifacts from the experience of those to be taught. Then, rather than focusing on the teacher's interpretation of items which learners know more fully than even the best-intentioned teachers, students are encouraged to name their own world in their own way. I think of Freire's story of the Brazilian peasant pictured in a photograph. The teacher, a well-intentioned liberal outsider, wants to characterize him as drunken and lazy, but the insiders describe something quite different—a man who desperately wants to provide for his family but at every turn over years of striving finds that he is beating his head against the wall of oppression and savage inequality with nowhere else to turn.

To move beyond what Freire pejoratively calls the "banking" mode of pedagogy to a problem-posing "pedagogy" requires political activism, because the banking notion of knowledge acquisition is so integrally tied to the dominant (and dominating) forms of social life. Students do need an experientialist curriculum, but one that centers inquiry and action together (praxis) on the experience of injustice—on first exposing it and then on working to overcome it. To engage in such work with students *is* the most important project of character education, because doing so requires the exercise of courage and commitment to overcome injustice. Through such work character is forged.

Summary and Conclusion

Each of the foregoing "speakers" illustrates a different orientation to curriculum that bespeaks a prevalent image of character education. The social behaviorist suggests that character worth emulation is right before our eyes, embodied in the activities of successful persons. We need to identify the ideals implicit in what successful persons know and do, and we need to design and organize learning activities to reach these purposes. The intellectual traditionalist argues that character is best formed by immersion in the great works because they put students in touch with fundamental questions and mysteries in a way that no other source can provide. The experientialist says that each person should follow his or her deepest concerns and interests, which will lead to becoming a curious problem solver and dedicated moral agent who trusts his or her own judgment based on experience. The critical reconstructionist sees character best formed in the struggle for equity and justice, as the consequence of imaginative, democratic, political action, not merely of adherence to precept or participation in "interesting" activities.

Each perspective also suggests considerations for educators and policymakers to relate to character education in their own experience. The social behaviorist recommends that educators should inquire seriously about what constitutes a morally successful person. The intellectual traditionalist encourages educators to reflect on powerful insights and understandings that they obtained from the great works. The experientialist wants educators to ponder the conditions and circumstances of the most profound learning experiences they have had as a basis for deciding how to influence the character of students. Finally, the critical reconstructionist asks that educators reflect on the experiences of discrimination they have known in an effort to sensitize themselves to the injustices faced by their students; efforts to overcome such injustices are the bases of character education.

My point in presenting the four perspectives is not that readers have to choose only one of them; neither is it the case that there are *only* four positions. My central hope is that as educators reflect on each of these perspectives they will discover more possibilities about how curriculum can provide social and intellectual experiences for students to use in constructing a moral sense of purpose to guide their lives. Educators can challenge their own views or ones they encounter by imagining how the intellectual traditionalist, the social behaviorist, the experientialist, or the critical reconstructionist might respond. Thus,

they will be in better positions to fashion educational experiences that
help their students develop character.

When I role-play each of the positions, I feel a strong kinship with
each. I believe that salient values of each are deeply embodied in my
own character. They provide the contradiction and conflict that help
me empathize with stalwart proponents of a single viewpoint and that
enliven my own internal dialogue about basic moral convictions. Empathy with a diversity of viewpoints and keeping dialogue alive contribute to the continuous construction of character in educators. Educators who engage in the life project of reconstructing their own
character are exemplars who can enable their students to do the same.
While each perspective presented here has a rightful place in the
worlds of educational theory and practice, I am convinced that social
behaviorist and intellectual traditionalist forms of character education
dominate our educational ethos today. Therefore, I want to call for
more balanced attention to experientialist and critical reconstructionist
forms of character education. I am increasingly convinced that all four
positions can enrich students' character development as we strive for
relevance in education. We must, of course, be mindful of the contradictions and complementarity that can result from combining dimensions of different perspectives. To tailor curriculum perspectives to the
ever changing situations of educational practice, however, requires the
highest degree of reflective action educators can muster. The best
starting point for such reflection is to examine carefully the curriculum
of the specific educational situation in which one works, and to identify the impact it has on the development of students' character. At the
same time we need to move beyond what *is* to consider what *ought to
be*, by engaging in ongoing dialogue about how curriculum can best
contribute to the social construction of character. While the guest
speakers presented in this chapter push us to consider four alternative
perspectives, this is only a beginning. New perspectives need to be created continuously to meet the needs of ever changing situations.

NOTES

1. Henry A. Giroux and David Purpel, eds., *The Hidden Curriculum and Moral Education* (Berkeley, Calif.: McCutchan, 1981).

2. William H. Schubert and Ann Lynn Lopez, *Curriculum Books: The First Eighty
Years* (Lanham, Md.: University Press of America, 1980); William H. Schubert, *Curriculum: Perspective, Paradigm, and Possibility* (New York: Macmillan, 1986). I believe that I
have come to know these perspectives also because they are deeply embodied within me.
When I teach about each of them, I find myself taking an advocacy role. Somehow they
have become more than four orientations to lecture about; they almost "want" to jump
out pedagogically when I speak to graduate and undergraduate classes or when I consult

with teachers, school administrators, policymakers, or teacher educators. So, over the years I have learned to role-play each of the "guest speakers" or "commentators" as I often refer to them. Now, when groups that invite me to speak have particular educational interests or questions, my "guest speakers" always seem to have responses, and they often disagree fervently with each other. Sometimes I feel as if these speakers are educational archetypes that well up within me wanting to speak. Having had little background in acting, I feel that I learn from these "guests" of my psyche, because I rarely plan what they say. Some audiences ask, tongue-in-cheek, if having multiple personalities is a prerequisite to role-playing the guest speakers. Nevertheless, I notice that students and other audiences are more likely to ask questions and challenge what I say, enriching our discussions, when I "bring" my speakers.

3. I hesitate to call the four perspectives "schools of thought" in some basic sense; instead I prefer the term "tendencies" or "orientations." As a consequence of experiences in presenting these orientations or tendencies to groups of educators, and in a desire to be pedagogic in textbook writing, I "invited" them to respond to the content of each chapter in my 1986 book, *Curriculum: Perspective, Paradigm, and Possibility*.

4. Ralph W. Tyler, *Basic Principles of Curriculum and Instruction* (Chicago: University of Chicago Press, 1949).

5. Franklin Bobbitt, *The Curriculum* (Boston: Houghton Mifflin, 1918); idem, *How to Make a Curriculum* (Boston: Houghton Mifflin, 1924).

6. Mortimer J. Adler, *Six Great Ideas* (New York: Macmillan, 1981).

7. Robert Ulich, "Comments on Ralph Harper's Essay," in *Modern Philosophies and Education*, edited by Nelson B. Henry, Fifty-fourth Yearbook of the National Society for the Study of Education, Part I (Chicago: University of Chicago Press, 1955), p. 255.

8. William J. Bennett, ed., *The Book of Virtues* (New York: Simon & Schuster, 1993).

9. E.D. Hirsch, *Cultural Literacy: What Every American Needs to Know* (Boston, Mass.: Houghton Mifflin, 1987); E. D. Hirsch, *What Every Third Grader Should Know* (Boston, Mass.: Houghton Mifflin, 1992).

10. Martin Swales, *The German Bildungsroman from Wieland to Hesse* (Princeton, N.J.: Princeton University Press, 1978).

11. Gilbert Highet, *The Art of Teaching* (New York: Vintage, 1950/1977).

12. John Dewey, *Democracy and Education* (New York: Macmillan, 1916/1966), p. 76.

13. John Dewey, *A Common Faith* (New Haven, Conn.: Yale University Press, 1934).

14. Dewey, *Democracy and Education*, pp. 219-223, 286-288.

15. L. Thomas Hopkins, *The Emerging Self at School and Home* (New York: Harper and Brothers, 1954).

16. Colin Greer and Herbert Kohl, eds., *A Call to Character* (New York: Harper Collins, 1995).

17. Joel Spring, *The Sorting Machine: National Educational Policy Since 1945* (New York: David McKay, 1976).

18. Jean Anyon, "Social Class and the Hidden Curriculum of Work," *Journal of Education* 162, no. 1 (1980): 67-92.

19. Jonathan Kozol, *Savage Inequalities: Children in America's Schools* (New York: Crown, 1991).

20. George S. Counts, *Dare the School Build a New Social Order?* (New York: John Day, 1932).

21. Carter G. Woodson, *The Mis-education of the Negro* (Washington, D.C.: Associated Publishers, 1933), p. xiii.

22. Paulo Freire, *Pedagogy of the Oppressed* (New York: Continuum, 1970/1992).

CHAPTER III

Research and Practice in Character Education: A Historical Perspective

JAMES S. LEMING

An important justification for the enterprise of educational research is that a clear relationship exists between research findings and the development of educational theory and practice. It is believed that through disciplined inquiry into important educational questions more defensible theoretical perspectives and better warrants for educational practice can be developed. Additionally, the argument goes, as one uses research to identify "what works" one can make more informed and therefore better decisions about the improvement of educational practice. In this chapter I will explore the historical relationship between research into character education and the development of theory and practice in the field. I will also discuss the implications of prior research programs for the future of theory, research, and practice in the current character education movement.

When discussing the broad-based effort of educators to influence the morals, values, and character of youth, I will use the following terminology. *Values education*, with a focus on moral as well as nonmoral values, will be used only when discussing values clarification. The term *moral education* will be reserved for use with the Kohlbergian approach with its focus on questions of moral obligations and moral values. *Character education* will be used in discussions of early (1920s and 1930s) and current character education movements.

Three Case Studies

In order to show how educational research has affected the development of theory and practice in moral/values/character education, I will analyze three significant character-related educational movements earlier in this century and the related research. The first of these was the character education movement of the 1920s and 1930s. The classic

---

James S. Leming is Professor of Education at Southern Illinois University.

Hartshorne and May *Studies in the Nature of Character*[1] was the most significant research during this era. The other two movements, values clarification and Lawrence Kohlberg's cognitive developmental approach to moral education, appeared concurrently in the 1970s and 1980s. Both were researched extensively. I will review the research programs developed during this period. Finally, I shall examine the current status of research in the character education movement.

STUDIES IN THE NATURE OF CHARACTER: THE HARTSHORNE AND MAY INQUIRY

At the 1922 meeting of the Religious Education Association a resolution was passed endorsing a research study to answer the question "How is religion being taught to young people and with what effect?"[2] In the spring of 1924 the Institute of Social and Religious Research, at the request of the Religious Education Association, agreed to fund research on this question. Hugh Hartshorne of the University of Southern California and Mark May of Syracuse University agreed to serve as co-directors. Eventually, the inquiry was housed at Teachers College, Columbia University under the immediate supervision of Professor Edward L. Thorndike. The agreement with Teachers College called for a three-year "inquiry into character education with particular reference to religious education."[3] The inquiry was set to begin September 1, 1924, with all funds supplied by the Institute of Social and Religious Research.[4] In 1926 the grant was extended for two additional years, making the grant a five-year study.

Whereas the motivation for and the original thrust of the inquiry was to examine influence of character and religious education on youth character, by the time Hartshorne and May designed the study, this goal had become a matter of only minor concern. Hartshorne and May's research design called for a primary study along with seven secondary studies. The primary study focused on the development of a large body of standardized test material for use in the field of moral and religious education. Tests were to be developed in the areas of knowledge and skills, attitude, opinion and motive, conduct, and self-control. Student character was assessed through innovative classroom tests of honesty (deceit) and altruism or prosocial behavior (service).

Of the seven areas that constituted the focus of the secondary study, only three were actually included in the study. The three secondary studies focused on the problem of traits—the interrelations of conduct, knowledge, attitudes, and opinions; the problem of causes and significance—the biological and social concomitants of conduct, knowledge, attitudes, etc.; and the problem of efficacy—the results of current techniques purporting to develop character and certain habits.

As the study evolved, the focus clearly shifted from a case of applied research to basic research. That is, instead of a study designed to focus on structures and processes as they appear in education practice with a view to developing knowledge that is useful to practitioners, the focus of the research was on the fundamental structure of character. Of the final 1,782 pages of text in the three-volume report, only 50 pages, or 3 percent of the total, reported data on the influence that character and religious education programs have on youth.

The sample, drawn primarily from private and public schools situated in eastern metropolitan areas of the United States, consisted of 10,850 students in grades five through eight. Hartshorne and May attempted to use representative samples combining various levels of socioeconomic status (SES), ethnic groups, types of communities, and intelligence levels.

The research design of the portion of the study that assessed the impact of religious and character education programs was flawed. When describing the small subsample of students enrolled in religious and moral education programs, the authors admit that the "educational agencies . . . were selected by accident rather than design."[5] Hartshorne and May appropriately warned against any attempt to generalize from their apparently atypical sample. Additionally, Hartshorne and May measured students' behavior on only two character traits (deceit and service). Character education programs of the time had a much broader focus. Hartshorne and May also did little to establish if these programs represented high-quality or poor-quality efforts at religious or character education.

Thus, the Hartshorne and May study was not, as sometimes reported, primarily a study of the character education movement of the 1920s and 1930s. By reading between the lines one can infer some of the puzzlement that the funders must have felt upon receiving the final report. Galen Fisher, the Executive Secretary of the Institute of Social and Religious Research, presents the following interpretation: "To lay minds this volume, at first glance, may seem overloaded with matter that has little to do with moral and religious education. . . . Such readers may profitably reflect that these preliminary processes are inevitable if character education is to evolve from guesswork to science. . . . It must be left to time and the experts to pass judgment on the daring work done by Professors Hartshorne and May."[6]

The findings of Hartshorne and May still reverberate today among those concerned with the education of character. The lasting significance of the study is due in no small part to the meticulous and careful job of instrument construction and the innovative methods of assessing character-related behavior in school settings. To date, there has been no similar inquiry that combines the quality of research and sample size employed in this study.

The findings of the study represented a potential double body blow to the enterprise of character and religious education. The primary finding regarding the nature of character was that children cannot be divided into honest and dishonest categories. It was found that honesty in one situation does not predict well to other situations. In other words, character was found to be situationally specific.

With regard to the efficacy of character and religious education in promoting character, the authors concluded that "the mere urging of honest behavior by teachers or the discussion of standards and ideals . . . has no necessary relation to conduct. . . . The prevailing ways of inculcating ideals probably do little good and may do some harm."[7]

The historical record is not clear as to the impact that this inquiry had on the practice of character and religious education. Even though there is good reason to believe that the movement was widespread and vigorous, educational historians have largely ignored it.[8] In three short histories of the character education movement there is no discussion of the impact of the Hartshorne and May inquiry on practice, or of reasons for the eventual decline of the movement.[9]

One common interpretation of the impact of the Hartshorne and May inquiry on the character education movement is seen in this statement: "From a research perspective the death blow to character education was delivered by Hartshorne and May's famous research on character."[10] To support this claim, Power, Higgins, and Kohlberg made an analysis of entries under "character" in *Education Index*. They found that the number of entries dropped 85 percent between 1930 and 1940.[11] In a similar analysis of published research articles devoted to character education, Stanhope found 480 articles on character education published between 1929 and 1938, but only 115 published between 1939 and 1948—a decline of 76 percent.[12] Based on the number of published articles on character education, interest in the subject had declined markedly by the decade of the 1940s.

However, the question that remains is, "Was the decline in published citations followed by a similar decline in the practice of character education in schools?" For example, the mid-1930s was a time of intense effort with regard to character education. A number of books intended to assist teachers in character education were published throughout the 1930s.[13] These authors did not view the Hartshorne and May findings as damaging to the cause of character education. Instead, the common interpretation was that the measurement field was still new and not completely reliable, and that the variables measured were few in number and did not include many of the important outcomes of character education. May and Hartshorne themselves suggested that current practice simply needed to be improved somewhat by focusing less on direct methods of instruction such as lecture and exhortation and more on indirect methods such as the creation of a positive school climate and service-oriented activities for students.[14] They did not seem to feel that the enterprise of character education should be abandoned.

A review of educational writing about character education in the decade of the 1930s shows no clear recognition that a death blow had been delivered to character education by Hartshorne and May's research. McClellan suggests that character education did not decline, but simply was transformed by the times: "Both the Second World War and the early stages of the cold war seemed to emphasize the importance of character . . . and schools offered a rich variety of activities to promote moral and civic growth."[15] Additionally, innovations related to character education, such as homerooms, student clubs, and grades on conduct or citizenship on report cards have persisted into the present era. What appears to have happened is that writing about character education gradually declined while many school practices related to character education slowly changed in response to shifts in societal and educational priorities.

If we look at the past through our current experience with basic research into educational questions, it is not surprising that Hartshorne and May's report had little impact on educational practice. Its length and the minor emphasis given to the impact on school curriculum would seem to insure that it would not achieve wide readership. In addition, the nascent field of educational research was not widely accepted by school personnel in the 1930s and 1940s. Even today it is a frequent lament among educational researchers that research findings seem to have little impact on practice.

Given the relative constancy of the teacher-centered method of instruction in American schools,[16] it appears unlikely that the use of the traditional direct method of character education changed substantially in the direction suggested by the May and Hartshorne study.[17]

Research on Values Clarification

The year 1966 signaled the beginning of a new period of interest in the values of youth. *Values and Teaching*, co-authored by Louis E. Raths, Merrill Harmin, and Sidney Simon, was the highly influential first statement of the theory and technique of "values clarification."[18] This approach to values education along with the cognitive developmental approach to moral education of Lawrence Kohlberg, dominated the field of moral or values education for the next twenty years.

It is difficult to judge exactly how much impact values clarification had on educational practice. It is clear, however, that the values clarification approach was far more popular with teachers than Kohlberg's approach. For example, one handbook of practical strategies for values clarification sold over 600,000 copies,[19] an almost unheard of figure for a textbook on educational methods.

During the culturally and morally turbulent era of the 1960s and 1970s, the proponents of values clarification interpreted the dramatic changes occurring in youth conduct to be the result of confusion in values. The proposed solution was not to attempt to restore a sense of traditional values to youth, but rather to assist them in clarifying their current values. To achieve this greater clarity, students were to follow the prescribed seven-step valuing process. The theory of values clarification held that "if we occasionally focus students' attention on issues in their lives, and if we stimulate students to consider their choices, their prizings, and their actions, then the students will change behavior, demonstrating more purposeful, proud, positive, and enthusiastic behavior patterns."[20] The teacher was urged to be only a facilitator of the valuing process and, for fear of influencing students, was to withhold his or her own opinions. Whatever value the students arrived at, they were to be respected by the teacher.

A vigorous research program evolved based on the values clarification approach. Between 1969 and 1985, seventy-four studies using school-aged youth were conducted where values clarification strategies served as the independent variable.[21] An equal number of studies utilizing adult samples were conducted. Of the studies utilizing school-aged subjects, sixty-eight were doctoral dissertations, five were published articles, and one an ERIC document. In general, the studies were of five weeks' duration or longer, consisted of a lesson per week, utilized a true or quasi-experimental design, were equally spread between elementary, middle or junior high school, and high school, and were carried out in a wide range of subject matter areas. A consistent pattern of findings emerged from these studies: only limited success was achieved in detecting significant changes in the dependent variables.[22]

Values clarification researchers utilized a wide range of dependent variables such as personal values, self-concept, attitudes toward the subject matter and the school, dogmatism, and value-related behavior. While the percentage of the studies finding the predicted results varies from dependent variable to dependent variable, the predicted change in a given variable is seldom found in more than 20 percent of the studies.[23] For example, in the fourteen studies that assessed increases in self-concept, only four found a statistically significant effect. Similarly, in the twenty-one studies that assessed changes in personal values as the dependent variable, only three detected statistically significant changes.

One would anticipate that such a pattern of findings would be unsettling to the proponents of values clarification and would result in the rethinking of the theory, the method, or the research design; however, the research findings apparently had no impact on the development of the theory or practice. In the second edition of *Values and Teaching*, published in 1978, twelve years after the first edition, the theory remained unchanged. Research studies conducted in the late 1970s and early 1980s continued to examine the same hypotheses and to use the same dependent variables as earlier studies.[24] The proponents began to change the theory and technique of values clarification only when subjected to devastating socio-moral critiques. It was not until ten years after the second edition of *Values and Teaching*, in 1988, that changes in the theory and practice of values clarification were finally proposed.[25] Typical of the proposed changes was the suggestion by Merrill Harmin that values clarification should now promote "practices that advance our (teachers') values and practices that advance the clarifying process."[26] How a teacher was to deal with the inevitable conflict between being an advocate for a set of moral behaviors and at the same time serving as an impartial clarifier of students' valuing processes was not spelled out.

One reason for the lack of impact of quantitative research findings on theory and practice in values clarification was that its proponents interpreted the existing research as supporting their claims. For example, in a 1977 article entitled "In Defense of Values Clarification" the authors state that "80 percent of the studies lend credibility to the assertion that the use of the valuing process leads to greater personal value (e.g., less apathy, higher self-esteem, etc.), and greater social constructiveness (lower drug abuse, less disruptive classroom behavior, etc.)."[27] This claim was made in spite of the fact that between 1973 and 1977 only 20 percent of the twenty-nine doctoral dissertations completed found a positive effect for values clarification.[28] Eleven years later, Merrill Harmin noted that "according to my reading of the available research, we can expect recommendations like the ones presented here to make a difference."[29] Rather than relying upon dissertation research and published articles, the proponents of values clarification tended to rely on "reports"—unpublished studies that typically did not control for potential sources of bias. Additionally, they tended to interpret trends in the data that were not statistically significant as supportive of the methodology.

The will to believe in the values clarification method, coupled with the willingness to suspend critical judgment in the interpretation of research, led many individuals, in spite of the evidence to the contrary, to believe the methodology was efficacious. In the end, however, it was not empirical research that resulted in the decline of values clarification; rather it was careful scholarly critique that exposed the major flaws in the moral perspective at the heart of values clarification. Critics pointed out the ethical relativism inherent in the approach, namely, that everyone's values resulting from the clarification process must be treated as acceptable. Additionally, critics identified striking similarities between Rogerian counseling and the values clarification process. Critics also demonstrated how the values clarification process frequently involved public intrusions into matters that posed potential threats to individual rights to privacy.[30] The power of these critiques, coupled with an emerging conservative political climate in the country, contributed to a state where values clarification became anathema in most schools. As Howard Kirschenbaum noted in 1992, values clarification had fallen so out of favor with educators that "some administrators today would rather be accused of having asbestos in their ceilings than of using values clarification in their classrooms."[31]

KOHLBERG'S COGNITIVE DEVELOPMENTAL APPROACH

In 1969, Moshe Blatt, a doctoral student at the University of Chicago, first demonstrated how Kohlberg's cognitive developmental theory of moral development could be applied to the practice of moral education. Blatt hypothesized that if children were systematically exposed to moral conflict accompanied by the presentation of moral reasoning one stage above their own, they would be attracted to that reasoning and attempt to adopt it for their own. He found that after a twelve-week program of systematically exposing students to moral dilemmas and "plus one" reasoning, 64 percent of his students had developed one full stage in their moral reasoning.[32] In the moral dilemma discussion approach that developed out of Blatt's research, the teacher's role was to serve as a facilitator of the student's reasoning—to assist the student in resolving issues of moral conflict and to insure that the environment in which the discussion took place contained the conditions essential for stage growth in moral reasoning.

Reviews of the extensive research on the use of discussion of moral dilemmas have reached similar conclusions,[33] namely, that in approximately 80 percent of the semester-length studies a mean upward shift of one-fourth to one-half stage in student reasoning will result when students are engaged in the process of discussing moral dilemmas where cognitive disequilibrium and exposure to examples of the next highest stage of moral reasoning are present. A review that utilized meta analysis techniques with data from James Rest's "Defining Issues Test" found that the mean effect size for studies using the dilemma discussion method was .41, a change equivalent to four or five years' natural growth.[34]

The achievement of predicted results in studies of the moral discussion approach must be interpreted cautiously. First, the stage growth detected as a result of moral discussion among school-aged subjects is in the stage two, three, and four range and it is small—usually less than one-third of a stage for interventions of at least one semester. Second, none of the "plus one" studies reviewed used any form of social or moral behavior as a dependent variable. Kohlberg and his associates did argue that moral reasoning and moral behavior were related at the principled level;[35] however, only weak associations between moral reasoning and moral behavior have been detected and these associations lack practical significance among school-aged populations.[36] One research study found that among fourth and eighth grade students stage 1 and stage 3 levels of moral reasoning are associated with fewer conduct problems than stage 2 reasoning.[37] Although Kohlberg was not proposing that behavioral development would mirror cognitive development at the lower stages, this finding raised the possibility that development in students' moral reasoning from stage 1 to stage 2 may actually be associated with a deterioration in student conduct. Thus, even though discussion of moral dilemmas proved to be successful in facilitating stage development, it provided little practical guidance for teachers in their efforts to influence students' personal and social behavior.

Although the research is largely supportive of the claim that discussion of moral dilemmas is successful at stimulating stage development, in the late 1970s Kohlberg's perspective on moral education underwent a major change. This change did not specifically grow out of the "plus one" research program, however, but rather out of a realization that the approach did not address the more practical concerns of parents and school personnel—student behavior and discipline. As Kohlberg noted in 1978, "I realize now that the psychologists' abstraction of moral cognition . . . is not a sufficient guide to the moral educator who deals with the moral concrete in the school world; . . . the educator must be a socializer."[38] It is clear that the major impetus to change in the cognitive developmental theory or moral education came from outside the "plus one" research program. Kohlberg's personal experiences with educational programs in prisons and tough schools, criticisms regarding the value neutrality of the approach, and Kohlberg's own increasing appreciation of the views of the French sociologist Emile Durkheim, were all powerful influences that led Kohlberg to shift his focus as a moral educator to the moral atmosphere of the school—the just community.[39]

Current Status of Research in Character Education

A perspective on the current status of research in character education can be gained by examining the current research from four sources that have served as significant outlets for the community of researchers working on moral, values, or character education: (1) *Journal of Moral Education*, (2) *Moral Education Forum*, (3) programs of the annual meetings of the Special Interest Group on Moral Development and Education of the American Educational Research Association, and (4) programs of the annual meetings of the Association for Moral Education. While these four sources certainly do not exhaust all possible outlets for research in this area, they are popular venues that researchers frequently seek out to communicate their research findings.[40]

Contents of the two journals and the programs of the two annual meetings were analyzed for the years 1993, 1994, and 1995. The total number of articles and papers or presentations for the four sources for these years was 411. The citations were categorized into one of five types of research. First, there were *psychological inquiries* into the nature of morality. Seeking to describe the nature of moral experience, these studies typically collected and analyzed data on morally relevant variables in order to develop a more complete understanding of the nature of moral development and moral experience. Second, a small number of articles or papers reported on the development or characteristics of new *measurement techniques* for quantifying variables relevant to the study of moral education. Third, there were *philosophical inquiries* into the nature of moral language and experience. These inquiries focused on language in order to achieve greater clarity regarding language and/or greater understanding of the philosophical assumptions underlying positions on moral education. Typically, these articles or papers were part of an ongoing debate that was as old as Plato and Aristotle. A fourth category consisted of articles or papers that *described, advocated, analyzed,* or *critiqued* moral education programs. Finally, there were articles or papers focused on *program evaluation,* attempting to answer the question of whether specific programs yield educationally significant outcomes.

The category for program description, advocacy, and analysis contained the largest number of articles or papers—172 of a total of 411 items (42 percent). The psychological inquiry category contained 152 items (37 percent). There were 52 items (12 percent) in the category for philosophical inquiries. Two categories were only minimally represented in these sources. Eighteen articles or papers (4 percent) focused on measurement techniques and seventeen (4 percent) assessed program effectiveness. Overall, only 8 percent of these articles or papers addressed questions concerned with assessment and program effectiveness.

The current character education movement lacks either a theoretical perspective or a common core of practice. The movement is eclectic both in terms of its psychological premises and its pedagogical practices. No common perspective exists to provide a basis for a coherent research program. Given the small number of quantitative inquiries into program effectiveness, it is not clear that research can inform practice at this time. It is also unlikely that theory can be built from practice unless the field begins to take research on program effectiveness more seriously.

Final Comments

I have argued that quantitative research has not been as important as other forms of inquiry in shaping the development of theory and practice in the area of moral/values/character education in this century. The forces that appear to have had the most dramatic effect on character-related educational movements have come from outside the ongoing quantitative research in the field.

Changes in the theory and practice of educational programs designed to affect the character of youth have resulted more from questions of values than from questions of data. In the case of the early character education movement, historical events, primarily the onset of World War II, had a major impact on its direction. In the case of values clarification and the cognitive development approach, the shift toward more conservative cultural values in the 1980s focused public attention on the lack of focus on "good conduct" in these approaches. When disciplined inquiry did appear to have an impact on the development of theory and practice in character education, it was scholarly critique rather than quantitative inquiry.

The conclusion reached here should not be interpreted as suggesting that research into program effectiveness in this area is unimportant. All educators have a moral responsibility to insure, to the extent possible, that their practices have, on balance, the maximum positive impact on individual development. However, researchers working in this area need to be aware that their goals and methods will not be judged solely on the basis of research design, quality, and results achieved. Equally important will be the judgment of careful scholarly critique. Ultimately, the force and direction of educational practice in the area of character education will be influenced only in part by the pattern of research findings. Instead, the future of character education will likely depend on the values that underlie the chosen approach and the degree to which those assumptions and values are perceived as congruent with the values and needs of the communities served. Research that supports program effectiveness is only one part of the warrant for character education programs.

NOTES

1. Hugh Hartshorne and Mark May, *Studies in the Nature of Character,* Vol. 1: *Studies in Deceit;* Vol. 2: *Studies in Self Control;* Vol. 3: *Studies in the Organization of Character* (New York: Macmillan, 1928-1930).

2. Hartshorne and May, *Studies in the Nature of Character*, Vol. 1, p. v.

3. Ibid., p. vi.

4. The Institute of Social and Religious Research was established and funded by John D. Rockefeller.

5. Hartshorne and May, *Studies in the Nature of Character*, Vol. 1, p. 339.

6. Ibid., Vol. 2, pp. v-vi.

7. Ibid., Vol. 1, p. 413.

8. For example, see Lawrence A. Cremin, *The Transformation of the School: Progressivism in American Education 1876-1957* (New York: Random House, 1961); Daniel Tanner and Laurel Tanner, *History of the School Curriculum* (New York: Macmillan, 1990); Joel Spring, *The American School*, 3rd ed. (New York: McGraw-Hill, 1994); Herbert M. Kliebard, *The Struggle for the American Curriculum* (New York: Routledge, 1989).

9. William E. Chapman, *Roots of Character Education: An Exploration of the American Heritage from the Decade of the 1920s* (Schenectady, N.Y.: Character Research Press, 1977); B. Edward McClellan, *Schools and the Shaping of Character: Moral Education in America, 1607–Present* (Bloomington, Ind.: ERIC Clearing House for Social Studies/ Social Science and Education and the Social Studies Development Center, Indiana University, 1992); Steven M. Yulish, *The Search for a Civic Religion: A History of the Character Education Movement in America, 1890-1935* (Washington, D.C.: University Press of America, 1980).

10. Clark Power, Ann Higgins, and Lawrence Kohlberg, "The Habit of the Common Life: Building Character through Democratic Community Schools," in *Moral Development and Character Education: A Dialogue*, edited by Larry P. Nucci (Berkeley, Calif.: McCutchan, 1989), pp. 125-143.

11. Ibid., p. 128.

12. Rebecca A. Stanhope, "Character Education: A Compilation of Literature in the Field from 1929 to 1991," Doct. diss., University of Pittsburgh, 1992.

13. For example, see Kenneth L. Heaton, *The Character Emphasis in Education: A Collection of Materials and Methods* (Chicago: University of Chicago Press, 1933) and Harry C. McKown, *Character Education* (New York: McGraw-Hill, 1935).

14. Mark A. May and Hugh Hartshorne, "Experimental Studies in Moral Education," *Religious Education* 22 (1927): 710-718.

15. McClellan, *Schools and the Shaping of Character*, p. 79.

16. Larry Cuban, *How Teachers Taught: Constancy and Change in American Classrooms 1890-1980* (New York: Longman, 1984).

17. May and Hartshorne, "Experimental Studies in Moral Education."

18. Louis E. Raths, Merrill Harmin, and Sidney B. Simon, *Values and Teaching* (Columbus, Ohio: Charles E. Merrill, 1966).

19. Howard Kirschenbaum, "A Comprehensive Model for Values Education and Moral Education," *Phi Delta Kappan* 73 (June, 1992): 772.

20. Raths, Harmin, and Simon, *Values and Teaching*, p. 248.

21. James S. Leming, "Values Clarification Research: A Study of the Etiology of a Weak Educational Research Program" (Paper presented at the Annual Meeting of the American Educational Research Association, Washington, D.C., 1987).

22. James S. Leming, "Curricular Effectiveness in Moral/Values Education: A Review of Research," *Journal of Moral Education* 10 (May, 1981): 147-164; idem, "Research on Social Studies Curriculum and Instruction: Interventions and Outcomes in the Socio-Moral Domain," in *Review of Research in Social Studies Education: 1976-1983*, edited by William B. Stanley (Washington, D.C., National Council for the Social Studies and Social Science Education Consortium (1985), pp. 123-213; idem, "Values Clarification Research"; Alan Lockwood, "The Effects of Values Clarification and Moral Development Curricula on School-Age Subjects: A Critical Review of Recent Research," *Review of Educational Research* 48 (Summer, 1978): 325-364.

23. Leming, "Values Clarification Research."

24. Idem.

25. Merrill Harmin, "Value Clarity, High Morality: Let's Go for Both," *Educational Leadership* 45 (May, 1988): 24-30; Kirschenbaum, "A Comprehensive Model for Values Education and Moral Education," pp. 771-776.

26. Harmin, "Value Clarity, High Morality."

27. Howard Kirschenbaum, Merrill Harmin, Leland Howe, and Sidney B. Simon, "In Defense of Values Clarification," *Phi Delta Kappan* 58 (June, 1977): 743-747.

28. Leming, "Values Clarification Research."

29. Harmin, "Value Clarity, High Morality," p. 30.

30. See Alan L. Lockwood, "A Critical View of Values Clarification," *Teachers College Record* 77 (September, 1975): 35-50; and idem, "Values Education and the Right to Privacy," *Journal of Moral Education* 7 (October, 1977): 9-26 for good examples of the critiques of values clarification.

31. Kirschenbaum, "A Comprehensive Model for Values Education and Moral Education," p. 773.

32. Moshe Blatt, "The Effects of Classroom Moral Discussion upon Children's Moral Judgment," Doct. diss., University of Chicago, 1969; Moshe Blatt and Lawrence Kohlberg, "The Effects of Classroom Moral Discussion upon Children's Moral Judgment," *Journal of Moral Education* 4 (February, 1975): 121-161.

33. Robert Enright, Daniel K. Lapsley, and Victor M. Levy, "Moral Education Strategies," in *Cognitive Strategy Research: Educational Applications*, edited by Michael Pressley and Joel R. Levin (New York: Springer-Verlag, 1983), pp. 43-83; Judith A. Lawrence, "Moral Judgment Intervention Studies Using the Defining Issues Test," *Journal of Moral Education* 9 (May, 1980): 178-191; Leming, "Curricular Effectiveness in Moral/Values Education"; idem, "Research on Social Studies Curriculum and Instruction"; Lockwood, "The Effects of Values Clarification and Moral Development Curricula on School-Age Subjects."

34. Andre Schlaefli, James Rest, and Steven Thoma, "Does Moral Education Improve Moral Judgment? A Meta-analysis of Intervention Studies Using the Defining Issues Test," *Review of Educational Research* 55 (Fall, 1985): 319-352.

35. Lawrence Kohlberg and Dan Candee, "The Relationship of Moral Judgment to Moral Action," in *Essays on Moral Development*, Vol. 2, *The Philosophy of Moral Development*, edited by Lawrence Kohlberg (San Francisco: Harper and Row, 1984), pp. 498-581.

36. Augusto Blasi, "Bridging Moral Cognition and Moral Action: A Critical Review of the Literature," *Psychological Bulletin* 88 (July, 1980): 1-45.

37. Herbert C. Richards, George G. Bear, Anne L. Stewart, and Antony D. Norman, "Moral Reasoning and Classroom Conduct: Evidence of a Curvilinear Relationship," *Merrill-Palmer Quarterly* 38 (April 1992): 176-190.

38. Lawrence Kohlberg, "Moral Education Reappraised," *The Humanist* 38 (November 1978): 14.

39. F. Clark Power, Ann Higgins, and Lawrence Kohlberg, *Lawrence Kohlberg's Approach to Moral Education* (New York: Columbia University Press, 1989).

40. The current character education movement lacks a research journal or professional meetings that feature educational research. At present there are two major character education meetings each year: the annual meetings of the Character Education Partnership and of the National Conference on Character Education. The programs of both of these meetings, while recognizing the importance of educational research, are primarily venues for the exchange of information about existing programs.

Section Two
TRADITIONALIST VIEWS OF CHARACTER AND CHARACTER EDUCATION

CHAPTER IV

Educating for Character: A Comprehensive Approach

THOMAS LICKONA

There are at least three compelling reasons for schools to engage in character education. The first is that we need good character to be fully human. We need strengths of mind, heart, and will—qualities like good judgment, honesty, empathy, caring, perseverance, and self-discipline—to be capable of love and work, two of the hallmarks of human maturity.

Second, schools are better places—certainly more conducive to teaching and learning—when they are communities of virtue in which qualities of character such as honesty, respect, diligence, and kindness are modeled, expected, taught, celebrated, and continually practiced.

Third, character education is essential to the task of building a moral society. It is painfully clear that our contemporary society suffers severe social and moral problems: the breakdown of the family, an epidemic of violence, the deterioration of civility, rampant greed at a time when one of four children is poor, dishonesty at all levels of society, a rising tide of sleaze in the media, a plague of problems stemming from the breakdown of sexual morality, widespread drug and alcohol abuse, the physical and sexual abuse of children, declining respect for life, and the moral schizophrenia of championing the rights of children after birth while permitting their violent destruction before birth. These societal problems have deep roots and require systemic solutions, but it is not possible to build a virtuous society if virtue does not first exist in

Thomas Lickona is Professor of Education and Director of the Center for the 4th and 5th Rs at the State University of New York at Cortland, New York.

the minds, hearts, and souls of individual human beings. The school, like the family, is one of the primary seedbeds of virtue.

What is character education? It can be defined as the intentional, proactive effort to develop good character. Qualities of good character are called virtues. Virtues such as the cardinal virtues of prudence, justice, temperance, and fortitude advanced by the ancient Greeks are objectively good human qualities. They are good for the individual— they help a person lead a fulfilling life—and they are good for the whole human community. The virtues provide the moral content that defines good character.

Every virtue has three parts: moral knowledge, moral feeling, and moral behavior. To possess the virtue of justice, for example, I must first understand what justice is and what justice requires of me in human relations (moral knowledge). I must also care about justice—be emotionally committed to it, have the capacity for appropriate guilt when I behave unjustly, and be capable of moral indignation when I see others suffer unjustly (moral feeling). Finally, I must practice justice by acting fairly in my personal relations and carrying out my obligation as a citizen to help advance social justice (moral behavior). Thus, in order to develop virtuous character, the young must come to know what the virtues are, appreciate their importance and want to possess them, and practice them in their day-to-day conduct. Character education thus conceived seeks to develop a morality of the head, the heart, and the hand.

What is a comprehensive approach to character education? It is one that seeks to develop full moral character—its cognitive, emotional, and behavioral aspects—and to do so through the total moral life of the school. This comprehensive approach challenges educators to look at school through a moral lens; to see and capitalize on the many opportunities school provides for influencing character development. From this perspective, the way adults treat students, the way students treat adults, the way students are permitted to treat each other, the way the administration treats staff and parents, the way sports are conducted, conflicts resolved, and grades given—all these send moral messages and affect character.

Drawing on our work with teachers and schools, our Center for the 4th and 5th Rs (respect and responsibility) at the State University of New York at Cortland offers a character education model that attempts to encompass the total moral life of the school.[1] This model consists of twelve mutually supportive strategies, nine for the classroom and three that are schoolwide. These twelve strategies are shown in the accompanying character education wheel (Figure 1). This framework, I believe, can help a school to be intentional in fostering character development in all that it does. In the rest of the chapter, I will briefly explain and illustrate each of the twelve strategies.[2]

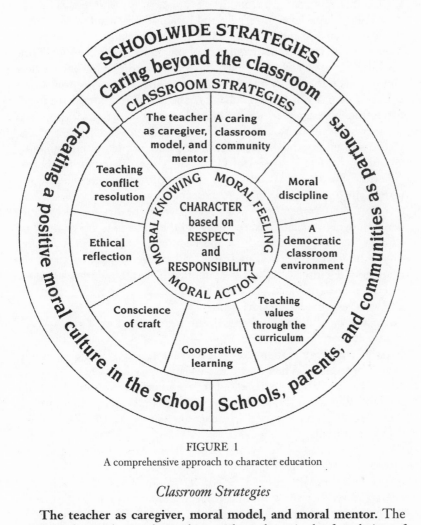

FIGURE 1
A comprehensive approach to character education

Classroom Strategies

The teacher as caregiver, moral model, and moral mentor. The quality of a teacher's relationships with students is the foundation of everything else a teacher may wish to do in character education. In their relationships with students, teachers can exert positive moral influence through three complementary roles. First, they can serve as *effective caregivers*—loving and respecting their students, helping them succeed at the work of school, building their self-respect by treating each student as having worth and dignity, and enabling students to gain a firsthand appreciation of the meaning of morality by being treated in a moral way. Second, they can serve as *moral models*—demonstrating a high level of respect and responsibility inside and outside the classroom and modeling moral concern by taking time to discuss morally significant events from school life and current events. Third, they can serve as *ethical mentors*—providing direct moral instruction and guidance through explanation, storytelling, classroom discussion, encouragement of positive behavior, and corrective moral feedback when students engage in actions hurtful to self or others.

What does this process look like at the high school level, where teachers often say the press of academics does not leave them time to attend to character issues? Hal Urban is an award-winning teacher of American History at Woodside High School in Redwood City, California, and author of the book *20 Things I Want My Kids to Know: Passing On Life's Greatest Lessons.*[3] In recent years, he has found his students showing a lack of basic courtesy in the classroom. He decided to address the problem directly at the beginning of the school year by giving his classes a handout titled "Whatever Happened to Good Manners?" He prefaced this by saying that he has found the classroom to be a more enjoyable place for all when everyone treats everyone else with respect and consideration.

Listed on the handout, under the heading "How Things Were Different Not Too Many Years Ago," were a series of Urban's observations of changing student behavior. For instance, "Students rarely came late to class. When they did, they apologized. Today many come late. Only rarely does one apologize." Another observation: "Students used to listen when the teacher was talking. Today many students feel they have a right to ignore the teacher and have a private conversation with their friends."

Under this list of behavioral observations were several questions, such as: "Why is this happening?" "Is a society better when people treat each other with respect?" "Is a classroom better when both students and teacher show mutual respect?" Each student was asked to think about these questions and write a paragraph in response. Mr. Urban then collected the students' written responses and used them as a springboard for a class discussion of manners.

Urban comments: "This simple exercise made a noticeable difference in the behavior of my students. Later in the semester, several students told me they wished all of their teachers would discuss manners

in the classroom, because it improved the atmosphere for learning."
At the end of the course one student wrote: "That manners page you
handed out really made me think. Sometimes we do rude things and
aren't even aware we're being rude." Mr. Urban's discussion of manners illustrates how the teacher can serve as a character educator by
acting as a caregiver, model, and direct moral guide.

Creating a caring classroom community. Many teachers do a conscientious job of fostering respect and caring in their relationships
with their students but feel much less successful when it comes to
establishing these values as operative norms in the student peer group.
That is a problem because the peer culture is a powerful influence on
student conduct and character. If teachers do not take the initiative to
shape a positive peer culture—one that supports the virtues adults are
trying to teach—the peer culture will often develop in the opposite
direction, creating peer norms that are antithetical to good character
(e.g., cruelty to schoolmates who are different, lack of academic responsibility, and disrespect for legitimate authority).

By contrast, when a teacher is successful in creating a moral classroom community, students can learn morality by living it. They receive respect and care from their peers and practice giving them in return. Through these repeated experiences, respect and care begin to
become habits—part of their developing character.

At any grade level, teachers can create this kind of positive moral
community in the classroom by helping students to (1) get to know
each other; (2) respect, care about, and affirm each other; and (3) feel a
valued membership in, and accountability to, the group.

This includes the teacher's being vigilant about peer cruelty, which
is on the rise nearly everywhere. In a third grade classroom I observed,
children excluded and repeatedly made fun of a girl named Rhonda,
who was shabbily dressed and had learning problems. No one would
eat lunch with her or play with her at recess. Rhonda's response was to
withdraw and regress to immature behavior such as "baby talk." One
day when Rhonda was absent the teacher asked Rhonda's resource-
room teacher, Laura LoParco, to speak to the class about this problem. Here is what Ms. LoParco said to help these children understand—and want to stop—the hurtful effects of their behavior:

What you are doing is hurting Rhonda here [pointing to her own head], in
her mind. You can't see the hurt, but it's very real. You can make her think that
she is stupid and the kind of person that nobody will like. That may stay in
her mind for a very long time, even years. It may affect her ability to learn and

her ability to make friends with other people. You have a decision to make: Do you wish to continue doing this?

The children said they did not wish to continue this behavior. After this discussion, students did in fact stop treating Rhonda cruelly, and many made an effort to talk and play with her.

Teachers are wise, however, to try to prevent peer cruelty from getting a foothold by being proactive in developing a supportive classroom community. How to do that is illustrated by a first grade teacher, Jan Gorman, at Meachem Elementary School in Syracuse, New York. For the first five weeks of school, she teaches a virtue a week, beginning with caring. She puts a large sign, CARING, on the board, along with a photograph depicting caring (two children working together). She then has a discussion with her children posing these questions: What is caring? Who can show caring? Where does caring take place? How can each of us show caring? In our classroom? In our school? In our families?

She makes a visual map of the children's ideas, which remains posted for the rest of the week. She then reads the class a children's book that conveys the importance of caring and leads a discussion of the story. During the rest of the day, she looks for opportunities to help children make connections between their own behavior and the virtue of caring. When a child behaves in a caring way, she compliments that child, sometimes calling the class's attention to the act of consideration or kindness. If a child behaves in an uncaring way, she speaks to the child privately, asking, "Did that show caring? Remember our story . . . remember our discussion." On each subsequent day of the week, she reads a different story about caring, has a class discussion, and again looks for opportunities during the day to reinforce the lesson.

"By the end of the week," Ms. Gorman says, "caring has been established as an expectation in my classroom." The following week, she takes another virtue—such as respect or loyalty—and repeats this process.

Moral discipline. Discipline must be a tool for character development, helping students develop moral reasoning, self-control, and a generalized respect for others. Rules should be established in a way that enables students to see the values (e.g., courtesy and caring) behind the rules. The emphasis should not be on extrinsic rewards and punishment but on following the rules because it is the right thing to do—because it respects the rights and needs of others. Consequences used to enforce rules should serve as a moral teacher, helping students understand how a given rule benefits self and others and strengthening the students' feeling of obligation to follow the rule in the future.

For example, Tom Izzo does substitute teaching at the high school level. He says, "At the beginning of each class, I tell my students that I expect them to treat their classmates, as well as me, with respect, and to be responsible for their own work and actions. I give them examples that illustrate these behaviors. For example, I tell them that no one is to speak when someone else—a classmate or me—is talking, because it is disrespectful and disturbs the lesson. If students misbehave in class, I ask them if they thought what they did was respectful or responsible—and why."

As an example of how this works, Mr. Izzo tells of an incident that occurred when he was substituting in a high school biology laboratory. One boy was copying answers from the person sitting next to him. Mr. Izzo pulled the student aside, and the following conversation ensued:

Teacher: Do you think you are following the rules I set forth at the beginning of class?

Boy: I don't know.

Teacher: I'll help you figure it out. Do you think copying someone else's work and using it as your own is being responsible?

Boy: I guess not, but it's no big deal.

Teacher: Let me give you another example. Imagine that you're a businessman working on a big report. One of your co-workers copies it and hands it in to the boss, taking credit for your idea. What would you think of that?

Boy: I see your point. It would make me mad.

Teacher: Do you think the man who copied the report was acting fairly or responsibly?

Boy: No. I never thought about it like that.

Mr. Izzo comments: "I tell my students that if they show people respect and are responsible, things will fall into place for them, and they'll have fewer hassles. Not only with teachers and other students, but also with people outside of school as well." In this way, he is teaching the important lesson that good character helps a person in life. The principal of this high school says he appreciates Tom Izzo as a substitute because he "can handle discipline problems on his own by simply talking to students." The students themselves are enthusiastic when they find out he will be teaching their class. Mr. Izzo shows how discipline problems can be a teachable moment—an opportunity for building good character.

Creating a democratic classroom environment. Creating a democratic classroom environment means involving students, on a regular basis and in developmentally appropriate ways, in shared decision making that increases their responsibility for making the classroom a good place to be and learn. A democratic classroom contributes to character because it provides a forum where any need or problem of the group can be addressed. It also provides a support structure that calls forth students' best moral selves by holding them accountable to norms of respect and responsibility.

The chief means of creating a democratic classroom environment is the class meeting, a face-to-face circle meeting emphasizing interactive discussion. Class meetings can deal with such issues as cutting in lunch line, put-downs, and homework problems, or they can help to plan upcoming events (the day, a field trip, a cooperative activity, the next unit). Most important, class meetings help students go beyond "saying the right words" to putting words into moral action.

For example, Patty Brody, a second grade teacher at a Catholic school in Syracuse, New York, called one of her first class meetings to deal with "chaos in the coat closet." It was January; the snows were deep; and at the day's end, there were angry words and jostling at the coat closet as children tried to find their boots, mittens, hats, and so on. Some children even missed the bus as a result of the confusion and conflict.

At their class meeting, Ms. Brody appropriately posed the problem in the collective moral voice: "How can we, working together, solve this problem?" After brainstorming possible solutions, the class decided that everyone should be assigned a hook; you would then put your things on or under your hook. "How are we going to make sure everyone does this?" Ms. Brody asked. A girl suggested a way that the class approved: If you didn't put your things where they belonged, you would have to keep them at your desk during the next day.

Ms. Brody then drew up a class agreement, had each of her thirty-four children sign it, posted it next to the coat closet, and set a time when they would meet again to see how their solution was working. She comments: "Since we adopted this plan, not a single person has missed the bus." Similarly, middle and high school teachers have used the class meeting to convert classroom management challenges (e.g., students talking out of turn, being tardy, not doing homework) into occasions for students to take responsibility for solving problems.

Teaching values through the curriculum. There are countless opportunities for teachers to use the ethically rich content of academic subjects—such as literature, history, science, and art—as a vehicle for teaching virtue. Mining the school curriculum for its moral potential requires teachers to look at their grade-level curriculum and ask, "What are the moral questions and lessons already present in the subject I teach? How can I make those questions and lessons salient for my students?"

A science teacher can design a lesson on the need for precise and truthful reporting of data (and how scientific fraud threatens the scientific enterprise); a social studies teacher can examine questions of social justice, actual moral dilemmas faced by historical figures, and current opportunities for civic action to better one's community or country; a literature teacher can have students analyze the moral decisions and moral strengths and weaknesses of characters in novels, plays, and short stories; a mathematics teacher can ask students to research and plot morally significant societal trends (e.g., violent crime, teen pregnancy, homelessness, children living in poverty). All teachers can engage students in the study of men and women who have achieved moral or intellectual distinction in their fields.

Teaching character through the curriculum also includes making thoughtful use of published character education curricula. The Heartwood Ethics Curriculum for Children (K-8) uses ancient and contemporary classics in children's literature from around the world to foster seven character qualities: justice, respect, honesty, courage, loyalty, hope, and love.[4] *Facing History and Ourselves*, a curriculum initially developed for eighth graders and later adapted to high school and college levels, uses history, film, and guest speakers to study the Holocaust—and has students look within themselves to probe the universal human tendency toward prejudice and scapegoating.[5] *Choosing to Participate*, which grew out of the Facing History curriculum, has students study all the ways people have historically participated—through human service, politics, social activism, and other voluntary activity—in creating a society that seeks justice and dignity for all its members; students are then encouraged to conceive and carry out social action projects of their own.[6] The *Art of Loving Well*, described by its creators as an "anti-impulse curriculum" for junior high and high school English and health classes, uses an anthology of short stories, poems, essays, and folk tales to help students reflect on romance, love, commitment, and marriage.[7] In a federally funded evaluation that used anonymous self-report questionnaires to survey several thousand students, 92 percent of the students who experienced the *Art of Loving Well* curriculum were still abstinent two years later, compared to 72 percent of the control group.[8]

Cooperative Learning. How can schools use the instructional process to develop character? Cooperative learning is one way. It gives students regular practice in developing important social and moral competencies, such as the ability to take perspective, work as part of a team, and appreciate others, at the same time that they are learning academic material. Cooperative learning also contributes to the development of a cohesive and caring classroom community by breaking down ethnic, racial, and other social barriers and integrating every student into the small social structure of the cooperative group.

For example, in a sixth-grade classroom in Montreal, Quebec, a teacher faced the most divisive group she had ever taught. The class was torn apart by racial conflict; blacks and whites exchanged insults and physically assaulted each other during recess and after school. The school psychologist observed the class and recommended that the teacher set up structured cooperative learning groups. Put together children who have trouble getting along, he said. Give them joint assignments and projects with roles for all members. Monitor them closely and teach them to monitor themselves. Most important, stick with the groups even if they don't seem to be working in the beginning.

The teacher started having students work together, usually in threes or fours, in all subjects for part of each day. They worked on mathematics problems in groups, researched social studies questions in groups, practiced reading to each other in groups, and so on. "It took them two months to really make this work," the teacher said, "but they finally got it together. Moreover, their test scores went up." Mastering the skills of cooperative learning is a gradual developmental process for both teacher and students, but the benefits for academics and character development, benefits that are documented at all grade levels,[9] justify the effort.

The conscience of craft. The literature on moral and character education often treats moral learning and academic learning as separate spheres. But academic work and learning have moral meaning. Work is one of the most basic ways we develop self-discipline and self-worth and contribute to the human community. It is a mark of people's character when they take care to perform their jobs and other tasks well. Thomas Green, a professor at Syracuse University, calls this a "conscience of craft"—the capacity to feel satisfaction at a job well done and to be ashamed of slovenly work.[10]

Teachers who effectively develop students' work-related character traits typically combine high expectations and high support. For example, Anne Ritter is the kind of teacher who believes that every child can learn. As a new teacher in her school, she taught a class of first graders, 85 percent of whom came from families below the poverty line. She astonished fellow teachers by getting 90 percent of her class up to grade level in reading and mathematics. Her comment: "It's the job."

When I visited her classroom, a list of classroom rules was writ large and posted in the front. The first rule was: "Always do your best in everything." On the wall was a sign: A PERSON WILL SELF-DE-STRUCT WITHOUT A GOAL. The "value of the month" featured on the class bulletin board was AMBITION, defined as "hard work directed toward a worthwhile goal."

Ethical reflection. This strategy focuses on developing several qualities that make up the cognitive side of character: being morally alert; knowing the virtues and what they require of us in concrete situations; being able to take the perspective of others; being able to reason morally; being able to make thoughtful moral decisions; and having moral self-knowledge, including the capacity for self-criticism.

Especially important is teaching students what the virtues are, how their habitual practice will lead to a more fulfilling life, and how each of us must take responsibility for developing our own character. The psychologist Patricia Cronin has designed a junior high school curriculum for doing this. "In these times of moral relativism," she writes, "children must be taught that right and wrong do exist, that there are moral standards that have defined human society since the origins of mankind."[11] The emphasis in Cronin's curriculum is on helping students increase their awareness of their own behavior, especially of how they treat themselves and others. Students are encouraged to set small daily goals for improvement in their practice of a particular virtue such as respect, cooperation, or generosity (e.g., to give help before it's asked, or to defend someone against negative gossip). At the end of the day, they self-assess and, if they choose, record their progress in a personal journal. This daily goal setting is considered important for self-awareness and good habit formation.

Teachers can also encourage ethical sensitivity and thoughtfulness by how they handle issues arising from the shared moral life of the classroom. For example, in a second-grade classroom in Auburn, New York, Mrs. Williams was conducting a chick incubation project. She suggested to her children that they might wish to open an egg each week to monitor the embryonic development of the chicks.

However, later that day, in his reading group, seven-year-old Nathaniel confided to the teacher: "Mrs. Williams, I've been thinking about this for a long time—it's just too cruel to open an egg and kill the chick inside!" Mrs. Williams listened with respect to Nat's concern, and said he could share his concern with the whole class.

When he did, there was some agreement that his point was worth considering. But many children said they were curious to see what the chick embryo looked like. Nat replied that being curious was not a good enough reason for killing a chick. "How would *you* like it," he said, "if someone opened *your* sack when you were developing because they were curious to see what *you* looked like?" Anyway, he argued, the library must have pictures of chick embryos; that would be a better way of finding out what they looked like.

Mrs. Williams asked the children to think about this issue overnight. By the following morning, the majority of the class had come to feel that Nat's objection should be honored; they decided not to open the eggs.

The potential moral learnings here were many: that all life, even that of a chick embryo, is to be taken seriously and respected; that just wanting to do something is not a good enough reason to do it; that the reasoned dissent of even one member of the group deserves a fair hearing from the rest; that an important moral decision should not be made in haste; and that, if possible, a conflict should be resolved in a way that tries to meet the needs of all parties. (In fact, the class did search out pictures of chick embryos in the library.) These moral learnings, and their contribution to each child's character as well as to the character of their classroom community, were possible because Mrs. Williams took the time to help her students think carefully about and deal sensitively with a real-life moral problem.

Teaching conflict resolution. Teaching students how to resolve conflicts without force or intimidation is a vitally important part of character education for two reasons: (1) conflicts not settled fairly will prevent or erode a moral community in the classroom; and (2) without conflict resolution skills, students will be morally handicapped in their interpersonal relationships now and later in life, and may end up contributing to violence in school and society.

There are a great many ways to teach conflict resolution skills in the classroom. Susan Skinner, a kindergarten teacher at Heathwood Hall Episcopal School in Columbia, South Carolina, uses two methods she finds effective. When two children have a conflict, she stops the action and uses it as a teachable moment. She invites two other children to come to the front of the class to role-play a positive solution to the conflict. She then asks the whole class for their suggestions. Finally, the two children who were involved in the conflict are invited to act out a positive solution that draws on what they have just seen and heard.

When one child has hurt another, Ms. Skinner teaches a reconciliation ritual that fosters the virtue of forgiveness. She instructs the offending child to say, "I am sorry—will you please forgive me?" If the victim judges the apology sincere, that child is instructed to respond, "I do forgive you." These behavior patterns have the best chance of becoming part of a child's character when they are learned early and practiced often. But effective training is still possible at the adolescent level, where the stakes are even higher because conflicts may explode into deadly violence.

Schoolwide Strategies for Character Education

Creating a positive moral culture in the school. The moral culture of a school is defined by its operative values, ones that are reflected in actual school practices and behavior (e.g., do people respect each other? help each other? pay attention to moral problems in the school environment?) Operative values are true norms—what people expect of everybody else and are willing to help uphold. The school's moral culture is important because it affects moral behavior (a positive moral culture pulls behavior up, whereas a negative pulls it down) and because it affects character development (a positive moral culture makes it easier to develop good character).

Creating a positive moral culture in the school involves defining, communicating, modeling, teaching, and consistently upholding the school's professed moral values in all areas of school life. The story of Jefferson Junior High in Washington, D.C. demonstrates this culture-building process. Ninety percent of its students come from single-parent families. "When I arrived," says the principal, Vera White, "parents and the community felt they were losing the children."[12] Theft and fighting were common, and twelve to fifteen girls got pregnant each year.

Ms. White met with faculty, parents, students, and members of the community. They decided they needed a multi-year plan. Year One would focus on setting objectives and strategies; developing "students' sense of responsibility for their own behavior" became the primary goal. Year Two would have the theme "attitude counts everywhere you go." Year Three would focus on conflict resolution training and Year Four on community service.

Personal responsibility is now the theme of daily morning meetings in homerooms and weekly grade-level assemblies. Students are expected to have assignment notebooks, to use them in every class, and to take their schoolbooks home with them each day. Jefferson's character-building effort has also incorporated three sexuality education programs, including Elayne Bennett's Best Friends curriculum,[13] all of which teach students the value of abstaining from sexual activity.

The school has also raised expectations for parents. "Our parents," Ms. White says, "must come to school for Back to School Night and for teacher-parent conferences during the year. Every parent is also asked to volunteer twenty hours of service to the school each year."

Since implementing its character program, Jefferson Junior High experienced a marked decline in thefts and fighting. Among the schools in Washington, D.C., it has been recognized for having the highest student academic achievement, the greatest academic improvement, and the highest attendance rate. It has won two U.S. Department of Education awards and now has a waiting list of 400 to 500 students. According to the principal, there were only two known pregnancies between 1993 and 1995.

Caring beyond the classroom. Character education must extend students' caring beyond the classroom into larger and larger spheres. Students can be helped to develop their awareness of the needs of others, the desire to help others, and the skills and habits of helping through exposure to inspiring role models and continuing opportunities for service in their schools and communities. Service opportunities with the potential to develop character are those that involve students in face-to-face helping relationships so that they experience the fulfillment of touching another's life.

An exemplary public school community service program can be found at the Shoreham-Wading River Middle School in Shoreham, New York. Since 1973, hundreds of sixth, seventh, and eighth graders have done community service, usually for one hour a week, as an integral part of the middle school curriculum. Students are involved in serving four groups: (1) young children in neighboring day-care centers, Head Start centers, and district kindergartens; (2) elementary school classes, where middle schoolers team up with younger children to lead a variety of learning activities; (3) handicapped children at a local hospital; and (4) elderly persons in adult homes and nursing homes. The transforming power of these face-to-face relationships is reflected in the comment of a boy who made regular visits to a school for the retarded: "When I used to see retarded kids, I was afraid of them. Now the retarded have become people to me, with needs and wants."[14]

Recruiting parents and the community as partners in character education. Three ideas here are key: (1) parents are a child's first and most important moral teachers, and the school must do everything it can to support parents in this role; (2) parents must in turn support the school's efforts to develop good character; (3) the impact of the school-parent partnership is enhanced when the wider community (e.g., churches, businesses, youth organizations, local government, and the media) promotes the virtues that make up good character.

Schools can support parents in their role as character educators in several ways. They can tell parents how vital they are in their child's character development. They can help parents understand how character is formed (by what children see, hear, and are repeatedly led to do). They can share what research shows regarding the difference that parents make in children's moral development and what parenting approaches are effective.[15] They should involve parents on the school's character education committee; survey all parents to seek their input; and clearly communicate the school's core values and character education plans to all parents. They can help parents participate directly in the character education of their children through school-based activities (e.g., Family Film Nights) and home-based activities suggested by the school. Home-based activities can be parent-initiated (e.g., topics for discussion at dinner or bedtime stories) or child-initiated (e.g., school assignments where children interview their parents concerning their attitudes about drugs, their views on friendship, what values they were taught growing up, etc.)

One of the areas where cooperation between home and school is especially crucial is sex education. Currently, sex is the area of young people's lives where they often display the poorest character—the lowest levels of respect, responsibility, and self-control. As a culture, we are gradually emerging from the sexual revolution to recover the wisdom that sexual self-control is part of good character, that chastity is in truth one of the virtues in the constellation of human virtues that serve the individual and common good. As the artist William Schickel has observed, "Chastity is a civic as well as a personal virtue. When a society loses chastity, it begins to destroy itself."[16]

Currently, many schools, even those committed to educating for character, lack a consistent educational philosophy governing their approach to sex education. In most areas of school life, teachers and administrators are likely to be appropriately directive, guiding students to morally correct conclusions (it's wrong to lie, cheat, steal, be racist, etc.) as character education recommends. But when it comes to sex education, they send a mixed moral message ("Don't have sex, but here's a way to do it fairly safely"), use the relativistic methodology of values clarification ("You have to clarify your personal values"), and end up being nondirective ("Make your own decision").

Two groups, the Character Education Partnership[17] and the Medical Institute for Sexual Health (MISH),[18] have each recently articulated principles of "character-based sex education" to try to help schools apply character education principles to the sexual domain. For example, several such principles set forth by the MISH publication are the following "national guidelines" (slightly abridged):

1. Premature sexual activity is destructive toward self and others. It poses a grave threat to young people's physical health, emotional well-being, and character development. It also harms the public health and the nation's moral character.

2. The destructive effects of adolescent sexual activity include pregnancy and its consequences (including children having children and more than 400,000 teen abortions annually), sexually transmitted diseases, emotional hurt, potential difficulty in future relationships, and the development of disrespectful and irresponsible behavior patterns that are antithetical to good character.

3. Sexual behavior is determined by values rather than by mere knowledge. Therefore, sex education must educate young people about the moral dimensions of sexual conduct.

4. To avoid premature sexual activity, young people need an understanding of the physical and emotional dangers of uncommitted sex; an understanding of the relationship between sex and love; a vision of the benefits of saving sex for the committed love relationship of marriage; and the strengths of character (such as prudence, self-control, modesty, and respect for self and others) needed to avoid and resist sexual pressures and temptations.

5. While condoms may reduce some of the physical risks of premature sexual activity, serious risks (pregnancy, disease, and negative psychological consequences) remain. Character-based sex education teaches young people the moral principle that it is never responsible to take serious, unnecessary risks with one's own or another person's physical, emotional, or spiritual welfare.[19]

Concluding Statement

A danger facing character education, as educational researchers David and Cheryl Aspy observe, is that severe social problems will be met with only weak educational efforts.[20] When weak efforts fail to ameliorate the problems, people will say, "We tried character education, and it failed." Character education efforts must be truly comprehensive in order to be commensurate with the seriousness of the moral problems that confront us. In the long run, this means that all groups that touch the values and character of the young must come together in common cause to elevate the character of our children and, ultimately, of society as a whole.

NOTES

1. For information about the Center for the 4th and 5th Rs and complimentary articles about character education, contact the Center: Education Department, SUNY Cortland, P.O. Box 2000, Cortland, N.Y. 13045; tel. 607-753-2455.

2. For a fuller presentation of the comprehensive approach, see Thomas Lickona, *Educating for Character: How Our Schools Can Teach Respect and Responsibility* (New York: Bantam Books, 1991).

3. Hal Urban, *20 Things I Want My Kids to Know: Passing on Life's Greatest Lessons* (Nashville, Tenn.: Thomas Nelson, 1992).

4. The Heartwood Institute, *Heartwood: An Ethics Curriculum for Children* (Pittsburgh: Heartwood Institute, 1994).

5. Facing History and Ourselves National Foundation, *Facing History and Ourselves: Holocaust and Human Behavior* (Brookline, Mass.: Facing History and Ourselves National Foundation, 1994).

6. Alan L. Stoskopk and Margot Stern Strom, *Choosing to Participate* (Brookline, Mass.: Facing History and Ourselves National Foundation, 1990).

7. *The Art of Loving Well: A Character Education Curriculum for Today's Teenagers* (Boston, Mass.: Boston University Loving Well Project, 1993).

8. Steven Ellenwood, "The Art of Loving Well," *Character*, 1, no. 3 (April, 1993): 4.

9. David Johnson and Roger Johnson, *Cooperation and Competition* (Edina, Minn.: Interaction Book Co., 1989).

10. Thomas F. Green, "The Formation of Conscience in an Age of Technology." *American Journal of Education* 94 (1985): 1-38.

11. Patricia H. Cronin, *A Manual for Character Education* (Chicago: Metro Achievement Center, 1995), p. 2.

12. Thomas Lickona, *Character Education Success Stories: What Do They Have in Common?* (Cortland, N.Y.: Center for the 4th and 5th Rs, 1996), p. 7.

13. Elayne Bennett, *Best Friends* (Washington, D.C.: Best Friends Foundation, 1995).

14. Shoreham-Wading River Middle School, *Children and Their Community* (Shoreham, N.Y.: Shoreham-Wading River Middle Schools, nd), p. 3.

15. See, for example, Thomas Lickona, *Raising Good Children* (New York: Bantam Books, 1983).

16. William J. Schickel, "The Case for Chastity, A Civic Virtue," *Ithaca Journal*, 13 November 1991.

17. Character Education Partnership, *Character-Based Sex Education in Public Schools: A Position Statement* (Alexandria, Va.: Character Education Partnership, 1996).

18. Medical Institute for Sexual Health, *National Guidelines for Sexuality and Character Education* (Austin, Tex.: Medical Institute for Sexual Health, 1996).

19. Ibid., p. 11.

20. Personal communication.

CHAPTER V

For-Character Education

EDWARD A. WYNNE

You get the best ability from children reared in an economic status without luxury, which admits them at an early age to the society of people responsible for a community. The community need not be a big one, merely responsible people doing public work.

> Alfred North Whitehead
> in *Dialogues with Alfred North Whitehead*,
> edited by Lucien Price (1954).

The concept of the construction of children's character is important to this anthology and is a central theme of this essay. And so it warrants a brief explication at this point. "Construction" implies some environments should be deliberately managed to form children's character. Some readers may see this as manipulative, totalitarian, or stifling. Yet, educators who want to help pupils acquire good character must manage school and classroom environments that are more likely to help produce outcomes associated with good character, in effect, to construct them.

The common ambivalence about managing environments is an important cause for many defects in contemporary character formation. The ambivalence inhibits adults who theoretically are responsible for helping children and adolescents acquire good character. These adults are afraid to act, or they act in excessively tentative ways.

Rousseau to the contrary, "good character" does not grow spontaneously, like wild flowers in a field, or turtles hatched from eggs.[1] Children learn good character as their latent emotional tendencies are shaped by participating in a series of overlapping communities. Such communities include the children's nuclear and extended families; congregations of religious believers; neighborhoods; clubs, athletic teams, and other informal organizations; schools; job sites; diverse

Edward A. Wynne is Professor in the College of Education at the University of Illinois at Chicago. His work focuses on how social environments in and around schools affect pupils' character.

63

communication networks, including our print and audio-video media. Finally, we have communities of the mind—popular, widely shared traditions and beliefs about the past, present, and likely future of our society—which serve to establish common networks of perception and expectation within or among diverse groups of citizens. All these communities provide children and adolescents with experiences and knowledge which cause them to learn good character.[2] The communities are created and maintained by the acts and decisions of adults.

Suppose that adults are reluctant or unable to create or maintain such communities. Such ineptitude may occur for diverse reasons: ignorance; the decay of adult character, for it takes good character to practice the self-control needed to maintain environments to form good character; or the unforeseen effects of material and technological change. Without such maintenance, children will learn bad—instead of good—character.

At this time, such fears of disorder are not mere speculations. The rates of white male adolescent deaths by homicide and suicide are now probably at the highest points since the first American settlements in 1607. The figures for out-of-wedlock births to white adolescent females are at an equivalent high point.[3] Such distressing data surely justify educators giving priority to contributing to the improvement of the character of American youth. And, beyond the formal data, there is widespread public concern over pupil conduct in and around schools.[4]

For simplicity, in this chapter I will designate persons, environments, and policies that help form good character with the adjective "for-character." And so the urgent tasks of for-character educators are to: clarify their understanding of what "good character" means; recognize how environments help or hurt character formation; analyze their current educational environments to assess their good and bad influences on character; devise ways to upgrade the for-character capabilities of the environments they control; recognize that upgrading will often involve soliciting the help of parents, colleagues, subordinates, superiors, and—depending on their age and capabilities—pupils; and start to put the changes into effect.

What Is Character? How Is It Formed?

The concept of character presumes that human beings possess internal emotional dispositions—traits or virtues. The traits are revealed in their regular behavior, or habits. The word character is derived from the Greek word "to mark." It signifies the permanence of such dispositions. Each person's total mix of dispositions is unique to that person, though many persons have certain patterns of traits that are similar to the patterns in many other persons.[5]

A learner's internal state is largely shaped by directing his behavior. The theories underlying such shaping may be termed "sophisticated behaviorism"[6] and/or social learning:[7] the systemic—but still semi-tacit—mobilization of the forces in the environment to form appropriate behaviors. I say semi-tacit because some persons have probably helped form that environment through deliberate choices. However, most persons in the environment are not actively conscious of such elements of "design"; the inhabitants just take their environment as granted, e.g., schoolchildren in a daily flag salute, or a family that has a practice of regularly eating dinner together.

For-character "forces" range from simple rewards and punishments, to the use of art, poetry, and literature, the design and management of diverse human groups, the regular practices of family life such as eating meals together, and the living and dead role models put before the young. Sometimes for-character environments are deliberately maintained; sometimes the process is unconscious; and sometimes it is a mix of deliberation plus the apparent release of controls over learners. (Ideally, such release occurs when the learner is practically habituated to good conduct.)

Consider the devices for-character schools might use to teach pupils the important trait of diligence.[8] Pupils would be assigned progressively more difficult assignments, and praise and criticism would be used to inspire increased effort and timely completion. Some assignments may be compulsory, and others voluntary. Gradually, the assignment load would be increased. The punishments for untimely work would become progressively severe. Extremely diligent students would receive extraordinary recognition. They might be eligible to join desirable or prestigious programs. The underlying for-character assumptions are that diligence is a good thing for the student in particular and for the society in general, and that displays of diligence in school make it more likely students will continue to practice that habit later.

The "For-Character" Approach to Education

The for-character approach to education is older than written history. Anthropological and archaeological studies disclose that even preliterate cultures have applied teaching methods congruent with for-character principles.[9]

For example, the anthropologist Margaret Read wrote an ethnology of the child-rearing practices of the Nogoni tribe in Malawi.[10] She told of a white traveler walking through the bush. He found himself behind a Nogoni teacher (working in a missionary school) who was reading a book as he walked. The traveler asked why the book was so engrossing. The native replied,

"This book has many good suggestions about education. They are just the kinds of ideas our tribe has always used."
"That's interesting. What is the book's name?"
"It is called *The Republic*. It was written by Plato."

And the rest of the ethnography demonstrated why and how the tribesman's perception was correct.

In literate societies starting in about 500 B.C., with Socrates (470-399 B.C.), Aristotle (455-380 B.C.), Xenophon (430-355 B.C.), Plato (427-348 B.C.), and Plutarch (46-120 A.D.), we can identify typical for-character themes, such as the practice of obedience and diligence by the young, the importance of providing the young with good examples. In China, somewhat equivalent themes can be found in the writings of Confucius (551-479 B.C.). These for-character themes have continued in a persisting stream, even into the United States in the nineteenth century with persons such as Horace Mann (1796-1854), and William T. Harris (1835-1908).[11]

No one ever contended that all schools were carefully run along for-character lines. Nor can it be denied that individual teachers, or even groups of them, have been occasionally lazy, sadistic, or simply ignorant. Furthermore, for-character schools often encompassed only a small fraction of the population—the aristocracy.[12] After all, in nonindustrial societies, "education" represents a double cost; teachers and pupils must be supported, and they are also withdrawn from most forms of immediately productive labor such as farming. Even when the training was "on-the-job," it involved extra costs, since supervisors or parents spent some of their time training others rather than simply overseeing production. Only recently have societies had the economic resources to support large groups of youths and adults as students and teachers. But, still, for all literate people, the formation of good pupil character was education's unquestioned goal of education.

This continuity is understandable. Over the more than twenty-five centuries involved, the human race has become the most successful of all animal species. This species, over those centuries, has increased its average life span about fourfold, and its total population a hundredfold. Indeed, during the lives of some of my readers, the human race will probably establish colonies in outer space. The educational principles which have prevailed through this whole era of notable growth surely have many inherent strengths.

A variety of studies have shown that a number of contemporary American public and private schools and teachers still persist in being traditionally character-oriented, despite the lack of intellectual sympathy for such approaches.[13] Thus, the biography of Jamie Escalante by Jay Matthews described a striking instance of a successful for-character teacher.[14] But such success is often ignored or misinterpreted by observers unsympathetic to for-character approaches. For example, many readers of the Matthews book to whom I have talked assume that Escalante's top priority was teaching his pupils calculus. They fail to recognize that, in reality, calculus was merely a means of teaching his pupils how to apply themselves to a difficult and traditional subject. Escalante might just as well have taught Latin or music.

The various education alternatives now proposed as substitutes for the for-character approach cannot equal its record of long-term success. The alternatives may even lead to regression. Nothing says that educational change must always be for the better.

BEING A FOR-CHARACTER EDUCATOR

As mentioned earlier, role modeling is an important part of the for-character tradition. The point is simple; the idea of being a good example is very ancient. Educators who hope to transmit good character should provide pupils with such examples; in working around pupils, educators should display virtues like diligence, honesty, kindness, thoughtfulness, courage, and loyalty.[15]

These for-character traits can be easily translated into professional practices such as being prepared for class; coming to work regularly and on time, avoiding clock-watching, and being ready to walk that extra mile. Design classes carefully and continuously work to improve them; hold high, but realistic, expectations for pupils; display courage by tactfully but firmly confronting students (and parents and colleagues) who subvert the learning process. Accept and solicit criticism with good grace. Show appropriate concern for students' emotional lives. Cooperate with colleagues; and, if your work environment seriously compromises your ability to practice virtue, look for a job elsewhere.

DESIGNING APPROPRIATE ENVIRONMENTS FOR
FOR-CHARACTER EDUCATION

For-character educators must first examine their existing academic environments to see if they encourage pupils to practice good habits. In what follows I suggest typical school and classroom practices or activities that may be seen either as inviting or subverting the display of each of four desirable traits: diligence, obedience, cooperativeness, and loyalty. "Pro" activities are those that invite or encourage behavior associated with each trait. "Con" activities are believed to have an opposite effect.

Some of the activities are congruent with many well-regarded educational practices (e.g., moving instruction along at a reasonable tempo). Others are more controversial (e.g., emphasizing appropriate tests, feedback, and recognition). But the for-character approach stresses not only the cognitive merits of such activities, but also their value in stimulating pupils' behaviors relating to each trait, in part to foster academic learning and in part to promote the trait as an end in itself.

DILIGENCE

Pro: Move instruction along at a reasonable tempo; provide notable, well-designed, and carefully monitored homework; use appropriate tests frequently and other systems to measure pupil effort and progress; provide notable recognition for diligent pupils and criticism for those who are disengaged. Use small groups to assist individual as well as collective responsibility. Maintain schoolwide policies that discourage pupils from getting "lost" and/or passed on even though their work is inadequate.

Con: Instruction moves at a slow tempo; there is little or no homework or homework is not promptly collected and graded; there are few or no ways of monitoring learning (e.g., tests, recitations); there is little or no recognition of pupils' success in learning and few or no criticisms of disengaged learners; recognition systems obscure pupils' personal responsibility; classes are grouped so as to frustrate individual responsibility for all pupils; automatic promotion.

OBEDIENCE

Pro: Develop written rules of behavior for the classroom and/or the whole school which prohibit all reasonably foreseeable forms of disruption and/or specify the behaviors required; regularly review and update rules; provide brief, clear statements of the rationales for the rules; provide clear, simple, sequenced, and unpleasant consequences for rule violations; routinely provide for punishment and counseling; publicly explicate rules to students as well as to families; systematically recognize individual pupils or groups of pupils whose obedience records are good; see that the staff regularly and fairly enforces rules.

Con: Rules are unwritten; if written, they are ambiguously phrased and not widely publicized; punishment is nonexistent or disjointed or lacks deterrent effects; rules are obsolete; and the staff does not regularly and fairly enforce rules.

COOPERATIVENESS

Pro: Establish activities in and around school and classrooms which encourage pupil cooperation with each other and with adults (e.g., extracurricular activities, competitive team sports, service clubs, dramatics; involve classroom and playground aides, crossing guards in such activities); use fundraising, community service, well-designed cooperative learning activities; provide for conspicuous recognition of individuals and groups who have performed excellent service.

Con: Fail to assign cooperative responsibilities to groups of pupils; do not monitor or recognize pupils' group activities; establish unrealistic goals for such activities; conduct ill-conceived cooperative learning activities.

LOYALTY

Pro: Organize classwide and schoolwide activities to encourage pupils to display loyalty to appropriate institutions and causes, e.g., the daily flag salute; an appropriate and often recited school pledge; wholesome, well-conceived assemblies honoring appropriate causes, such as Martin Luther King's birthday; have the curriculum in literature and history solicit such loyalty, e.g., keep revisionism under control ("revisionism," in this context, means historical materials with an undue interest in deprecating the contributions of previous traditional leaders and notable past achievements); talk up school spirit; assign a mentor to each pupil.

Con: Display cynical attitudes about most popular and historic institutions; regard ceremonies as trivial; conduct poorly designed ceremonies; overemphasize roles of loners in history; fail to recognize the anti-loyalty messages in certain texts and literature.

Such a listing of "Pro" and "Con" activities could be extended to include those associated with other character traits such as courage, charity, honesty, and courtesy.

THE ROLE OF ART AND CEREMONIES

Art and ceremonies have always played an important role in affecting character formation. Researchers have recognized such patterns in traditional settings and even in contemporary schools.[16] However, it can be helpful for contemporary practitioners if this matter is directly approached. But we first need some definitions.

"Art," means music, poetry, rhetoric, costumes, and the graphic and plastic arts. The artistic creations may range from high or classic art—like the Parthenon in Athens, or the United States Capitol, or Vergil's classic mythic poem, *The Aeneid*, celebrating the founding of Rome—to popular or folk art—even including pupils' drawings or team cheers. Sometimes the art is overtly symbolic. Sometimes it is less formally evocative. In any event, such creations—or borrowings— should help honor and intensify communities and the personal virtues they encourage. "Ceremonies" are deliberately staged public occasions. Communities use ceremonies to honor persons or traditions which exemplify their ideal virtues.

Almost all schools engage in certain forms of ceremonies, and use ceremonies and art to identify their values and communities, e.g., the daily flag salute (using the symbol of the flag, and the rhetoric of the Pledge of Allegiance), graduations, assemblies, and the celebration of certain occasions. From my research and that of my students, it seems that a certain number of for-character schools in the Chicago area stress art and ceremonies in managing their environments.[17] They hold pep rallies, parades, and dances, display purposeful posters and student art throughout the building and classrooms, integrate art and music with assemblies and academic work, and create occasions for students to wear special clothes or uniforms in school. (Obviously, some private schools have modest advantages in the matter of ceremonies; many church-related schools can use prayer, religious music, the clergy or other devices to enrich such occasions.[18])

There is a simple and vital test of the character focus of a school's ceremonial life: Does the school have essentially one single graduation ceremony, which excludes most of the schools' students from significant forms of participation and observation?

I estimate that perhaps 75 percent of Chicago area public schools hold "excluding" graduations—graduations where most nongraduates have little contact with the ceremonial process. However, an important part of the graduation is to recognize all graduates, particularly graduates earning special honors, so that other students may want to

win such recognition in the future. Schools with nonexcluding graduations can hold two successive "graduation" ceremonies—one for the
graduates and all other students and the other for the graduates and
their families. Or they can devise other compromises. The point is
that the elaborate honoring process typical of graduation is largely
designed to motivate potential future graduates to strive for graduation, and to earn special honors. If nongraduates have no advance contact with the honoring process, much of the motivational potential of
the graduation ceremony is wasted. It is like giving secret praise to
successful pupils. Other pupils do not realize they can win praise, or
know what kinds of conduct can earn praise.

A school that fails to recognize the true potential of its graduation
ceremonies is likely to miss the point of many other for-character
activities. Conversely, if a school deliberately takes the trouble to plan
inclusive graduations, probably its overall for-character policies are
strong. It is a for-character school.

The connection between ceremonies and pupil discipline is also
relevant. Schools cannot conduct elaborate ceremonies without good
pupil discipline. Otherwise, the unusual nature of such activities—
when 2,000 students may be brought together in one large facility—
may be a license for disorder. For-character schools, which naturally
include pupil discipline among their goals, can easily stress ceremonies
and discipline. Conversely, schools that fail to give regard to discipline
have trouble in conducting ceremonies.

Evaluating For-Character Activities

Character-forming techniques can be evaluated by collecting data
to answer a series of questions such as:

1. Are educators conscious of the traits the school or classroom
should be trying to transmit, e.g., kindness, diligence, obedience?

2. Are educators themselves encouraged to practice such traits
around the school? How? Do they actually practice them?

3. Are students regularly encouraged to practice such traits in the
school and in classrooms? On what occasions? How do we recognize
individual pupils or groups of pupils who show excellence in applying
such traits? Can such policies or activities be improved? How?

4. How often, if at all, are pupils regularly formed into persisting
small (and larger) communities in and around the school? Communities may range from a small group in a class, to a small high school

club, to the whole school. To what extent, if at all, do adults monitor or "construct" such communities to ensure they act in congruence with basic for-character goals?

One Example of Evaluation

Let us evaluate one commonly prescribed for-character activity in operation—the much lauded practice of "cooperative learning." The examination will provide thought-producing information about a widely prescribed for-character activity, and also suggest the novel challenges often arising in analyzing and evaluating such activities.

"Cooperative education" is often recommended as an important form of for-character education. However, my perspective, from innumerable evaluations of cooperative learning practices, is far more pessimistic. Such pessimism is shared by some authorities.[19] Over twenty-five years, I have questioned thousands of my pupils (in group interviews) about their cooperative learning experiences in elementary and high school. Not what the literature recommends, but what is really typical in my students' diverse schools and classrooms. The aim was to examine the learning demands such activities generated for students. The assumption was that traits underlying cooperation—being solicitous about the welfare of other team members, striving to allocate work fairly—would only be formed if appropriate demands were made during the activity, and support provided. The students' replies to such questions were relatively precise.

High proportions of the pupils had regularly engaged in cooperative learning activities. But most of the groups only "cooperated" for brief periods of time—ten minutes, a half hour. Such arrangements can be legitimate learning activities, justified novelties, or digressions. However, the activities cannot be occasions for shaping important for-character traits, for they lack the complexity or power that pervades long-term relationships.

Many students remembered that they occasionally participated in more complex cooperative learning activities, which persisted over many hours or weeks. Students usually assumed such activities would receive academic "grades" that counted toward their final grades. Without such grades, most students regarded such activities as low priority—and reported that they then focused on their graded work. In effect, little for-character learning will occur in a lengthy cooperative project to which students give low priority. (Some authorities disagree with such contentions.[20])

The students reported that teachers assigning elaborate cooperative projects often did give students individual grades. In most such cases, each student's individual grade for the project was the same as all the other team members. Some authorities in cooperative learning recommend such equalization procedures, and others disagree. I object to such procedures, partly because of (1) my own theoretic leanings, and (2) the many students I have interviewed who have been subjected to such equalization and have strongly resented it. They recall cooperative learning as a time of victimization; a time when the "motivated pupils" were exploited by less engaged or less responsible students. The less engaged students simply avoided the work. Then, circumstances inevitably coerced the motivated pupils into doing everyone's work. The typical cooperative classroom project, far from making serious students cooperative, made them more desirous for personal responsibility. They were "taught" poor character traits. They hated having significant assignments to do with other, randomly chosen people.

Of course, it is possible to design grading systems which overcome such handicaps. However, my research has consistently found that either most teachers giving cooperative assignments do not know of such systems, or fail to use them. Under these circumstances, many (and perhaps most) elaborate cooperative learning assignments probably have deleterious effects on character.

Research on Character Formation

Do for-character approaches "work"? If such activities are conducted as prescribed, will students develop, and retain, notably better characters? What does the sum of the data show? This is an extremely complex question.

Through all of history, the process of character formation has been notoriously imperfect. Young persons reared in excellent environments have gone bad. Concepts such as "black sheep" suggest the recognition of such occasional aberrations. And, conversely, some youths reared in "anti-character" environments have been of good character, despite many obstacles. Abraham Lincoln was notably studious as a young man and adult, even though his environment was relatively bare of books. Presumably, there are certain semi-random—or genetic—forces, that can occasionally overcome the main currents of even the most purposive environments. Or one may talk about regression to the character mean, after several generations of notable character successes (or failure?).

There are many confounding issues affecting formal research on such issues. Sometimes graduates from different character formation systems are compared to see if different effects occur. Graduates of private, church-related schools, for instance, are compared to graduates of public schools. In such comparisons we must consider selective recruitment; persons who choose to join different character formation systems are often different even before they enter.[21] They already have some predisposition to display the traits that environment cultivates. Therefore, we have to try to compare output, holding constant differences in input.

Again, a significant body of long-standing research claimed that many for-character learnings were not very (or not at all) "generalizable."[22] Just because some pupils learned not to steal while in their classroom did not mean they will not steal in the local candy store. However, some later researchers, whose work has not received appropriate attention, reached different conclusions.[23] They reported that for-character learnings are far more generalizable than was previously believed.

Finally, we must also weigh the theoretical case against for-character policies. It is indisputable that the character of persons reared in different environments are affected by such environments. A person's attitudes towards monogamy (versus polygamy), or tribal cannibalism, or the routine application of extraordinary torture to certain enemies are largely determined by the environments where he or she was reared. There is such a thing as national character. Environments affect the modal character of the people born and living in them, and also help clarify the inhabitant's definition of "good character."

In the short run, our policies regarding character formation may be largely based on highly qualitative analyses, relying on history, anthropology, or reflection, compared to definitive, numerical data. But even with such cumbersome tools, many groups have achieved notable for-character effects. For instance, after World War II, the United States and some of its allies adopted notably more forgiving—realistic?—attitudes towards their former enemies than was typical in previous wars. Such a generous disposition had much to do with the reconciliation and comparative peace which prevailed after that war. It may be that this peace is partly the outcome of deliberate efforts to reform national character in America. Similar constructive changes have occurred over many years regarding race relations in the United States. And schools and colleges have been one of the forces involved in stimulating such effects.

The distressing data on rising youth disorder sends one clear message. The United States in general, and our schools in particular, must redirect their priorities toward more for-character policies. Perhaps the research about forming character is somewhat inconclusive. However, societies engaged in educational reform often have to make do with imperfectly tested expedients. For instance, as noted, American schools presumably made constructive contributions to a shaping of a national climate that helped reconcile us with Japan and Germany. And, at this moment, most of us do not even recognize what those educational contributions were. And so it seems that, even with imperfect knowledge—but with as much reflection as possible—educators and schools should become more engaged with the character problems of youth.

NOTES

1. Jean J. Rousseau, *Emile* (New York: Dutton, 1948).

2. Yehudi Cohen, *The Transition from Childhood to Adulthood*. (Chicago: Aldine, 1964); James S. Coleman and Torsten Husén, *Becoming an Adult in a Changing Society* (Paris: OECD, 1991); John Dewey, *Democracy and Education: An Introduction to the Philosophy of Education* (New York: Macmillan, 1916); Shmuel N. Eisenstadt, *From Generation Unto Generation* (New York: Free Press, 1968).

3. William J. Bennett, *Index of Leading Cultural Indicators* (Washington, D.C.: American Enterprise Institute, 1994); Jane Stallings, "Ensuring Teaching and Learning in the 21st Century," *Educational Researcher* 24, no. 6 (1995): 4-8; Edward A. Wynne and Jacques Benninga, "Keeping in Character," mimeographed (Chicago: College of Education, University of Illinois, 1996).

4. Stanley Elam, Lloyd C. Rose, and Alec M. Gallup, "The Phi Delta Kappa/Gallup Survey, The Public's Attitude Towards Public Schools," *Phi Delta Kappan* 76, no. 1 (1994): 41 et seq.; Jean Johnson and John Immerwahr, *First Things First: What Americans Expect from the Public Schools* (New York: Public Agenda Foundation, 1994).

5. Richard S. Peters, *Authority, Responsibility, and Education* (New York: Atherton, 1996); Plato, *The Republic*, trans. Allan Bloom (New York: Basic Books, 1991).

6. Burrnus F. Skinner, *Beyond Freedom and Dignity* (New York: Knopf, 1971).

7. Albert Bandura, *Social Foundations of Thought and Learning* (Englewood Cliffs: Prentice-Hall, 1986).

8. Edward A. Wynne and Kevin Ryan, *Reclaiming Our Schools: Teaching Character, Academics and Discipline*, 2nd ed. (Columbus, Ohio: Prentice-Hall, 1993).

9. Edward D. Meyers, *Education in the Perspective of History* (New York: Harper and Row, 1960).

10. Margaret Read, *Children of Their Fathers* (New York: Holt, Rinehart and Winston, 1968).

11. Lawrence A. Cremin, *American Education: The Colonial Experience* (New York: Harper and Row, 1978); Joseph Kett, *Rites of Passage* (New York: Basic Books, 1977); David Tyack and Elizabeth Hansot, *Managers of Virtue: Public School Leadership in America* (New York: Basic Books, 1982); and Stephen Yulish, *The Search for a Civic Religion* (Lanham, Md.: University Press of America, 1980).

12. Rupert Wilkinson, ed., *Educating Elites* (New York: Oxford, 1969).

13. Edward A. Wynne, *Looking at Schools: Good, Bad, and Indifferent* (New York: Lexington, 1980); idem, *A Year in the Life of an Excellent Elementary School* (Lancaster, Pa.: Technomics, 1993).

14. Jay Matthews, *Escalante: The Best Teacher in America* (New York: Holt, 1988).

15. Edward A. Wynne, "The Moral Character of Teaching," in Alan Ornstein, ed., *Teaching: Theory into Practice* (Boston: Allyn and Bacon, 1995), pp. 190-202.

16. Wynne and Ryan, *Reclaiming Our Schools*, ch. 10.

17. Ibid.

18. Nancy Lesko, *Symbolizing Society* (New York: Falmer, 1988).

19. Marian Matthews, "Gifted Students Talk about Cooperative Learning," *Educational Leadership* 50 (March, 1992): 48-50; and Robert Slavin, *Cooperative Learning: Theory, Research and Practice* (Englewood Cliffs: Prentice-Hall, 1991).

20. David Johnson and Roger Johnson, *Learning Together and Alone: Cooperative, Competitive and Individualistic Learning* (Englewood Cliffs: Prentice-Hall, 1991); and Alfie Kohn, *Punished by Rewards* (New York: Houghton-Mifflin, 1993).

21. Ernest Pascarella and Patrick Terenzini, *How College Affects Students* (San Francisco: Jossey-Bass, 1991).

22. Hugh Hartshorne and Mark A. May, *Studies in the Nature of Character:* Vol. 1, *Studies in Deceit*; Vol. 2, *Studies in Self-Control*; Vol. 3, *Studies in the Organization of Character* (New York: Macmillan, 1928-1930); and James S. Leming, "The Search for Effective Character Education," *Educational Leadership* 51 (November, 1993): 63-71.

23. J. Philliphe Rushton, Charles J. Brainerd, and Michael Preisly, "Behavioral Development and Construct Validity," *Psychological Bulletin* 94 (1983): 18-38.

CHAPTER VI

Schools, Character Development, and Citizenship

JACQUES S. BENNINGA

Some 2300 years ago, Aristotle offered the following advice:

We become just by the practice of just actions, self-controlled by exercising self-control, and courageous by performing acts of courage. . . . Hence, it is no small matter whether one habit or another is inculcated in us from early childhood; on the contrary, it makes a considerable difference, or, rather, all the difference.[1]

The truth of this statement is nowhere better exemplified than in a revealing piece of research conducted by Stanford University psychologist Walter Mischel and reported by Daniel Goleman in his book, *Emotional Intelligence*. In that study, four-year-old children were given a choice. They could either have one marshmallow now, or, if they waited a short time they could have two. The researchers were looking for the effects on later adjustment of children's ability to delay gratification. And they found them. By the time these four-year-olds were ready for high school graduation, the effects of this single trait were evident. Those who at age four had resisted the temptation to satisfy their need immediately were, years later, more competent socially and academically than those who did not resist. They did not give up in the face of difficulty, were more self-reliant, confident, trustworthy, and dependable, whereas the children who grabbed the one marshmallow were more shy, stubborn, indecisive, and resentful. The children who were able to delay gratification at age four scored an astounding one standard deviation, approximately 200 points, above the others on the Scholastic Aptitude Test.[2] Research such as this should give direction to those who ask questions such as how we ensure that children grow into adults who maintain responsible jobs, participate in community improvement, pay taxes, get married, and raise responsible children of their own. If, as

Jacques S. Benninga is a Professor in the Department of Literacy and Early Education, School of Education and Human Development, California State University at Fresno.

Aristotle suggested, the actions of adults to inculcate well-chosen early habits in children have direct implications for children's future behaviors, then adults must see it as their duty to become more directive.

Focus on Academic Achievement Is Not Sufficient

For years America has struggled to identify factors influencing the decline of academic achievement of our youth. From major national reports to discussions at the school site level, this lack of achievement has claimed our attention. We are alarmed by international comparisons which document that other countries require up to twice the amount of core academic instruction that we require,[3] and that even students in vocational tracks are expected to function at higher levels in reading, mathematics, and history than American students in similar tracks.[4] We rightfully assume that all students are capable of higher achievement and better performance and we have the conceptual basis to support this assumption. For example, for at least twenty years we have known that any child can learn if provided with appropriate conditions for learning, and that schools, if they choose to do so, can provide the best of education for virtually all of their students.[5] We are presently engaged in a national debate about how to restructure learning environments for this purpose.

Certainly, American students are just as capable as students in any other country. But the answers to the question about how to educate students for responsible adulthood may lie as much in the *values* we teach as in the emphasis we now give to academic achievement. For example, Berliner and Biddle report data collected from personnel directors of major industries.[6] These employers were asked to list the five most important and the five least important skills needed by their employees. The surveys suggest that the habits and motivation of workers are more important to employers than the technical skills workers bring to their jobs. Berliner and Biddle conclude that "if schools are truly to serve the needs of business, it appears they should concentrate less on skill training and more on the values that students will need when they enter the workplace."[7]

No reasonable person, and certainly not those personnel directors, would suggest de-emphasizing academic standards for students. But if we are truly committed to educating students for responsible citizenship, we must devote equal attention to developing positive character traits such as persistence, temperance, and civic mindedness. Educating children with these traits requires work, and while no simple solutions exist, we do have perspectives, albeit conflicting perspectives, that provide direction.

One such approach we might call the "modern" position, a position optimistic about the merits of giving students a major say in their own moral education. This position is often critical of overt adult direction or monitoring. A second approach we might call the "traditional" position, a 'position which expects adults to shape and determine the immediate behavior of the young, that is, to form their character. The traditional position asserts that as children mature, a strong base of positive habits and beliefs in moral values must be established. I will consider each approach separately later in this chapter. But first I consider the roots of the differences between them.

Ethics and Political Theory: Differing Ways of Viewing Society

Rational educators rely on a conceptual basis for understanding workable theories and strategies to counteract the troubling trends in youth behavior that confront us each day as we open the morning newspaper. It is not news that the rise of youth delinquency, out-of-wedlock births, and other youth disorders, including suicide, are troubling indicators of the status quo.[8] We search for reasonable approaches that will help all children achieve and that will further the goals of the society in which they will live. But often our underlying perspectives conflict in purposes and means, and if educational theories conflict, how then do we get from the structuring of wholesome classroom and school environments to the construction of a good society?

The answer may come from an understanding of the connections, and the differences, between the study of ethics and the study of political theory in relation to education. Both ethics and political theory spring from the same well, both have their origins in the thought of the ancient Greeks, and both are important sources of insight for educators and policymakers as they attempt to create meaningful experiences for children that will lead to their becoming healthy and productive citizens. Yet ethics and political theory differ, sometimes confusing those very same educators and theorists.

The study of ethics deals with issues of right and wrong and with moral obligations. Ethics asks, What is it to be a human being? How can we improve the way we behave and how can we make adequate or satisfactory judgments about others? Related to ethics is political theory, which likewise attempts to answer these questions, but on a broader scale. To the Greeks, the city, the human collective, was like the human soul, only increased in magnitude. Political theory, therefore, deals with how we might best organize society. It is not difficult to imagine that rules and obligations that regulate human interaction can lead to a just society. However, we encounter a difficulty as we leap from goals for individuals, particularly children, to broader societal goals which usually focus on the development of healthy adults and moral communities.

This difficulty is sometimes obscured by the individuals representing their respective positions. That is, some experts on educational reform focus on immediate issues—the processes related to teacher interactions with children and resultant classroom ideas and strategies (e.g., self-esteem and cooperative learning strategies). The expectation is that such activities, in and of themselves, will positively impact long-range student achievement and behavior. Other experts focus mainly on the end results, the products such as democratic education, that will (or should) in time produce a better society. One approach deals with educational change at the microcosmic (classroom) level; the other at the macrocosmic (societal) level. But it sometimes seems that these processes and end results are interchangeable, creating confusion between what are felt to be the goals of a good society and the specific interventions that might take us there. Such reasoning suggests that if adults have certain rights (e.g., one person, one vote), children also should have those rights. While this perspective may be appropriate theoretically, it denies recent advances in child development and child psychology which clearly point to the qualitative differences between children and adults. Processes that work for adults are not necessarily applicable to children.

Nowhere is this issue better exemplified than in recent public service television spots for the United Negro College Fund in which small children are pictured piloting advanced aircraft, sitting behind corporate desks, and teaching in a university classroom while the announcer suggests, "A mind is a terrible thing to waste." The clear point behind these gripping presentations is that children are only *potentially* capable of doing the jobs suggested by the images, but certainly not ready in those early stages of life for the responsibilities that are inherent in those adult positions. They need encouragement and training to realize their potentials but their minds are not those of adults; they are not miniature versions of what they will become. Rather they are, as we now know, thinkers of a qualitatively different sort than the thinkers we hope they will become.

Often, as we will see, this point is overlooked by educational policy analysts, the modern educational political theorists, who believe that from a definition of the best environments for adults (the end results) we can infer direct implications for restructuring classrooms and schools. In the following sections I provide an overview of some of the germinal ideas that have shaped mainstream educational thought in the twentieth century and contrast those ideas with a more traditional perspective on the formation of character.

Modern Education and the Teaching of Morality

John Dewey (1859-1952), a major force in twentieth-century philosophy, was arguably the most dominant force in American education in this century as well; the father of Progressive Education, he received accolades for his work as well as criticisms of it. Dewey shared with the nineteenth-century philosopher G.W.F. Hegel (1770-1831) the idea that the moral process is one without fixed origin and fixed ends; that moral judgments are to be regarded as hypotheses for experimentation rather than as absolute principles. Thus, hypotheses about proper classroom instruction must be formulated; these then lead to practical experimentation and experiences for children which are then evaluated to formulate new hypotheses and experiments, and so on. It should come as no surprise, therefore, that Dewey saw himself as an experimentalist, trusting his scientific approach to education, his notion of "deliberately conducted practice," as the most far-reaching and fundamental method for the reconstruction of social life in classrooms, schools, and society.

This conception of education as an evolving process of experimentation followed naturally from his philosophy, and Dewey deserves credit for advocating the application of the exact methods of science to the problems of education. Still debated today are his criticisms of education in the early decades of the twentieth century: too much abstraction in the curriculum; not enough firsthand, hands-on experiences with real life activities; too much emphasis on constraining children to accepted social attitudes rather than making schools the centers for the reconstruction of social life; and too little attention to the development of social goals of responsiveness and cooperation in learning.[9]

Lamentably, Dewey's criticisms have remained with us while the theoretical base he proposed has been largely ignored. Many of today's educational writers have continued the criticisms, focusing their writings on them, but proposing untested and inadequate strategies to rectify the problems they criticize. Thus the spate of articles in educational journals devoted to developing children's self-understandings, their self-concepts, the clarification of their values, strategies such as whole-language for reading, full inclusion in classrooms for children with very special needs, nonrepression, and democratic participation in classroom decisions. In the words of one biographer, Dewey's leadership was that of a "reverently misinterpreted prophet."[10] Toward the end of his career he warned his followers against the "aimlessness and dangerous permissiveness of the notion of the child-centered school," but his words were largely ignored. Indeed, the eminent educational historian Lawrence Cremin wrote in 1959 words that ring true today.

His writings have been translated into a dozen different languages; many are still in print; almost all are widely available. Yet contemporary educational discussion is filled with the shoddiest misconceptions of what he said; and disciples and critics alike have purveyed the grossest caricatures of his work.[11]

The Perils of "Democratic Education"

Despite such criticism of Dewey, the field is littered with books and articles based on personal interpretations of his ideas. Many theorists have favored general, emotive terminology like "educating for democracy" (Dewey's famous and complicated educational book was titled *Democracy and Education*), without evaluation of the policies advocated to advance such ends. The notions identified above (e.g., self-esteem programs, whole language, inclusion and other forms of heterogeneous groupings) are all advanced to further democratic understandings, but few have undergone rigorous evaluation to determine their effects, and their effects are often undesirable. But that does not seem to matter to some. In the words of educational theorist Amy Gutmann, democratic education "commits us to accepting nondiscriminatory and nonrepressive policies as legitimate even when they are wrong."[12] Even when such practices lead to lower academic achievement, she states, they are necessary to advance the "virtues of citizenship," and even when student participation threatens to produce disorder within schools, it may be defended on "democratic grounds."[13] The examples that follow may provide some indication of what educators proposing such ideas have in mind.

Values clarification. In our era, educators such as Raths, Harmin and Simon and researchers such as Lawrence Kohlberg have proposed approaches to democratic education in the form of consensual methods to teach morality.[14] The values clarification approach of Raths, Harmin, and Simon is aimed at helping students clarify "what their lives are for, what is worth working for."[15] In this approach students are presented with dilemmas and asked, individually and/or in small groups, to respond to those dilemmas with the expectation that this procedure would help them define their own values and make them aware of and more sensitive to others' values as well. Students proceed through a series of seven steps to clarify these values, from choosing their own beliefs and behavior (steps 1, 2, 3) through prizing and affirming them (steps 4 and 5), and then acting on them (steps 6 and 7). The teachers, on the other hand, are cautioned to avoid moralizing, criticizing, offering their own values, or evaluating the responses. To be appropriately democratic, they are warned against leading children to preordained notions of right and wrong. A well-known typical problem is the "Lifeboat Dilemma" where students must decide which of ten people they will save.

Though hugely popular in classrooms throughout the country for most of the past thirty years, this approach has been soundly criticized in the last decade. Because of its controversial content, values clarification often offends community standards,[16] and because of its relativistic process, it undermines accepted values,[17] does not induce a search for consensus, does not stress truth and right behavior, and does not distinguish morality as a generalizable system of norms from morality as a system based on personal preference or whim.[18] Substantial evaluations of values clarification programs indicate that they have little impact on student values and appropriate behaviors.[19] Today, even the authors of this approach are in retreat.

Kohlberg and moral education. From 1958 until his death in 1987, Lawrence Kohlberg conducted research on children's moral reasoning which resulted in a definition of six successive stages of moral reasoning and judgment each with its underlying conception of justice and each more adequate than the preceding one for resolving justice problems.[20] Kohlberg concluded that, as individuals move upward through his six stages, their moral perspectives broaden as they become more morally mature. Thus, whereas children of six or seven years evaluate their own actions only as to the effects on themselves, students at higher stages, at ages twelve to fifteen, for example, become increasingly skilled at taking the perspectives of others as they make judgments. The first three of Kohlberg's stages, which encompass the bulk of children's school years, are dominated by notions of right and wrong based on what others might do to them or think of them. Their thinking is dominated by forces and significant people external to themselves and has consequences which affect them directly. It is consistent with their development, therefore, for them to look outside themselves to significant others for justification of right and wrong actions. Kohlberg's theory thus seems more in accord with notions of externally directed education and, therefore, his resultant educational interventions may have missed the mark.

In applying his theory to education, Kohlberg stated that as individuals move upward through his stages of more adequate moral thinking, the moral perspectives they are cognitively capable of integrating become increasingly broad. That is, children become better able to reason how others may think about the same issues and to relate others' thinking to their own. But this ability is limited by their cognitive growth, and that is exactly where the educational implications of the theory may have gone astray. Kohlberg advocated the creation of "just communities" in high schools, communities that would address naturally arising moral issues with students and teachers each having one vote in deciding how the issues would be resolved.[21] Topics of discussion in such just communities might include school rules, and issues such as lying, stealing, using drugs, and disciplinary procedures, with the emphasis placed on consensus and majority rule rather than on top-down directions from experienced adults. Such strategies are cause for concern. For example, Wynne described a *New York Times* article about one such discussion in a high school in which the students had an elaborate debate about whether to bring knives and have sex on a school picnic (they eventually voted both down).[22] Howard describes one elementary classroom where the students decided that a student who was guilty of spitting on a classmate was to be punished by standing in the middle of his classmates who would each, in turn, spit on the offender (a more experienced teacher intervened and stopped the punishment).[23] Clearly these tactics, though compatible with the democratic process, were more detrimental than helpful, and most adults would describe them as examples of majority rule gone awry.

An example of a democratic school. Examples of democratic education are not limited to interactions within classrooms between teachers and their students, but also involve whole schools. In their book, *Democratic Schools*, Apple and Beane present several such programs.[24] In one chapter, Bob Peterson, a fifth grade teacher in a public elementary school in Milwaukee, described his school as a "two-way bilingual, multicultural, whole language school governed by a site-based council."[25] The definition of democratic education in this school is rather unique. The focus of La Escuela Fratney (formerly the Fratney Street School) seems to be a constant battle with the local public school system of which it is a part. The curriculum, classroom management procedures, and parent involvement strategies all are at odds with ways of operation in the "dominant culture."

For example, La Escuela Fratney teaches students to be anti-racist by focusing primarily on the contributions of "people of color" through their music, art, stories, poetry and literature, giving each "geopolitical group" (i.e., African-American, Hispanic, Native American and Asian-American) extensive exposure during kindergarten through grade five, and thoroughly integrating instruction on non-European cultures into many subject areas. When a white parent questioned the absence of the pledge of allegiance in classes, she was told by a young Puerto Rican teacher that the pledge "reminded her that Puerto Rico has endured decades of U.S. colonial rule without 'liberty and justice for all.'" That ended the discussion. The pledge and national anthem might "violate what many consider one of the fundamental building blocks of democracy—the equality of all people—in its continued emphasis on European points of view."[26]

As for the academic program, the school staff believe that education should be "based on the experience of the children." Thus these five-to-ten-year-olds think, investigate, and write about their community, reconfirming "their own and their families' worth." As an accommodation to the "political pressures" imposed by the district administration, La Escuela Fratney teaches spelling, but little other mention is made about the academic achievement of the children in this mostly minority school. The school has hired a full-time "self-esteem specialist" to work with the students on "self-management skills" because the students, some of whom have transferred from other schools where they had been treated "like mindless sheep," could not handle rights "as simple as being able to take a pass and go to the bathroom on their own."[27] Nonetheless, after several years of operation, chronic discipline problems persist, because, according to Peterson, "our culture does a great job of teaching children to be disrespectful of people on the basis of a host of attributes."[28]

Though many parents were involved in the establishment of La Escuela Fratney, parental participation dropped off after the school opened. The parents who remained active were mostly white and middle class. To solve this problem the school established a quota for their management council and hired two part-time parent organizers. In a section of his chapter called "What Have We Learned?" Peterson concludes that grass-roots movements such as the one at Fratney can produce "real change," and that successful school reform is "part of larger societal change efforts."[29] No mention is made of the effects of such a program on the future achievement of the students or speculations about their future adjustment or character development. Rather the tone of the chapter suggests a rather hostile, anti-American bias and a selfish lack of understanding of the basic principles of child development as related to elementary education. This, then, is promoted as an exemplar of "democratic education."

The Long Reach of Traditional Character Education

The more traditional approaches to character education have their roots in the foundational writings of our Western heritage. From the dictates of the ten commandments through the writings of the Greek philosophers, to the more modern philosophies of Immanuel Kant and Mortimer Adler, a well-established body of thought has directed our relations with others, including the process of educating our youth. For most of that history, the concept of character formation, the duty of the older generation to form the character of the young, has been a basic principle structuring moral education. Such a consistent tradition is difficult to ignore, and no current research supplants it.

For example, Aristotle wrote about the development of excellence, stating that to become excellent at any craft, including becoming virtuous, we have to exercise, or practice, those behaviors that will lead us there. Sarah Broadie, interpreting Aristotle, states that "learning that there are things which one is expected to do even when all concerned are aware that one does not feel like doing them is perhaps the only way we have of learning from scratch that there are things worth doing and aiming for which are not immediately pleasant. This is our way into an active sense of 'noble.'"[30] Thus, the early formation of proper habits and the development of character traits such as honesty, kindness, courage, perseverance, and loyalty, provide the foundation for how we later internalize that things are good beyond our immediate needs and desires for them.

The eighteenth-century philosopher Kant expanded on this concept. He wrote about the duties and obligations of moral people. According to him, moral actions must be performed from motives of duty, from an obligation to act in accordance with universally agreed upon principles of right and wrong, and not, presumably, from a classroom discussion about who should stay alive in a lifeboat. Kant speculated that if we all followed his reasoning, good people would arrive at similar conclusions when faced with moral decisions. Thus emerged the famous Kantian categorical imperative—one should act in such a way that one could wish the outcome of one's action to become a universal law of human conduct.[31] In other words, our actions, to be truly moral, need to be formalized, articulated, and generalized. For example, in donating clothing or food to the needy, we are acting on the rule—the moral duty—that one is obligated to help others in need.

These notions of character can only come to us through direct training, or as Piaget suggested, through cultural transmission. Indeed, throughout the history of our country, Americans have always had faith that their schools could "close the floodgate of corruption and ... arrest the torrent of public immorality"[32] through character education, believing that the nation could not survive unless its citizens were virtuous as well as intelligent. The recent emphasis on self-discovery, values clarification, and consensual morality thus may be only a blip in an otherwise long and consistent history of more directed teaching for character formation.

Character education is both an old and new concept, deriving its roots from the writings of both Plato and Aristotle. As demonstrated by the quotation at the beginning of this chapter, character can be observed in an individual's behavior. People with good character habitually display such behavior. Thus an approach different from what was called the "modern" or "progressive" attracts advocates of character formation. Teachers concerned with character formation aim to teach students to behave morally through direct example. They set high standards and encourage persistence, honesty, kindness, and other observable good conduct. To combat rising tides of teenage disorder—crime, pregnancy, substance abuse, and suicide—these educators take a public stand to form positive character traits in their students, traits such as the core "Six Pillars of Character" growing out of the Aspen Summit Conference on Character Education in 1994: trustworthiness, respect, responsibility, justice and fairness, caring, civic virtue and citizenship. Examples abound:

- The Reverend Jesse Jackson is heading a national effort to combat disorder in schools "driven by drugs and guns and perverse values." Jackson is asking black parents to sign pledges to take their children to school, meet their teachers, read their children's report cards, and turn off their television sets at home for at least three hours every night.

- The Million Man March on Washington in October 1995 urged black men to atone for past grievances against them (e.g., lack of commitment to their families, lack of modeling for their children, lack of productive focus in their lives) and to commit themselves to reinvolvement with their families and communities.
- The Cincinnati Public Schools have adopted a stricter disciplinary code leading to more suspensions and expulsions with the majority of parents of all demographic groups supporting the policy; in the Commonwealth of Virginia parents are required to sign a copy of the school rules or face a possible $50 fine; in Patterson, N.J. parents of truant children are forced to attend school with their children; Wisconsin's Learnfare Program withholds a portion of the welfare payment to families whose teenage children miss more than two days of school a month; Los Angeles now expels students *from the district* for bringing guns to school; over one hundred school-site councils in Chicago have installed dress codes for students, including the banning of gang colors and uniform-style dress; Houston has a "zero-tolerance" plan which mandates expulsion in certain cases for chronic troublemakers.
- Cedar Hill (Texas) School District passed a resolution encouraging the teaching of traditional moral values; one hundred New Haven ninth and tenth grade students are enrolled in a three-year experiment called "Character First"; Nashville (Tenn.) is piloting a character education program for Kindergarten through grade four called "Project: Solution"; Fresno (Calif.) has adopted nine core character traits for both students and adults; and Clovis (Calif.) has developed an elaborate statement on character education for students that is focused on a core of seven central traits.

No doubt, policies such as these have been implemented as a reaction to the more ad hoc, "reconfirming" approaches described earlier. Whatever their strengths or drawbacks, these policies were most likely conceived to reassert the responsibility of adults for the character formation of children. Whether implemented knowingly or not, however, they have their roots in the best of recent research on the role of parents and, by extension, teachers in child development. That research has been summarized by William Damon in his book, *Greater Expectations*.[33]

Damon argues that, contrary to popular conceptions, children thrive on accomplishment, not on empty self-esteem messages; they

do not become overburdened by reasonable pressures related to worthwhile activities, including demanding schoolwork; they are tough and
resilient and are motivated to learn through both extrinsic induce-
ments (e.g., teachers' expectations, rewards, pressure, encouragement,
grades) and intrinsic motivations; they need guidance, and that guidance can best be provided by able, caring, concerned adults.

In addition, moral awareness is active at birth and develops throughout life. Reactions such as empathy, fear of punishment and disap-
proval, guilt, anxiety, shame, and pride in accomplishment seem to be
inherent in all humans, including young children.[34] But only proper
adult interaction, guidance, and feedback ensure that these native qualities will result in well-balanced, productive, morally mature adults.
Such interaction is provided through thoughtful parenting and well-
planned schools.

One District's Traditional Character Education Program

The Clovis Unified School District is a medium-sized school district in California's Central Valley that has had a consistent character
education focus for over thirty years.[35] The guiding philosophical orientation for the district's goals is "Sparthenian," their interpretation of
the best of two ancient Greek cultures, Athens and Sparta, representing an emphasis on three domains: mind, body, and spirit. The district
has publicly articulated its mission and assessed its progress through
establishing specific, measurable goals and performance standards in
all areas of the program and across grade levels including not only academics, but also extensive and inclusive co-curricular, community
involvement, and school management programs. It annually publishes
the progress of individual schools and compares those results to district expectations. The district believes that education that helps children experience academic competence also aids in the formation of
good moral character.

This strong focus on character education in Clovis was the topic of
a *Wall Street Journal* article in which the writer commented that Clovis
"believes good values go beyond knowledge; they are ingrained habits
embraced through experience."[36] Students in Clovis earn points for
activities that develop their mind, body, and spirit. Thus they can
apply for an on-campus job like library monitor or groundskeeper;
they cooperate by vying for a bi-weekly custodian's rating by keeping
their classrooms clean; they read stories in English classes that exemplify the district's set of seven values; and teachers prod students to

exhibit self-control and politeness. Rules are strict, with stringent dress codes and a no-quit policy for electives after the first week. All the schools are involved in these programs, with high school students serving as models and mentors for the elementary children. One fifth grade teacher, realizing that the character and skills of his students were shaped by what he did as well as by what he said, told the reporter that he had given up cursing at umpires at sporting events and doesn't buy beer anymore. "How can I let one of them see me with a six-pack at the grocery store?" he asked.

Results of this comprehensive program are impressive. Incidents of vandalism and stealing are low; academic achievement is solid; student participation in after-school activities is very high, approaching 90 percent; and many of the schools, including two of the three high schools as well as many of its elementary and middle schools, have won the prestigious National Exemplary School Award sponsored by the U.S. Department of Education.

The effects of this district's program on elementary students and their teachers have been evaluated.[37] In a four-year evaluation, children's social attitudes and behaviors and the perceptions of the school's program by teachers in one of the schools were compared with a set of schools in another California district which stressed cooperative activities, intrinsic motivation, and student autonomy. When compared with the responses of teachers in the comparison schools, the responses of the Clovis teachers indicated that their school was more businesslike, creative, and innovative. Clovis teachers felt that the parents at their school were more involved and supportive and that their principal was more supportive and accessible. The Clovis school was felt to have a more traditional focus, a more pleasant atmosphere, and better relations between teachers and students. Students in Clovis also scored higher on measures of self-esteem in the third and fourth grades than did students in the comparison schools.

Other effects on children were not so clear. That is, these two differing, well-thought-out approaches, did not produce students who differed significantly on measures related to resolving individual or group social problems, and both groups of students were indistinguishable on measures such as concern for others and liking for school. What is significant is that a school that emphasizes traditional programs of academic achievement and character education seems to foster unanimity of purpose between its students, parents, teachers, and community.

Recognizing and Rewarding Character Education

A logical question is how to begin creating a school program with a central focus on character. How can one know that what is being planned is consistent and effective? Education is, after all, an applied field. It is the job of the educator to take the best of our collective knowledge and apply it to the real world of children. Unless a district and its schools are able to translate their mission and philosophy into practice, those statements are nonfunctional and may be counterproductive to their intended purposes. Philosophy, as shown, gives meaning and direction to actions, and in its absence, teachers and students are left to the whim of whatever is fashionable. Thus the mission and philosophy of a school take on added significance as they are used to justify classroom and school practices. School programs that are clear and open about their purposes are most likely to offer their students the balance of experiences necessary for character development.

But individuals in schools must be motivated to engage in such elaborated explanations and need to take their work seriously. Without some recognition for their efforts, many may find these tasks burdensome, and carelessly implemented programs can result. On the other hand, school faculties that anticipate public affirmation and recognition for their efforts are encouraged to devote extra time and energy to ensuring quality programs for their students. The ripple effect of such recognition can inspire efforts in other schools.

One such encouragement to action has been established in Fresno County, California. For the past nine years, a group of educators there have implemented a voluntary evaluation of character education programs in elementary and middle schools. Known as the Values and Character Recognition Program, it was inspired by the For Character Program described by Edward Wynne of the University of Illinois at Chicago in a visit to Fresno in 1985.

Each year schools in this large geographical area are offered the opportunity to submit an application asking them to document how they address a series of open-ended questions related to the enhancement of moral and character education. Applications are sent in alternate years to either elementary schools or middle schools in the county. Participation is, of course, voluntary. The questions are generic; their purpose is to evaluate the quality of activities provided for the students in each school.

Responses in five broad areas are called for. It is expected that each of the schools returning the application will demonstrate evidence of performance in each area by their responses on the application and at the time of the follow-up site visit. The questions posed and the types of responses given by award-winning schools are indicative of the high quality of involvement of many schools serving students at all socio-economic levels. Requirements in the five areas are that:

- each school describe the kind of student it wants to develop and the conceptual or philosophical rationale that underlies its program; each application must provide evidence of broad-based participation in the planning of its programs/activities and show how the programs/activities reflect the described rationale.
- each school cite specific activities which offer evidence that instruction in the area of character and values education is part of the curriculum in the classroom and in the whole school.
- in each school the rules of conduct, disciplinary procedures, and standards and expectations for all students are clearly understood and communicated effectively and positively; teachers, parents, and students must all be involved in the development of the rules.
- each school offer a rich variety of activities, both academic and co-curricular, through which students contribute in meaningful ways to the school and to others; each school must have an active student government.
- each school recognize student achievement in formal and meaningful ways at the school and classroom levels.

School programs that include a wide scope of student activities and encourage broad participation can best provide essential opportunities for students to learn to be considerate and helpful to others, to respect the rights and opinions of others, and to respect the institutions of American society. Such activities provide a relevant context for school personnel to work with students in nurturing values, social awareness, and prosocial conduct. Schools providing such opportunities and encouragement for student involvement are apt to have fewer discipline problems, less student-to-student conflict, and more cooperation between peers and members of the school staff.

A typical school may include as documentation for its program its student-parent handbook, past copies of its school/classroom newspapers, photographs or announcements of special programs and activities, and other evidence that the school administration and students have, over time, given careful attention to its programs. A team of reviewers screens all applications and chooses the finalists, after which separate teams of validators make site visits to each of the schools to obtain firsthand information on whether what was reported in the application is actually taking place. The schools receiving this award are justifiably proud of their accomplishments and serve as models for other schools in their district.

CHARACTERISTICS OF AWARD WINNING SCHOOLS

Schools winning the Values and Character Recognition Award share certain similarities. Each school has an overtly stated philosophy. For example, one school stated as its purpose the preparation of "productive, contributing members of society . . . who, through their actions and conduct exhibit qualities perceived by the school and community to be positive traits of character." Another school focused on "the four characteristics associated with being an effective human being: (1) an intellectually reflective person, (2) a person en route to a lifetime of meaningful work, (3) a good citizen, and (4) a healthy person." In that school, the staff "believes in a highly ordered and academically rigorous instructional program that promotes student achievement and self-reliance in all curricular areas while developing a sense of responsibility and personal and civic values."

These winning schools make deliberate efforts to involve teachers, students, and parents in planning and implementing the school curriculum. One school conducts a yearly survey, polling parents to ascertain their feelings regarding school and district policies, procedures, and programs; and all schools communicate frequently and thoroughly with parents through meetings, newsletters, notes, and a variety of parent/teacher committees. In addition, many of these exemplary schools publish and disseminate a student/parent handbook outlining goals, operational procedures, standards of acceptable conduct, and rules and policies. Almost all of the schools recognized as exemplary have a stringent dress code for students, and increasingly many require students to wear uniforms.

What is most impressive about these schools is the extent to which they have developed meaningful activities for student involvement outside the regular academic program. Though per-pupil funding for California's schools is well below the national average, these schools offer instrumental music and choir programs; school-sponsored clubs and activities such as peer counseling, community service, and leadership; and support for students in intra- and inter-district competitions. Individual students as well as whole classrooms are publicly recognized for activities such as contributions to school beautification and to clean campuses, acts of kindness and responsible behavior, participation in monthly theme activities related to character, and community service such as Coats for Kids and canned food drives.

For example, one large inner-city elementary school initiated both a Young Gentleman's Club and a Young Ladies Club in addition to its other character-promoting activities. Each of these clubs includes high-, low-, and average-achieving students selected by their teachers as in need of the structure provided by the clubs. Club activities include learning how to dress appropriately, use conventional manners and etiquette, fill out job applications and interview for positions, and regular visits to various businesses and agencies in the community. Marvin Howard, faculty coordinator of these clubs, described the activities of the clubs as follows:

On field trips the boys must wear a white shirt, tie, black slacks and black shoes. They must maintain a C average and exhibit good social and behavioral skills. . . . The goal is to get them thinking about professions and careers, and both clubs are designed to build character, self-esteem, values, and to develop life-long social skills. They have been interviewed four times on television, have received certificates from the Mayor, the Board of Education, have participated in the Veterans Day Parade, have attended a luncheon with County Supervisors, been written up in the *Fresno Bee*. A scholarship has been provided at Fresno City College by a club sponsor for eligible participants who graduate from high school. The scholarship is $1000 and is being matched by the college. This is a positive incentive to encourage our youngsters to complete school and continue on to higher education. The self-esteem and confidence have improved so drastically that teachers and parents have commented on their positive attitude.

Conclusion

In a very concrete manner the staff of these excellent schools understand that they act as one important preparatory base, along with families, in securing the next generation for fruitful participation in our democratic society. A long philosophical and practical tradition exists to support the efforts of these schools. That tradition should not be ignored, particularly when more modern efforts, the so-called democratic school experiments, have not shown themselves to have greatly improved our society and its youth.

In many ways, effective schools have the same characteristics that research has found in highly effective parents.[38] Similarly, the less effective schools share characteristics of less effective, *laissez faire*, parents.

Well-grounded schools set high expectations and encourage children's sense of competence and self-reliance. They rely on extrinsic control, clarity of communication, and nurturance to shape the character of their students. They are primarily concerned for the well-being of the children and take great pleasure in their accomplishments. Schools with these characteristics are more apt to graduate into society students who are accomplished academically and who demonstrate the habits and character traits that lead to productive citizenship.

NOTES

1. Aristotle, *Nicomachean Ethics* (New York: Bobbs-Merrill, 1962), pp. 34-35.

2. Daniel Goleman, *Emotional Intelligence: Why It Can Matter More Than IQ* (New York: Bantam, 1995), pp. 81-82.

3. National Education Commission on Time and Learning, *Lessons from Abroad* (Washington, D.C.: U.S. Department of Education, 1994).

4. Albert Shanker, "An 'Average' Standard," *New York Times*, 29 October 1995, E7.

5. See, for example, Benjamin S. Bloom, *Human Characteristics and School Learning* (New York: McGraw-Hill, 1976), p. 7; Sam Stringfield, Mary Ann Millsap, Elios Scott, Rebecca Herman, "The Three Year Effects of 10 Promising Programs on the Academic Achievement of Students Placed at Risk" (Paper presented at the Annual Meeting of the American Educational Research Association, New York, 1996).

6. David C. Berliner and Bruce J. Biddle, *The Manufactured Crisis: Myths, Fraud, and the Attack on America's Public Schools* (New York: Addison-Wesley, 1995), pp. 88-89.

7. Ibid., p. 89.

8. Rates for these disorders are at an all-time high. See, for example, the epilogue in Gertrude Himmelfarb, *The Demoralization of Society* (New York: Vintage, 1996) for an overview of these and other statistics in America and Great Britain from the 1920s to the 1990s.

9. An excellent overview of Dewey's work is provided in Merle Curti, *The Social Ideas of American Educators* (New York: Pageant, 1959), ch. 15.

10. Martin Dworkin, ed., *Dewey on Education* (New York: Bureau of Publications, Teachers College, Columbia University, 1959), p. 9.

11. Ibid., "Foreword."

12. Amy Gutmann, *Democratic Education* (Princeton, N.J.: Princeton University Press, 1987), p. 288.

13. Ibid., p. 288.

14. Louis E. Raths, Merle Harmin, and Sidney B. Simon, *Values and Teaching* (Columbus, Ohio: Charles E. Merrill, 1966); Lawrence Kohlberg, *The Philosophy of Moral Development: Moral Stages and the Idea of Justice* (New York: Harper and Row, 1981); idem, *The Psychology of Moral Development: The Nature and Validity of Moral Stages* (New York: Harper and Row, 1984).

15. Raths et al., *Values and Teaching*, p. 7.

16. Martin Eger, "The Conflict in Moral Education: An Informal Case Study," *Public Interest* 63 (1981): 62-80; William J. Bennett, *The Devaluing of America: The Fight for Our Children and Our Culture* (New York: Summit, 1992).

17. Diane Ravitch, *The Schools We Deserve: Reflections on the Educational Crises of Our Times* (New York: Basic Books, 1985).

18. Fritz K. Oser, "Moral Education and Values Education: The Discourse Perspective," in Merlin C. Wittrock, ed., *Handbook of Research on Teaching*, 3rd ed. (New York: Macmillan, 1986), pp. 917-941.

19. James S. Leming, "Curricular Effectiveness in Moral/Values Education: A Review of Research," *Journal of Moral Education* 10 (1981): 147-164; idem, "In Search of Effective Character Education," *Educational Leadership* 51, no. 3 (1993): 63-71; Alan L. Lockwood, "Effects of Values Clarification and Moral Development Curricula on School-Age Subjects: A Critical Review of Recent Research," *Review of Education Research* 48 (1978): 325-364.

20. Kohlberg, *The Philosophy of Moral Development*.

21. Robert W. Howard, "Lawrence Kohlberg's Influence on Moral Education in Elementary Schools," in Jacques S. Benninga, ed., *Moral, Character and Civic Education in Elementary School* (New York: Teachers College Press, 1991), pp. 43-66.

22. Edward A. Wynne, "Character and Academics in the Elementary School," in Benninga, ed., *Moral, Character and Civic Education in the Elementary School*, p. 142.

23. Howard, "Lawrence Kohlberg's Influence on Moral Education in Elementary Schools," p. 62.

24. Michael W. Apple and James A. Beane, eds. *Democratic Schools* (Alexandria, Va.: Association for Supervision and Curriculum Development, 1995).

25. Bob Peterson, "La Escuela Fratney: A Journey toward Democracy," in Michael W. Apple and James A. Beane, eds., *Democratic Schools* (Alexandria, Va.: Association for Supervision and Curriculum Development, 1995), pp. 58-82.

26. Ibid., p. 67.

27. Ibid., p. 70.

28. Ibid., p. 71.

29. Ibid., p. 80.

30. Sarah Broadie, *Ethics with Aristotle* (New York: Oxford University Press, 1991), p. 109.

31. John Hospers, *Human Conduct: An Introduction to the Problem of Ethics* (New York: Harcourt, Brace and World, 1961).

32. Curti, *The Social Ideas of American Educators*.

33. William Damon, *Greater Expectations: Overcoming the Culture of Indulgence in America's Homes and Schools* (New York: Free Press, 1995).

34. Ibid., p. 135.

35. Richard K. Sparks, Jr., "Character Development at Fort Washington Elementary School," in Benninga, ed., *Moral, Character, and Civic Education in the Elementary School*, pp. 178-194.

36. Sonia L. Nazario, "Right and Wrong: Teaching Makes a Comeback as Schools See a Need to Fill a Moral Vacuum," *Wall Street Journal*, 11 September 1992, pp. B4, 5.

37. Jacques S. Benninga, Susan M. Tracz, Richard K. Sparks, Daniel Solomon, Victor Battistich, Kevin Delucchi, Ronald Sandoval, and Beverly Stanley, "Effects of Two Contrasting School Task and Incentive Structures on Children's Social Development," *Elementary School Journal* 92, no. 2 (1991): 149-167.

38. Eleanor Maccoby, *Social Development: Psychological Growth and the Parent-Child Relationship* (New York: Harcourt Brace Jovanovich, 1980), pp. 382-383; Diane Baumrind, "The Development of Instrumental Competence through Socialization," in Anne D. Pick, ed., *Minnesota Symposium on Child Psychology*, vol. 7 (Minneapolis, Minn.: University of Minnesota Press, 1973).

Section Three
EXPANSIVE VIEWS OF CHARACTER AND CHARACTER EDUCATION

CHAPTER VII

Connections between Character Education and Multicultural Education

GENEVA GAY

What is the relationship between character education and multicultural education? Is it one of irreconcilable differences, or natural complements? Does it represent unavoidable tensions between absolute and relative standards of goodness and virtuous human behavior? Is one destructive and the other constructive, and if so, which one? Is one a directive for the future and the other a historical memory? Does character education promote the values and principles on which the United States is founded while multicultural education challenges and even violates them, as some critics such as Arthur Schlesinger and Chester Finn contend? If character education is conceived as teaching a single standard of normative behavior based only on cultural values derived from Greco-Roman origins, and assumed to be universally applicable, then it is highly contestable from a multicultural education perspective. If multicultural education is merely glorifying the ceremonial customs, rituals, and artifacts of ethnic groups, or the rejection of principles of democracy, then it is in conflict with any reasonable conception of character education. Neither of these polarized conceptions provides a useful framework for pursuing a constructive relationship between these two endeavors.

Other conceptualizations discussed here suggest that multicultural education and character education are more complementary than conflicting. They contend that the relationship is one of generalities and

Geneva Gay is a Professor in the Department of Curriculum and Instruction, College of Education, University of Washington in Seattle.

specificities, of text and context, of principle and practice, of idea and action, of personal and social dimensions. Character education deals with general values and attributes of individual behavior such as honesty, truth, responsibility, and integrity. It suggests that these are universally understood, and that they transcend time, place, and circumstance. Ryan and Lickona make this point when they explain that the moral values upon which character development rests are "objectively grounded in human nature and experiences."[1]

Multicultural education poses the question: "Honesty, truth, and responsibility about what, when, and for whom?" It particularizes these generalized virtues to sociopolitical issues specific to ethnic and cultural diversity within the United States. While multicultural education contextualizes and situates character development within a particular sociocultural and political milieu, this fact does not suggest that its underlying values are situational. Instead, it accepts the basic values which constitute the idealized social character of the United States (e.g., democratic principles), but challenges practices which deny them to certain groups because of race, ethnicity, and socioeconomic status. For example, African Americans, people who are poor, and women have not been treated with the same kinds of opportunities, respect, honor, and dignity as middle class European-American males. Multicultural education demands that these discrepancies cease, and that the privileges embedded in the social character of the United States be applied equally across ethnic and cultural groups. Therefore, it shares with character education the claim of "universality of some values," when allowances are made for the scale and locality of their application.

Whereas character education is often centered in "individual attributes and actions," multicultural education emphasizes the "social and the collective." It evokes the promises and perils of the social character of the United States (as symbolized by principles of democracy) in justifying its vision, and its calls for group action and social reform to achieve its goals and objectives. In this sense, multicultural education is consistent with conceptions of character development as "a social and not an individual phenomenon," since "there is no such thing as a solitary, a private human being."[2] As a social edict multicultural education challenges "the societal power structure that has historically subordinated certain groups and rationalized the educational failure of children from these groups as being the result of their inherent deficiencies."[3] At its core are those attributes of the nation's social character which constitute "social justice and equality."

Some of the more specific intersections between character education and multicultural education are discussed here to further illustrate these general relationships. The explanations are developed primarily from the perspective of multicultural education. This emphasis seems reasonable since many of the other chapters in this volume deal in detail with character education from an individual perspective. The perspective of multicultural education complements and expands these other discussions. It also helps to dispel assumptions that character education and multicultural education are contradictory, incompatible, and inevitably contentious.

Common Concerns

Both character education and multicultural education are concerned with the development of *habituated moral and ethical behavior.* In more conventional language, they are committed to teaching students to routinely do "the right thing." Because this "doing right" is persistent and consistent, it is more an attribute associated with a "total way of being" than a set of isolated or selective behaviors. Thomas Lickona explains further that "character consists of operative values, values in action." Its development progresses as a value becomes a virtue, and the expressive behaviors of individuals are consistent with their virtues. A virtue is "a reliable inner disposition to respond to situations in a morally good way."[4] Good character is generally understood to include such virtues as honesty, loyalty, respectfulness, fairness, responsibility, dependability, caring, unbiased, openmindedness, courage, and compassion.

Multicultural education applies these general virtues in the context of ethnic, cultural, and racial diversity. By so doing, it contributes significantly to making character education meaningful to the sociocultural, political, and philosophical specifics of society in the United States. It promotes fairness, equality, respect, and caring across ethnic groups. Developing knowledge, attitudes, values, and skills to relate to, interact with, and promote equity for diverse ethnic and cultural groups, individuals, and experiences is, according to Sonita Nieto,[5] character development for citizenship in the culturally pluralistic society of the United States. Carl Grant[6] extends this notion of multicultural education as the characterization of a philosophical disposition, a value orientation, a total way of being in relationship to cultural diversity and the active promotion of social reconstruction. These orientations are necessary because the potential of the country's social character has not been fully realized for all groups. Social, cultural, ethnic, and gender inequities, injustices, indignities, and discriminations still exist. Contextualizing character education thus fits well with how Henry Johnson conceptualizes its ultimate purpose. He suggests that "if our aim is character . . . as a positive notion of consistent being and acting, as the realization of the growing potentialities of a coherent self, we cannot avoid taking account of the concrete social and cultural matrix in which character develops."[7]

Honesty and caring are two other key anchor points of both character education and multicultural education, which serve well to illustrate the connection between them. To describe an individual as an "honest person" is to evoke an element of his or her way of behaving that is characteristic, habitual, and dependable. It signals one who does not lie, cheat, steal, or deceive in any circumstances. Honesty within the context of multicultural education means teaching historical, social, political, and cultural *truths* about the cultures, contributions, struggles, and experiences of ethnic groups in the United States. These "stories" are not romanticized by inflating the positive aspects, or sanitized by downgrading the negative. Instead, accomplishments and problems, along with yet unrealized possibilities, are viewed as essential to authentic portrayals of the lives and cultures of individuals, groups, and the nation. This process involves dispelling cultural hegemony, debunking ethnic and racial stereotypes, and resurrecting the stories of ethnic groups and individuals that have been "lost" or ignored in mainstream historical records and cultural priorities. Essential to the latter is accessing the insider's perspective, the internal voice of ethnic group members. Thus, including the personal memories of individuals who lived the experience is fundamental to telling the truth about the internment of Japanese Americans during World War II, the enslavement of Africans, and the displacement of Native Americans because of European immigration.

The commitment of multicultural education to telling the truth about ethnic and cultural diversity also means bringing multiple ethnic perspectives and experiences to bear upon the analyses and interpretations of sociopolitical issues such as power, resistance, privilege, and progress. It symbolizes the general character traits of flexibility, openmindedness, and informed decision making. The necessity of multiple perspectives in capturing the truth about the United States and individuals' stories was argued cogently in a 1972 statement issued by the American Association of Colleges for Teacher Education (AACTE). Entitled "No One Model American," it appealed to educators to embrace, preserve, and promote cultural pluralism as a fact of life, a basic quality of United States culture, and a valuable resource to enrich knowing, learning, and living.[8]

Using multiple ethnic perspectives in analyzing sociopolitical issues is necessary because no single "truth" about such issues is absolute or universal. Truth—or knowledge—is always socially and culturally constructed, and influenced by time, context, situation, person, and position. For example, sexism has different meanings for Latinos, Filipinos, and European Americans, for women of poverty and economic privilege, and for women in different historical periods. Europeans migrating from the Eastern to the Western coast of the United States in the nineteenth century were indeed pioneering unknown terrains. Yet, the same terrains they were "discovering and conquering" were already known intimately by many native tribal groups. For them, the arrival of the Europeans soon became an intrusion, and a serious disruption (and ultimately, destruction) of their life styles. Cultures, values, attitudes, behaviors, ethics, and moralities clashed. These various orientations and experiences caused the different travelers to see and relate to each other quite differently. Each one's perspectives offer some degree of truth about the nature and effects of these cultural encounters, but neither is complete without the other. The coming of other ethnic groups, such as the Chinese, African Americans, Mexicans, and Mormons provided additional perspectives on the truth about populating the Great Plains and Pacific coastal regions of the United States. Multiple perspectives such as these serve as avenues through which more ethnic groups and their histories and contributions can be rightfully included in the "cultural capital" taught in schools, and in the democratic community envisioned in the nation's social ideals and political promises.

Caring is another central feature of character education and multicultural education. It is based on the fact that humans are social beings, and therefore highly interdependent. The development of their personal character and the quality of their lives occur within the context of "community" and relationships, and are based on how well these are negotiated with respect and integrity. As the world becomes more and more technologically and socially complex with conflicting desires, wants, and claims, the challenge of achieving qualitative and uncontested community membership is compounded. Moral independence, as well as physical, social, and cultural interdependence, is paramount for individual and civic achievement. Being in a community makes demands upon individuals from different ethnic, cultural, and social backgrounds with respect to "roles to play, perspectives to consider, commitments to fulfill, relationships to care about, responsibilities to juggle. . . . [These demands] are the social matrix in which we live and have our moral being. . . . When we interact with others in positive ways, we become attached to them, learn to value . . . [their] worth and dignity, and come to know and feel from within our essential interdependence and responsibility for each other."[9] This is a salient testament to the reciprocal and complementary relationship between character education and multicultural education.

Embedded within caring conduct are elements of respect, responsibility, and compassion. Nel Noddings describes these needs and mandates as an "ethic of relation." This ethic emphasizes reciprocity between care givers and recipients, moral belief and behavior, and the contextual and situational factors of caring expressed in actions. It "does not posit one greatest good to be optimized, nor does it separate means and ends . . . [or] regard caring solely as an individual attribute."[10] Rather, caring is a form of social moral action. Thomas Lickona suggests that respect and responsibility are the bedrock of caring, and that they comprise the fundamental moral agenda of public schools. He explains further that "these values constitute the core of a universal, public morality. They have objective, demonstrable worth in that they promote the good of the individual and the good of the whole community . . . [and] are necessary for healthy personal development, caring interpersonal relationships, a humane democratic society, [and] a just and peaceful world."[11] This simultaneous pursuit of "the good" for the individual and the collective (person and society) represents a crucial linkage between character education and multicultural education.

Respect is the feeling or emotional dimension of the caring aspect of both character development and multiculturalism; it is valuing and honoring the worth and dignity of others. Responsibility is its action dimension; it means working for the betterment of others. In character education this "morality of responsibility" mandates social action, but it does not dictate *the right* specific action to take. Instead, "it calls us to try, in whatever way we can, to nurture and support each other, alleviate suffering, and make the world a better place for all."[12] The "morality of responsibility" in multicultural education requires that students engage in actions which promote social justice—politically, culturally, and educationally—for diverse ethnic and racial groups. This involves respecting one's own and others' cultural differences, developing a social consciousness about ethnic issues and experiences, being morally committed to ethnic, racial, and gender equity. It also involves striving for full acknowledgment of the pluralistic nature of our society and for changes in our institutions that will truly reflect that pluralism. These goals and skills comprise the "caring" components of multicultural education, and parallel the attributes of individual caring identified by Noddings and Lickona.

A classic example of the ethic and obligation of moral action embedded in character development and multiculturalism is the Civil Rights Movement. Maxine Greene explains why:

Finding freedom repeatedly held away from its objectives . . . [the activists] came together to name the obstacles—the unjust laws, the segregation codes, the fire hoses, the clubs, the power structures themselves. *Having named them, having found them obstacles to their own becoming . . . they took action together to overcome. They came together, in town after town, on road after road, in "speech and action"; they chose themselves, in all their diversity, as morally responsible for kindred goals* . . . the thousands of young and old people who marched and suffered for what they had appropriated as cause were pursuing a life project whose name was freedom. They were choosing a way of being in the world[13] [emphasis added].

These individuals were driven to communal action by the impulse of the moral and legal imperatives of justice, freedom, equality, dignity, and human and civic entitlements for themselves personally, and for everyone else similarly denied their rights. Their actions and the images they convey are cogent illustrations of the clarion call to both the individual and the collective for the action that moral conviction—character—invariably commands.

Multicultural education requires ethical conduct of educational leaders, students, institutional structures, and instructional programs. No person or part of the educational enterprise is exempt from promoting or benefiting from cultural pluralism. To be caring, concerned, and fully entitled citizens, all students need to learn about ethnic groups which comprise the United States, their contributions, critical issues, and social problems. This requires systemic school reform and a comprehensive pedagogy that incorporates cognitive, emotional, social, personal, political, and moral learning. In multicultural education students acquire knowledge about diversity, develop respect and appreciation for it, and do not behave in demeaning and discriminatory ways toward people who are racially, ethnically, and culturally different. They are committed to equality in both their ethics and actions. Consequently, the ultimate goal of multicultural education is for everyone to genuinely accept cultural diversity, and integrate it into their intellectual, personal, social, and political behaviors in everyday living.

Character Education in Multicultural Context

Suggestions for how the educational process should be constructed to develop skills commensurate with these goals and purposes encompass all the features considered necessary for moral agency. These include *moral knowing* (awareness of moral issues and values, perspective taking, reasoning, decision-making strategies, imagination, and judgment about cultural diversity); *moral feeling* (conscience, attraction to the good, empathy, and self-control); and *moral action* (competence, will, courage, and habits to function well in culturally pluralistic settings).[14] One illustration of how these may be implemented in school programs is Christine Bennett's[15] conception of multicultural education as encompassing the overlapping dimensions of ideology, knowledge acquisition, internalized personal convictions, and *commitment to action*. Another example is found in James Banks's[16] recommendations for teaching students skills in social criticism, decision making, political efficacy, and personal empowerment for the express purpose of eliminating racism, sexism, and other inequities in political, economic, cultural, and educational opportunities. These emphases are necessary because acquiring knowledge about and appreciation for cultural diversity is no guarantee that people will "necessarily be moved to help put an end to prejudice and discrimination or to solve basic problems of inequality."[17] In other words, proclaiming beliefs in and merely teaching values associated with democracy devoid of their concomitant behaviors is meaningless. The high level of agreement among multiculturalists on the importance of social action skills governed by an ethic of equality and the recognition of cultural diversity as a creative and generative resource for society and individuals indicate that these are core values and essential components of multicultural education.

Typical multicultural action proposals also include suggestions for teachers to personify multicultural principles and ideals in their own personal and instructional behaviors; for students to demonstrate their knowledge of, appreciation for, and commitments to cultural diversity and sociopolitical equality; and for broadening the base of social change through creating networks, collaborations, partnerships, and coalitions among different kinds of proponents of change. These types of action meet the conditions of a caring character that Nel Noddings describes as *socially engaged relating and responding*, and which involve modeling, dialogue, practice, and confirmation.[18]

Advocates argue that character development and acceptance of cultural diversity must be substantive components and outcome expectations of the entire spectrum of teaching and learning. As Henry Johnson explains, "There are moral and ethical dimensions in every sort of human experience as it is lived. Deliberately to reduce human experience to neutral terms, so that subject matter drawn from it no longer represents a form of moral experience, is to destroy simultaneously both the educational content of any area of study and the principal element in anything that can be called human life."[19] Similar arguments are made about culture and diversity. They are so deeply ingrained in the human condition, personal identity, and the sociopolitical life of the United States that failure to acknowledge them distorts individuals and society. Rejecting or demeaning the cultural heritage of individuals constitutes an act of psychological and moral violence to their human dignity and worth.[20] Portrayals of United States history, life, and culture are incomplete and dishonest when ethnic and cultural diversity are ignored. Consequently, no dimension of true character development on either the personal or social level can be successfully achieved without dealing with diversity. Multicultural education facilitates this by teaching students knowledge, values, and skills appropriate for quality living in a racially, ethnically, and culturally pluralistic nation and world.

At the level of principle, then, character development—that is, "doing right"—for the culturally pluralistic society of the United States, includes a combination of *egalitarian* ethics, morality, and behaviors evident in personal, social, and civic conduct. The actual forms these behaviors take vary somewhat by the particular sociocultural and interpersonal interactions in which one engages because the participants and dynamics of these interactions change frequently. This is inevitable because people do not live in abstract, static moral universes. Therefore, it is important to recognize how efforts at character development in the United States are affected by the country's sociomoral traditions and its racial and cultural composition, are grounded in democratic principles and visions, and are hampered by inconsistencies between philosophical ideals and social realities. The same is true for multicultural education. It grew out of the tensions and visions of the Civil Rights Movement of the 1960s, with its struggles to eliminate racial discrimination in housing, public accommodations, voting, employment, and education.[21] The Western cultural ideals of representative democracy, enfranchisement, and civic entitlement are persistent and pervasive themes stressed by those who advocate making education more culturally inclusive, accessible, and egalitarian for ethnic and racially different students. These ideals form the rationale, direct the goals, establish the contours of the essential content and methodology, and anchor the criteria for quality control of multicultural education.

The foundational principles of the United States as declared in the Declaration of Independence and the Constitution—freedom, equality, justice, community, and the uncontested human rights of dignity, respect, and protection of the law—represent an ethical code of conduct. They obligate individuals and institutions to behave *consistently* in accordance with them. John Dewey made this point when he explained that democracy is a "mode of associated living, a conjoint communicated experience," not merely a form of government.[22] As such, it requires individuals to understand their interconnectedness, to learn to work together, and to take actions to advance the common good for the greatest number. Given the incredible diversity of the participants in this "associated living," the degree to which it functions effectively is the ultimate testament of the civic and personal character that is reflected in behavior.

The challenges this diversity poses for creating the inclusive, egalitarian, representative, and smoothly functioning community envisioned in the democratic ideal are more moral and ethical than legal. They involve resolving cultural conflicts, sharing power and resources, and striking a balance between rights, privileges, and responsibilities. There also is a perpetual search for ways to make good prevail over evil, right over wrong, honesty over dishonesty, respect over disrespect, compassion over apathy, benevolence over selfishness. The need to nurture simultaneously the one and the many is a preeminent theme throughout the philosophical conceptualization of constructing a democratic community. Herein lies validation for both character education and multicultural education, and their inextricable interconnection in practice.

All of these moral challenges have personal and social, universal and particularistic, philosophical and pragmatic dimensions. In order to be effective citizens in a culturally pluralistic society, individuals need to "do right" for themselves according to their own cultural group's values, as well as "do right" toward others whose standards are different from their own. These requirements place character education and multicultural education at the center of school programs and practices, and in a complementary relationship to each other. Both are needed to ensure that students learn how to improve their own personal development, while contributing to the betterment of the civic and social order.

Conclusion

The common concerns for habituated moral and ethical conduct—for doing the right thing, telling the truth, caring about others, and engaging in transformative social action—represent significant philosophical connections between multicultural education and character education. Their expected outcomes also are fundamentally the same—that is, individuals and sociopolitical structures which behave in ways that *honor* the human rights, dignity, contributions and capabilities of all people regardless of their race, class, ethnicity, gender, national origins, and language. They differ only in arenas of operations, degrees of specificity, and referent groups.

While character education deals with principles of respect, justice, and equality to be applied generally in all situations, multicultural education is concerned with developing respectful, just, and equitable conduct in specific ethnically and culturally diverse situations, issues, and relationships. For example, character education may consider individuals who speak out against oppression in any form and place, without targeting specific incidences of it, as having a commitment to equality. By comparison, multicultural education sees deliberate actions to resist racial discrimination in employment and education as behavioral manifestations of a commitment to equality.

Consequently, multicultural education provides a specific *operational context* (e.g., ethnic and cultural diversity) for the *philosophical text* of character education in the United States. They complement each other in efforts to recover and realize what Lickona calls a "foundational understanding." That is, "just as character is the ultimate measure of an individual, so it is also the ultimate measure of a nation."[23] The knowledge, values, habits, and skills represented by multicultural education are necessary if the individuals in the pluralistic society of the United States are to genuinely exhibit "good character" by demonstrating *coherency* between their democratic ideals, their ethical and moral edicts, and their sociopolitical behaviors.

To achieve these outcomes, character education and multicultural education should be central features of all curricula designed for students in kindergarten through grade twelve and for teacher education. They should permeate the teaching of skills in critical thinking, problem solving, and social action. They should be embedded in the content of the social and natural sciences, the humanities, mathematics, technology, the fine arts, and business courses. Invariably, in the performance of their duties teachers must deal with issues of fairness, justice, honesty, equity, dignity, and morality as they work with an increasingly diverse student population. In order for teachers to meet these challenges successfully, multicultural and character education must be salient features of both their content specializations and professional education courses. Neither has to necessarily take the form of free-standing courses and programs of study that exist separately from other knowledge, disciplines, and skills taught. Instead, they can permeate everything else, be taught throughout the K-12 curriculum and the teacher education curriculum, and be developed in conjunction with each other.

NOTES

1. Kevin Ryan and Thomas Lickona, "Character Development: The Challenge and the Model," in *Character Development in Schools and Beyond*, edited by Kevin Ryan and George F. McLean (New York: Praeger, 1987), p. 18.

2. Henry C. Johnson, Jr., "Society, Culture, and Character Development," in *Character Development in Schools and Beyond*, edited by Kevin Ryan and George F. McLean (New York: Praeger, 1987), p. 61.

3. Jim Cummins, "Foreword," in Sonia Nieto, *Affirming Diversity: The Sociopolitical Context of Multicultural Education* (2d ed.) (New York: Longman, 1996), p. xvi.

4. Thomas Lickona, *Educating for Character: How Schools Can Teach Respect and Responsibility* (New York: Bantam Books, 1989), p. 51.

5. Nieto, *Affirming Diversity: The Sociopolitical Context of Multicultural Education*.

6. Carl A. Grant, "Education That Is Multicultural—Isn't That What We Mean?" *Journal of Teacher Education* 29 (1978): 45-49.

7. Johnson, "Society, Culture, and Character Development," p. 69.

8. "No One Model American" (Washington, D.C.: American Association of Colleges for Teacher Education, November 1973).

9. Ryan and Lickona, "Character Development: The Challenge and the Model," p. 29.

10. Nel Noddings, *The Challenge to Care in Schools: An Alternative Approach to Education* (New York: Teachers College Press, 1992), p. 21.

11. Lickona, *Educating for Character*, p. 43.

12. Ibid., p. 45.

13. Maxine Greene, *The Dialectic of Freedom* (New York: Teachers College Press, 1988), p. 101.

14. Ryan and Lickona, "Character Development: The Challenge and the Model"; Lickona, *Educating for Character*.

15. Christine I. Bennett, *Comprehensive Multicultural Education: Theory and Practice*, 3rd ed. (Boston: Allyn and Bacon, 1995).

16. James A. Banks, "Approaches to Multicultural Education," in *Multicultural Education: Issues and Perspectives*, 2d ed., edited by James A. Banks and Cherry A. McGee Banks (Boston: Allyn and Bacon, 1993), pp. 195-214.

17. Bennett, *Comprehensive Multicultural Education*, p. 15.

18. Nel Noddings, *Caring: A Feminine Approach to Ethics and Moral Education* (Berkeley: University of California Press, 1984).

19. Johnson, "Society, Culture, and Character Development," p. 88.

20. Young Pai, *Cultural Foundations of Education* (New York: Merrill/Macmillan, 1990).

21. James A. Banks, "Multicultural Education: For Freedom's Sake," *Educational Leadership* 49 (1991/92): 32-36.

22. John Dewey, *Democracy and Education* (New York: Macmillan, 1924), pp. 101, 115.

23. Lickona, *Educating for Character*, p. 22.

CHAPTER VIII

Chemistry or Character?

HUGH SOCKETT

Production of Ritalin, widely prescribed to treat Attention-Deficit/ Hyperactivity Disorder (ADHD) has more than quadrupled in the last four years. ADHD (or ADD) "seems to have become the 'disorder of the 90s,' embraced by parents and teachers as the explanation for why Johnny can't sit still and concentrate, a condition easily 'fixed' by taking a smart or magic pill,"[1] reminiscent of the soma-stuffed children in *Brave New World*. Some two million children nationwide are presently taking this drug, and boys are diagnosed as ADHD three times as often as girls. An epidemic of ADHD has hit children in our schools.

A decade or more ago, Johnny would have been described by such epithets as careless, impolite, lacking determination, persistence, and self-control, impatient, rude, and without respect for other people. His behavior would have been explained by a lack of character training and/or character education. He was badly brought up. Nowadays he is drugged to get his behavior to correspond to acceptable norms. This presents three kinds of problems for character educators which provide the framework for this discussion.

First, there is the problem of definition: What is the difference between what a psychiatrist and an educator might say, when confronted with Johnny and his behavior? Character educators, in my view, need to assert the primacy of the educational description of the behavior of such children over the psychological description. We should reject the view that children diagnosed as ADHD children *can't* be attentive, control themselves, or persist in things, and so need to be drugged. Rather, we have yet to find out how to *teach* them how to develop capabilities of attention, control, and persistence as a part of their moral education.

Second, there is the problem of understanding. What is needed to develop moral agency in children places huge demands on teachers' understanding. This means not just learning how to teach all children

---

Hugh Sockett is Professor of Education and Director of the Institute for Educational Transformation at George Mason University, Fairfax, Virginia.

the personal capabilities lacking in the diagnosed ADHD child, but to be able to explain the child's behavior in educational terms to parents, doctors, counselors, principals and, of course, the children themselves.

Third, there is a problem of social context. Living in a culture in which we reach for explanations that do not respect moral autonomy, we believe in the therapeutic or the clinical as solutions for our weaknesses. This provides teachers, principals, parents, and the children themselves with ways to circumvent moral responsibility for their actions. So we need a clear idea of what the social and institutional context of schools should look like for the development of character, especially for those children labeled ADHD.

The Problem of Definition

Character as one element in moral agency. Contemporary character education is usually defined in terms of virtues. "Lack of character," often the impetus for promulgation of character education, is found in numbers of children indulging in activity generally antipathetic to contemporary mores—they take drugs, engage in premarital sex, have little regard for others, and so on. So character education, in its contemporary manifestation, is synonymous with moral education in general. And that makes good political sense given that the word "moral" seems to attract public opprobrium. We can continue to give children a moral education under the label "character education."

The problem with that strategy is that it conceals the way in which a person's "having character" is only one part of his or her moral agency, not a synonym for it. This may explain the absence from contemporary character education of any serious concern with what moral philosophers have called the will. Richard Peters, in a much neglected paper on the psychology of character, set out an interesting Kantian analogy comparing full moral agency to the democratic state.[2] A moral agent was like a state with three functions—legislative, judicial, and executive. The legislative function is similar to a person establishing a basis of moral principles such as honesty and fairness, that is, the rules governing his or her life. The executive function is like that by which a person implements these principles (e.g., with determination, patience). The judicial function is similar to the individual weighing up the consequences of moral actions in different contexts and situations (e.g., resolving dilemmas). The analogy draws the attention of educators specifically to this "executive" part of moral agency, that is, all those matters concerned with carrying out what one believes and having the personal capabilities to do so. These are precisely Johnny's weaknesses. Weakness of will, notably described in Aristotle's discussion of *akraisia*, is a failure of character. Strength of will could be the (narrower) object of character education. Johnny's behavior is called ADHD by the psychologist, and a weakness of will or character by an educator. This difference needs explanation.

THE PSYCHOLOGICAL DEFINITION

Examine the ADHD definition of the child's behavior. ADHD is regarded as a neurological syndrome, not a learning or language disability (like dyslexia), or a brain condition (like epilepsy), nor a lack of education. Children with this syndrome, it is said, are prevented from *normal* functioning at school and at home. Their behavior, defined as attention-deficit-hyperactive disorder, can be modified to acceptable social norms either by drugs (like Ritalin, the para-amphetamine methylphedinate-hydrochloride) or by interventions such as behavior modification, or both.[3] The normal is defined as those patterns of order and purpose in the school and the home against which the disorder is diagnosed: "School," as Silver puts it, "is the lifework of children and adolescents."[4]

Johnny's behavior is described in the criteria for ADHD set out by the American Psychiatric Association: *Inattention, Hyperactivity*, and *Impulsivity*.[5] *Inattention* includes such behaviors as "fails to give close attention," "makes careless mistakes in schoolwork," "has difficulty in sustaining attention in tasks," often "does not seem to listen," "does not follow through and fails to finish," "has difficulty organizing tasks and activities," "often avoids or expresses reluctance about, or has difficulty engaging in, tasks that require sustained mental effort (such as schoolwork or homework)," "loses things," is distracted and forgetful. *Hyperactivity* is distinguished when Johnny "often fidgets with hands or feet or squirms in seat," "leaves seat in classroom or in other situations in which remaining seated is expected," "often runs about or climbs excessively," "has difficulty playing or engaging in leisure activities quietly," "acts as if driven by a motor," and "talks excessively." *Impulsivity* describes Johnny when he "often blurts out answers to questions," "has difficulty waiting lines or awaiting turns," and "interrupts or intrudes."

THE EDUCATIONAL DEFINITION

How would we describe Johnny and his problems, educationally? Though we might use some of the same words as the psychologist, we lack (a) a developed conceptual framework within which to describe the personal capabilities of will Johnny has not acquired or been taught, and (b) an account of the necessary and empirical conditions for their development and how he is to learn them—for none of them is innate. This defining framework will describe the executive side of moral agency, the narrower sense of character as iterated by Peters, which illuminates the problems Johnny faces. Conceptually, this framework is in three domains: (1) capabilities of *heed* (such as concentration, carefulness, conscientiousness, vigilance), (2) capabilities of *endeavor* (such as persistence, perseverance, doggedness); and (3) capabilities of *control* (such as self-restraint, patience, punctuality).[6] The task is to begin to pry open these categories and examine the educational tasks.

Heed. To pay heed to something is to give it one's attention. Attention is integral to many different personal capabilities, two of which can serve as examples—concentration and carefulness.

No one who reflects on his or her personal history should forget the problems of learning to concentrate. It is easier to acquire the habit of concentration if it can be learned through working on things which we value or are interested in. It is the capability of giving something our exclusive attention. Individuals differ, of course. Some "lose" concentration when the phone rings; others remain focused while the television blares. Concentration is not just intellectually useful; it is morally significant, for example, when we listen with respect to other people. Young children manifest early a proclivity for exclusive preoccupation with things they find of interest if left to themselves and with appropriate challenges. Presumably this is the seed from which the ability to concentrate springs. Parents sometimes drag their youngsters to the table to eat, taking them away from projects in which they are absorbed. Unwittingly, parents undermine thereby the development of this embryonic ability to concentrate by changing the child's agenda. But we don't only distract children by occasionally interfering with their projects. Homes and classrooms are often chock-full with objects, procedures, or rituals that distract their attention.

Being careful is another element in the category of heed. We learn to be careful by working with those things about which we care. This is manifest not only in interpersonal relationships, but in our work or leisure, for example, in our attention to arts and crafts. Taking care expresses our responsibility—moral or prudential—for persons or things. But it is not just a disposition; it involves levels of personal capability relevant to that which is being cared for. Young children need to be trained in caring for their pets, however much they care for them. Young parents have to be taught how to care for their babies. It is not enough that they simply care about them. They have to have acquired skills which require detailed committed attention.

Endeavor. The second of these categories of will points up a central personal capability, namely the general ability to strive for something difficult. Endeavor presupposes difficulty. Determination and persistence, as examples of endeavor, describe a person's behavior which goes beyond mere trying to what we might call striving. Yet again, the object has to be perceived as worth striving for, even though a person can be coerced into being determined or persistent, as military training indicates. Fundamental to striving for anything is facing up to difficulty, and difficulty is not just a part of school-life. It is part of the human predicament. Yet sometimes teachers and parents do not want children to face difficulties or to have to strive. Some believe that children need do in schools only "what is expected of them." Provided they are conscientious, in other words, students will not have to experience any challenge in learning. For the pedagogy will be painless, since the teacher is technically expert enough to tailor the curriculum to the child's ability. Others think that learning just needs to be "fun," and that will create the motivation to learn. On either of these views, students will not experience the need to strive and will therefore get no practice in being determined or persistent. When confronted by situations of difficulty, they will most likely give up (or complain about a B grade).

Control. Control, as self-control, is actively being passive. Two examples of control will suffice—self-restraint and patience. When we restrain ourselves, we may appear to be doing nothing. Self-restraint is "not acting" in contexts which invite action. Tempted, pushed, cajoled, or bullied, we may get angry and lose our temper if we lack this capability. Yet being self-restrained is not always the right thing to do. In teaching children self-restraint, one is not teaching submissiveness to the will of others, or the immorality of anger. George Orwell, for example, lost control when he saw boys blowing up frogs with bicycle pumps, and this expression of moral outrage no doubt taught the youths some kind of lesson. This corner of the executive side of moral agency is revealing because it indicates so clearly that being moral is a practical business of action. And, though you may judge that something needs morally to be done in terms of your beliefs and principles, you won't be able to carry your conclusion out if you lack the character, the wherewithal in terms of determination, persistence, and so on to get it done. Patience, unlike self-restraint, is connected to the use of one's time, and Jackson claims it is what children learn primarily in schools.[7] Yet patience, too, has its limits. One may have more important things to do than wait in a line. At a different time, there may be nothing more important right now than patiently explaining something to a child.

This outline of a conceptual framework covering some personal capabilities of the will and character describes the executive side of moral agency. Each category (heed, endeavor, and control) needs to be examined especially with an eye to specifying what the conditions are for the acquisition of those capabilities specific to the category. It will then become possible to examine a definition of the ADHD syndrome, regard each specification of undesirable behavior as matters of character, see them as the personal capabilities necessary to the exercise of moral agency, and, as such, *work out how we can teach them to children.*

The Problem of Understanding

Armed with this moral, rather than psychological, framework of understanding children's personal capabilities (or their lack of them) we can identify three critical areas of understanding for teachers in matters of educating the will: children's interests and values, facing difficulty, and judgment and control.

Children's interests and values. Definitions of ADHD are developed against the norms of order in home and school.[8] Johnny, on the educational definition, does not need treatment: undisciplined and uneducated, he will see no point in adhering to these norms and still less to paying attention to what the teacher or the parent wants. Pat Wilson writes interestingly of the connection between interest and discipline.[9] He suggests that we educate children by taking their interests and showing them what is of interest in their interests. Learning in this way, they acquire the habits of self-discipline needed to pursue those interests.

Clearly we cannot regard schooling as detached from life. How seriously we take individual children's interests at school has to be understood against the institutional arrangements in their families as well as schools. Mostly, we will cope with children whose interests and values have rarely been taken seriously so that we can hardly expect such children to be disciplined in pursuit of educational goals. Other people's norms have always been foisted on them, so the attractions of education are not glittering prizes.

This is most pertinent when we seek to teach children to concentrate or to be careful. If the objects of either capability are of no interest to the child, why should he or she strive to concentrate or to take care? It is manifestly false that "school is a child's work," if by that we mean that they have selected it and value it. They are compelled to go to school and have little choice of curriculum. However, while it is not logically possible to force someone to care about something, it is no doubt possible to coerce them into learning to concentrate, for example, through offering an extrinsic reward, or through some kind of disciplinary format which is more unpleasant than doing "what is expected." The problems are obvious, educationally. Offered a reward, a person may "go through the motions," but remain uncommitted to the value of the object. Coerced, a person may succumb, develop avoidance strategies, or simply rebel (and get labeled ADHD). In being taught to concentrate or to take care, children must value the relevant objects.

Whether this argument is correct or not, it is clearly a moral and educational account of a child's behavior very different from a psychological explanation which treats the school's norms of order as an unquestionable given. Deviance from those norms is often seen as malicious or involuntary. I suggest it is neither. It is at least as coherent to say that children are reacting against the fact that no one takes their interests seriously and, since they are then subject to strategies of coercion, they rebel. They rebel, of course, because children are no fools. The challenge to the character educator thus becomes very profound, namely, to find ways of teaching children to develop these personal capabilities (like concentration, care, patience, self-restraint, etc.) in situations they value. For example, rock climbing is a good place to learn to concentrate. Carefulness can be learned in being given responsibility for younger children. Presently, character educators are anxious to integrate their work into existing curricula. Whether these curricula are the best vehicles for children to learn these personal capabilities depends on whether children value the curriculum content.

Facing difficulty. Imagine first a young child, striving and struggling to figure out how to fit those variously shaped objects into the right holes in the top of the box. It does not require empirical test, in my view, to assert that we will undermine his ability to pay heed to something, to give it full attention, to concentrate on it, to learn to be careful, to control himself, and so on if we constantly distract him, by inviting him to watch TV, by dragging him to lunch table, or whatever. Not only are we breaking up the beginnings of his abilities to focus on

something; we are implicitly enticing him away from a struggle with
the difficult. The educational task is to find ways to help children face
difficulty and help them through difficulty. Many curricula have arbi-
trary difficulty. Real difficulty is where the achievement or mastery of
the difficulty matters to us, something that even the very young can be
helped to face up to. In matters of character education, difficulty is a
critical curriculum element, for the human predicament is complex
and challenging. How can we as teachers prevent the child from
assuming that the difficult is not really valuable? How can we provide
constant opportunities for challenge, intellectual, moral, and physical,
which engage the child's will?

Judgment and control. Presenting issues in moral education through
dilemmas for children to wrestle with overemphasizes the role of judgment and reason in moral life. But, as teachers, we have to understand
that the judgments moral agents constantly make (where our moral life
has not become a matter of habit) are strongly connected to our ability
to execute them. The obvious general description of the ADHD child
is a lack of self-control, and consequentially a lack of judgment.
Nowhere is the need for balance between judgment and self-control
more apparent than in situations requiring the exercise of self-restraint
and patience, as qualities of will. This is very complex: for while we see
how critical it is for the young to develop the connection between talk
and action (e.g., in choosing what to do or making judgments about
complex situations), there seem to be no pedagogical rules to follow.
We know self-control is not innate but don't know how to teach it. We
realize the significance of (moral, practical) judgment, but don't know
how to make it an authentic (rather than a classroom) feature of a character education curriculum.

Unless we grapple with these sets of problems, how can we explain
to parents, children, and others what we, as educators, see as what we
need to teach Johnny?

The Problem of Context

Context refers (a) to the institutional conditions established in
families and schools for the development of these personal capabilities
and (b) to the social influence of the use of the ADHD description on
the moral responsibility of teachers and parents.

The institutional conditions of family and school. In a recent study on children reading for pleasure a team of teachers in a small rural elementary

school in Virginia invited children to describe the contexts in which they preferred to read.[10] Some chose sitting with parents or grandparents, some chose to read to each other, some to read to an older sibling, some to read to a younger sibling, and one girl chose to read by herself on a chair in the school hallway. The variety of physical environments selected ("my magic closet," "the garage," etc.) was astonishing. These children were, of course, setting their institutional conditions for concentration. Postmodern families, with a household of conflicting agendas, often offer a huge range of choices to children to ensure that they are "occupied, busy, and out of trouble." This often results in children flitting from activity to activity like butterflies without developing any habits of persistence or carefulness. Are there institutional conditions of home and school, especially for young children, which are basic to ensuring the development of will? If so, what are they?

The social effects of the ADHD diagnosis. Let us assume that there *are* some (we don't know how many) children with severe behavior disorders of the ADHD variety (call them syndromes, if you like) which appear to have an abnormal chemical/biological origin. Although the chemistry of the condition is not clear, it is treatable with drugs. It is morally difficult to use chemical treatments for antisocial behavior without excellent justification. But the growth in the prescription of Ritalin for antisocial behavior invites educators and teachers to see ADHD as an explanation for their inability to work with a child. They are likely to see increasingly in children behavior which is "treatable," rather than struggling with the problems of educating the child. The ADHD diagnosis not only removes the need for them to struggle; it removes from them any responsibility for the disordered behavior. If my child's "bad" behavior is the result of some condition over which I, as parent or teacher, am presumed to have no influence or control, then I am absolved from moral responsibility for what the child does, in the same way that my child's epilepsy cannot be described as my fault. I cannot be described as having failed, for the child's condition has prevented him or her from being in my control. The child becomes a patient, not a student.

Conclusion

Much deeper conceptual analysis and empirical work is needed, for example, through theories of volition on these matters.[11] I have sketched a conceptual framework which offers an educational antidote to the ADHD description on matters of the will, that is, in precisely those areas in which Johnny is diagnosed as having a syndrome. I have raised several conceptual and empirical questions in seeking to elaborate why it is the educational definition that must be preeminent. But we have hardly started work on it. Meantime the pill-popping version of social control persists, and the development of autonomous rational human beings gets more difficult day by day.

NOTES

1. Marylou Tousignant, "Children's Cure or Adults' Crutch?" *Washington Post*, 11 April 1995, p. B1.

2. Richard S. Peters, "Moral Education and the Psychology of Character," *Philosophy* 37 (January, 1962): 37-56. Highly traditional forms of education, sometimes benignly, sometimes not, coerce children into accepting its values and internalizing them, thereby creating the capabilities alongside a commitment to intrinsic value.

3. Edward M. Hallowell and John J. Ratey, *Driven to Distraction* (New York: Pantheon Books, 1994); Larry B. Silver, *Attention Deficit Hyperactivity Disorder* (Washington, D.C.: American Psychiatric Press, 1993).

4. Silver, *Attention Deficit Hyperactivity Disorder*, p. vii.

5. American Psychiatric Association, *Diagnostic and Statistical Manual of Mental Disorders*, 4th ed. (Washington, D.C.: American Psychiatric Press, 1994).

6. Hugh T. Sockett, "Education and Will: Aspects of Personal Capability," *American Journal of Education* 92, no. 2 (1988): 195-214.

7. Philip W. Jackson, *Life in Classrooms* (New York: Teachers College Press, 1990).

8. Silver, *Attention Deficit Hyperactivity Disorder*.

9. Pat S. Wilson, *Interest and Discipline in Education* (London: Routledge and Kegan Paul, 1972).

10. Shaw Armstrong, Deborah Burrow, Terri Ganow, Theresa Gaskin, and Mildred Left, "Reading, Risking, Reflecting," Master of Education Project, Institute of Educational Transformation, George Mason University, 1994, Chapter 4.

11. Lyn Corno, "The Best-Laid Plans: Modern Conceptions of Volition and Educational Research," *Educational Researcher* 22, no. 2 (1993): 14-22.

CHAPTER IX

What Inner-City Children
Say about Character

BEVERLY CROSS

In the mass media, American young people are often portrayed as entangled in a destructive downward spiral involving drugs, peer pressure, sex, immorality, pregnancy, violence, gangs, crime, and alcohol. Character educators tend to agree and blame the problems on a lack of good character among youth. Although much is written about the characters óf our young people, we less frequently have an opportunity to hear from them. To bring the voices of children and youth into the current discussion on character education, I recently conducted a series of conversations with inner-city students to ascertain their views of "character." From these conversations, I can report that inner-city children and youth have acquired a vocabulary that matches, in many respects, that used by teachers and writers who discuss the goals of character education.

Over a six-month period in 1996, I interviewed eighty-five students from inner-city schools in a large midwestern public school system. Of the eighty-five, twenty-nine were elementary school students, forty-eight were from middle schools, and eight were from high schools. Seventy-five students were African American, nine were European American, and one was Latino. These students attended school in a district that is 59 percent African American, 26 percent European American, and 11 percent Latino.

My conversations with small groups of students ranged from thirty minutes to one hour. I sat with the young people in their classrooms or libraries to listen to their frank conversations. To get the conversations going I asked such questions as "What are the general characteristics of good and bad people?" "What lessons did you learn about good character at home?" "What lessons did you learn about good character at school?" My purpose was to create a context in which the

---

Beverly Cross is Associate Professor in the Department of Curriculum and Instruction at the University of Wisconsin—Milwaukee.

students felt free to express their own ideas and tell their own stories. I wanted the children to describe something of their everyday lives in a casual, open, nonevaluative environment. Their responses to my questions were lively, quick, and certain.

During the interviews I made copious notes in shorthand to record verbatim what the students said. After each session I prepared transcripts of the interviews, which I then studied in order to identify common themes in the responses. What follows are my perceptions and inferences derived from my review of these transcripts. First, I present six statements that summarize my interpretations of the students' comments in the language they used. Second, I identify some key problems related to character education in inner-city schools—problems that were called to my attention as I studied the transcripts.

Children's Perspectives on Character Education

1. *We can make distinction between good and bad character.* The children held clear and certain conceptualizations of character generally conceived of as good or bad, appropriate or inappropriate, acceptable or unacceptable. The words they used were not greatly different from those used by advocates of character education. When asked what good and bad people are like, the children responded quickly. Good people are loving, caring, compliant, honest, generous, respectful, kind, nice, helpful, friendly, and disciplined. They have morals, they share, they play fair, obey adults, do chores, and stay on task. Bad people, on the other hand, hurt and kill others, drink, lose control, are disrespectful, steal, lie, use drugs, damage property, get into gangs, commit robberies. They are mean and they don't share.

The children's vocabularies were not markedly different from the lists of character traits often presented in the literature as representing what is seen as important by scholars in the field. For example, a working paper of the U.S. Department of Education presented four different descriptions of character.[1] Many of the characteristics cited match those identified by the children and youth whom I interviewed: kindness, helpfulness, honesty, self-discipline, respect for others, fair play, obedience to authority. Other phrases crept into the students' conversations about "good people," include such ideas as having a family, being interesting, having a good personality, making right choices, thinking positively, listening to other people's problems, and volunteering. Not all of these are cited by character educators, but on the whole the vocabularies of students and educators are very similar.

2. We have learned that good character and good school behavior are similar. Many behaviors mentioned by the children—being competitive, staying on task, respecting adults, raising your hand, handing work in on time, getting good grades, reading and writing, thinking smart, going to college and getting a good education, never getting suspended, staying in school, comprehending [school work], being good at sports, working together—suggest the extent to which they regard appropriate school behaviors as reflecting what good people are like. The emphasis that teachers place on behaviors that facilitate learning, control the learning environment, and lead to the achievement of school goals seems to be translated by the children into images of what good people everywhere are like and also how they themselves should act in various social contexts.

3. The things we learn about character in school are different from what we learn at home. Although it is difficult for children to pinpoint exactly where they acquire particular understandings about character, my interviews suggested that they did in fact make such distinctions and that there was relatively little overlap between what was learned at home and what was learned at school. That does not mean, however, that what was learned in school contradicted what was learned at home. The learning was highly contextual and reflected the two major social environments in which the children learn and live. For example, in their homes they learned about what is expected of them in their homes and communities, such as distinguishing right from wrong, acquiring good manners, completing chores, being street wise, defending themselves, acting appropriately in public, and being polite to guests. Unlike what was learned at home, what was learned in school tended to emphasize what *not* to do, for example, don't do drugs, don't shoot people, don't steal, and don't disobey adults.

4. The school environment taught us much of what we learned about character. The power of an implicit curriculum in shaping the character of students was evident in our conversations. Much of what students identified as having been learned in school was apparently learned by functioning in their school environments. Their understanding of competition, cooperation, the importance of getting an education, of staying on task, and of discipline are all examples of what children appeared to have learned from the implicit curriculum. What children learned in school shaped their understanding of character, but there was no formal program of character education in the schools these children attended.

5. *Families, friends, and other personal relationships are more important to us than our material possessions.* I wanted to find out whether these children were as materialistic as the media lead us to believe. I asked them what they would take with them if they were selected to go on the next space shuttle mission because I thought this would reveal what they valued most. Their immediate responses included "my mom," "my brother and sister," "my dad," "my friends and my teachers." Only after mentioning the people close to them did the children talk about personal items to take with them. Younger children mentioned a puppy or a teddy bear. Older children said they would take pictures of family and friends, electronic games, roller blades, or stereo systems. They seemed to value most the relationships they had with people and the interconnectedness this afforded them.

6. *We have ideas about creating a better world.* When I asked the children to imagine they were creating a new community of their own and to identify the rules they would expect community members to live by, their rules were concise, real, and explicit. They cited rules like be respectful, work, be nice, help people, care for people, take advantage of school. The significance of context and experience was reflected in such rules as no drugs, no shooting, no gangs, no guns or violence, no killing, no stealing babies, keeping the peace, and respect for others' space. A few said they would want to be able to dress in gang colors without being shot. Rules such as these have significance in the lives of inner-city children. A contextual lens clearly informed the way these children perceived character.

Problems for Character Educators in Inner-City Schools

What the students said certainly does not inform every aspect of problems related to character education in inner-city schools. Their words do, however, raise critical and essential questions for educators who are shaping programs in character education. If it is true that character education is important because it is perceived to be "(1) necessary to a complete education, (2) linked to better academic achievement, and (3) connected to the well-being of society in numerous ways."[2] then the following inferences drawn from my conversations with the children seem crucial to inform discussions about character education.

1. *Inner-city children say the "right things" about character and do so without benefit of formal character education programs.* Although the students I spoke with had not experienced any formal character education

program, they were able to refer to dominant social mores and to name traits of good character like honesty, respect, generosity, discipline, and obedience to authority. Apparently, they had retained messages about character education from an implicit curriculum in the school rather than from a particular character education program. It would seem that daily exposure to norms and expectations meant to guide student behavior had provided students with at least the vocabulary of character education. It is also possible that their understandings of "good" and "bad" character were affected by their perceptions of the real and perceived power structures in their schools as well as the nature of gender roles and relationships. In this school district, as in many urban systems, other social and political pressures—for example, the uneven distribution of high-quality curricula across racial groups—could have influenced the students' views of character.

The conversations I had with students raised questions about how messages concerning character are transmitted to children and about the power of schools as social institutions. They also raised the question of what kinds of programs in character education could counteract the superficial mimicking of the "right" phrases that so many students displayed in my conversations with them. The children did not hesitate to recite messages they had absorbed about character, but they were uncritical of them. They voiced the desire to live up to standards they accepted uncritically. If the only purpose of character education were to indoctrinate students, there would be no need of specific programs since that purpose is already being served, judging from the conversations I studied. The challenge faced by teachers and policymakers is to design programs that take students beyond lipservice adherence to platitudes and slogans.

When I heard students responding to my questions with slogans like "stay in school," "say no to drugs," "get an education," "stay on task," which they recited like 2 x 2 = 4, I realized that their brief comments were isolated from any academic content or cognitive process. Their responses did not appear to be anchored in the sort of analytical thinking or critical inquiry that educators advocate.

I began to see the dangers—and the power—that lie in transmitting platitudes to students. What role do slogans about character formation play in the manipulation of children? Are the stakes higher for inner-city children whose experiences are already strongly shaped in schools by assumptions related to race and class? What linkages are there between what the children say and what they do? What opportunities are there for character education programs to move children beyond mere recitation to a genuine critique of social, political, and economic forces that shape how we live our lives? Do some character education programs represent an effort to sustain the status quo with respect to a hierarchically differentiated society? Should not character education lead to a more equitable society?

2. *The values cited by the children are largely designed to control their behaviors, to change those behaviors, and to create miniature adults.* The perspectives on character that had been transmitted to the children I interviewed emphasized being obedient (do what adults say, don't lose control, don't break or damage property, and never get suspended), maintaining the status quo (make right choices, think positively, and comprehend [school] work—in short, do as you are told), and submitting to socialization (competing, staying on task, raising your hands, handing work in on time). They were designed to fit children into the microcosmic society of schools and later into the larger society of adults. Children were being taught, it seems, to behave in particular ways that create passive, noncritical human beings who do not challenge social injustices or ask why our society is organized as it is. The students certainly were not being challenged to consider their roles in recreating society or to contemplate different perspectives on the organization of society. It would seem that the overwhelming emphasis when it comes to character development has been on producing conventional-thinking adults.

I began to question how the often-reported fear that teachers supposedly have of inner-city children was informing what the children were being taught about character. Were educators using this hidden curriculum to control children rather than, at a minimum, to create an environment conducive to learning and, more significantly, to engage them in a critique of society? Were their teachers using platitudes to distance themselves further from the lives of the children by defining the conditions of the social order that placed the students beneath them by class, race, and intellect? Were teachers' efforts degrading students by making them feel they were at a particular social level and implying that if they displayed certain character traits they could rise to higher social levels?

3. *The students' perspectives on character were rooted in negative views of urban communities, of families, and of the experiences of children.* What the children with whom I talked had retained about character development was based primarily on what not to do. They showed no signs of questioning whose voices were represented in determining what constitutes good character or how the structure of society creates

dominant social norms. What they seem to have learned appears to be derived from negative assumptions about their families and communities—assumptions that work to devalue both. For example, they seem to have acquired many ideas ("don't do this; don't do that") that may have originated in assumptions that shootings, robberies, killings, violence, and drugs dominate their neighborhoods. Apparently, they had not been asked to challenge their own voicelessness and that of their families and communities, or the complicity of schools in shaping their character around dominant perspectives, or the views held in their schools about their communities and families, or the detached relationship between schools and communities. Admittedly, I did not ask them to challenge schools and societies as hierarchies that hold authority over them, that transmit a single, universal truth, and that create a single reality. I cannot, therefore, predict how they might have responded to such challenges. However, from the conversations to which I listened it seemed clear to me that the overarching message these children derived was "your families and communities (and implicitly you) are 'messed up,' and the schools can fix it all if you adopt these particular perspectives." It seemed to me as though they had learned to ignore how social, political, and economic policies often hurt their families and communities while they were being socialized to march to the dominant drum.

Concluding Statement

The students I interviewed seemed to be keenly aware of ideas pertaining to character. They seemed to have learned a great deal about character at home and at school. Although they have not had the benefit of direct teaching about character in their schools, their teachers and just being in school have played significant roles in shaping their ideas about character. As I listened to the students and studied the transcripts of my conversations with them, it seemed clear to me that what these young people had to say about character is something educators should take into account as they consider how best to shape the character of children.

NOTES

1. Ivor Pritchard, *Character Education: Research, Prospects, and Problems* (Washington, D.C.: Office of Educational Research and Improvement, U.S. Department of Education, April, 1988).

2. Ibid., p. 1.

CHAPTER X

School as a Caring Community: A Key to Character Education

ERIC SCHAPS, VICTOR BATTISTICH, AND DANIEL SOLOMON

Some fifteen years ago, we at the Developmental Studies Center began working intensively with educators at a small number of elementary schools on the Child Development Project (CDP)—a comprehensive reform aimed at enhancing students' prosocial development. In the course of this work, the concept of the school as a "caring community" gradually emerged as central to our understanding of what makes for effective character education, and it has continued to serve as a fundamental guiding principle in our current work with a much larger number of schools around the country. Along with several other educational researchers,[1] we believe that this construct of school as community provides a powerful framework for looking at educational practice, and especially for practice aimed at helping children to become caring, principled, and self-disciplined.

We assume, along with Connell,[2] Deci and Ryan,[3] and their associates, that children have basic psychological needs for belonging, autonomy, and competence, and that their level of engagement with, or disengagement from, school is largely dependent on the degree to which these needs are being fulfilled there. Our basic assumption is that when children's needs are met through membership in a school community, they are likely to become affectively bonded with and committed to the school, and therefore inclined to identify with and behave in accordance with its expressed goals and values.

In its early years, our work on school change rapidly evolved to address students' intellectual development as well as their social and ethical growth. We came to believe that if schools are to foster long-term learning and growth in all three of these domains, they must provide two sets of "essential conditions" to the full range of students they

The authors are all connected with the Developmental Studies Center in Oakland, California. Eric Schaps is the President of the Center. Victor Battistich is the Deputy Director of Research and Daniel Solomon is the Director of Research.

serve: (1) *opportunities for membership in a caring community of learners*; and (2) *important, challenging, engaging learning opportunities*. The second of these conditions is only briefly discussed below; the first is the main focus for this chapter.

Sense of Community as One of Two Essential Aspects of Effective Schooling

We have come to believe that in most school settings, the creation of important and engaging learning opportunities, and opportunities for membership in a caring community of learners are so strongly interdependent that each is actually indispensable to full realization of the other. Both sets of conditions must be deliberately built into the structure, organization, and pedagogy of the school to enable children to learn across the major domains of development, and to keep them eager to learn.

Important and engaging learning opportunities. What are these, and why do children need them? "Important" learning opportunities help students acquire the skills, knowledge, and commitments they need to assume adult roles and responsibilities. "Engaging" learning opportunities are relevant to students' concerns, interests, and experiences— they tap children's intrinsic motivation to learn. How to make learning both important and engaging has been the focus of much of the current wave of reform efforts, and this goal has been central in our work as well, although it is not discussed here.

Opportunities for membership in a caring community of learners. What does it mean for children to be part of a "caring community of learners"? It means they are valued contributing members of a group dedicated to shared purposes of helping and supporting each other as they work, learn, and grow together. It means that they care about their learning and care about each other.

At the heart of a caring community of learners are the following:

- *Respectful, supportive relationships among students, teachers, and parents.* Supportive relationships—not competitive, punitive, judgmental, or exclusionary ones—allow all members of the school community to best contribute to children's learning. Children can venture opinions, make mistakes, tackle new subjects, and otherwise take all the risks that true learning entails. Educators can help each other deal with the daily demands of their work and the risks of changing professional practice. Parents, especially those who otherwise might feel vulnerable or ill at ease, can feel welcome and valued when taking active roles in the school and in their children's education.

- *Emphasis on common purposes and ideals.* Part of being a community is having a sense of common purpose; part of feeling included and valued in a community is living by that common purpose. When a school community deliberately emphasizes the importance of learning *and* the importance of behaving humanely and responsibly, students have standards of competence and character to live and learn by.

- *Frequent opportunities to help and collaborate with others.* We learn by doing; we learn to do things well by doing them often; things done often can become second nature. So it follows that children should often have opportunities to collaborate with or help others (for example, in academic group·work, community service, or tutoring)— and they should be encouraged to reflect on the ins and outs and ups and downs of these interactions. They will learn how to work well with others, and for the welfare *of* others, and why it feels good to do so.

- *Frequent opportunities for autonomy and influence.* We are invested in the choices we make for ourselves; we feel little intrinsic responsibility when choices are made for us. When children genuinely have a say in the life of the classroom—class norms, study topics, conflict resolution, field-trip logistics, and so on—then they are committed to the decisions they have been trusted to make and feel responsible for the community they have helped shape.

How Sense of Community Influences Children's Development—A Conceptual Model

As shown in Figure 1, various experiences associated with a caring school community are predicted to help students to: (1) satisfy basic psychological needs; and (2) develop their intellectual and sociomoral capacities, including their knowledge of academic subject matter, their reasoning and thinking skills, their conceptual understanding, their empathy with others, their social skills and social understanding, and their understanding of the values of the community. We assume that the development of these intellectual and sociomoral capacities also contributes to the satisfaction of basic psychological needs, particularly children's sense of autonomy and of efficacy.

According to the model in Figure 1, when their basic needs are met, children will become attached to the school community. This

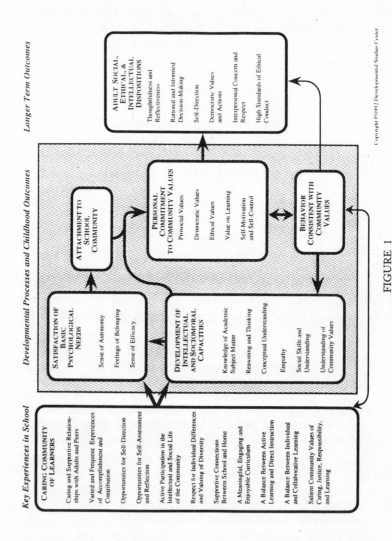

FIGURE 1

Conceptual Model of Effects of School Community

attachment, combined with the intellectual and sociomoral capacities already listed (including understanding of the community's values), will lead children to feel personally committed to the values promoted and endorsed in that school. In the school communities that CDP endeavors to establish, these include prosocial and ethical values, democratic values, the values of learning, self-motivation, and self-control. Children who develop commitments to these values will tend to behave in ways consistent with them. Such behaviors in turn help to solidify children's commitments to community values, to further develop relevant capacities, and to reinforce the school factors that, in combination, constitute a caring community of learners.

Children who develop long-term commitments to these values are likely to become adults with consistent ethical and intellectual dispositions—to be thoughtful and reflective, to make rational and informed decisions, to be self-directing, to maintain and act on democratic values, to be concerned for and respectful of others, to avoid courses of action that are harmful to themselves or others, and to maintain high standards of ethical conduct. These adult dispositions are also influenced by the behavior patterns developed by children, largely indirectly (through the effects of that behavior on solidifying the commitments to community values) but also, to a degree, directly.

The CDP Program and Its Effects on Community

The CDP program focuses on making deep, comprehensive change in the classroom, in the school at large, and in the links between home and school. The program has been described in detail elsewhere.[4] In brief, it includes:

- a reading and language arts curriculum based on high-quality children's literature drawn from many cultures, designed to help children see that reading can be both fun and informative, encourage them to explore the values and behaviors of characters in a wide variety of fictional situations, and sensitize them to the needs and perspectives of diverse others;
- cooperative learning, in which students are organized into small collaborative groups, both to master academic material and to learn to work with others in fair, caring, and responsible ways;
- an approach to discipline and classroom management which engages students in creating a warm and friendly classroom that stimulates learning and helps strengthen students' capacities to be self-disciplined;

- an extensive menu of home-school activities that invite families to shape and participate in the social life of the school, and share in and support their children's learnings; and
- school service programs, such as a Buddies Program that pairs older and younger students and helps them build caring, helpful relationships with each other.

Beginning in 1982-83, we worked with teachers at three elementary schools to implement the CDP program over a seven-year period. We evaluated the program's effectiveness by following a longitudinal cohort of students in these schools, and in three other schools that were very similar to the CDP schools prior to the introduction of the program, from their entry into the schools in kindergarten through their departure after sixth grade. As we refined our thinking and adapted program activities during the initial years, it became clear that what served to integrate the program elements was the creation of a caring community of learners—a community that meets students' fundamental needs for autonomy, competence, and belonging, and in which they come to understand through direct experience the importance to life in a democratic society of such values as fairness, caring, and responsibility.[5]

INITIAL RESEARCH

Our initial research on community therefore focused, first, on whether the CDP program—as implemented by collaborating teachers—created among students a sense of the classroom as a community; and, if so, on how the sense of community was related to students' attitudes, values, motivation, and behavior.

Our initial self-report measure of students' sense of the classroom as a community included items representing two elements: (1) students' perceptions that they and their classmates cared about and were supportive of one another (e.g., "Students in my class work together to solve problems." "The students in this class really care about one another." "My class is like a family."); and (2) students' perceptions that they had an active and important role in setting norms for the classroom and in making decisions (e.g., "In my class the teacher and students plan together what we will do." "In my class the teacher and students decide together what the rules will be." "The teacher in my class asks the students to help decide what the class should do.") We administered this measure to students when they were in fourth, fifth, and sixth grades. Program students scored significantly higher than comparison students on the measure of community each year, with the difference in mean scores ranging between one-third and one-half a standard deviation.[6]

As expected, sense of community was found to be significantly related to many positive student outcomes, either on its own or in combination with the intervention program.[7] These included both personal and social qualities (e.g., social competence, conflict resolution skill, empathy, and self-esteem) and school-related variables (e.g., liking for school, motivation for learning, and reading comprehension).

The findings from our initial research on community were limited to a small number of schools in a single suburban school district, with a largely white, middle-class student population. We wondered about the extent to which schools serving more diverse and disadvantaged student populations could be characterized as caring communities and, if so, whether community would be associated with a similarly wide range of positive effects. Theoretically, at least, the more diverse the population, the more difficult it might be to establish a sense of community. Yet doing so may be critical to maintaining social cohesion as our society becomes increasingly diverse. Similarly, the benefits of participating in a caring school community may be particularly great for those students who traditionally have not been well served by our schools—the socioeconomically disadvantaged and socially disenfranchised.

RECENT STUDY OF 24 SCHOOLS

Our recent research[8] has involved a more extensive examination of the effects of community at twenty-four elementary schools in six school districts across the United States—three on the West Coast, one in the South, one in the Southeast, and one in the Northeast. The schools in this sample (four from each district) were quite diverse, and included schools in large cities, smaller cities, and suburban and rural communities. They ranged in size from schools with fewer than 300 students to those with enrollments over 1,000. The student populations at these schools also varied greatly in their socioeconomic and ethnic composition, and in their academic achievement.

Teachers in half of these schools—two in each district—worked to implement a refined version of CDP. The other two participating schools in each district, selected to be demographically similar to those implementing the program, served as a comparison group. Baseline assessments were conducted in the program and comparison schools during the 1991-92 school year, prior to the introduction of CDP in the program schools in the fall of 1992. Annual assessments were conducted in each of the subsequent three years, during which the program was being gradually implemented in half the schools. The major assessment procedures included classroom observations, teacher surveys, and student surveys.

We assessed students' sense of the *school* as a caring community using the measure of student autonomy and influence in the classroom from the original study, an expanded measure of classroom supportiveness, and a new measure of the supportiveness of the school environment at large that included items like "People care about each other in this school." and "I feel that I can talk to the teachers in this school about things that are bothering me." The overall measure of students' sense of the school as a caring community included all three components.

RELATIONSHIPS OF SENSE OF COMMUNITY TO SCHOOL AND CLASSROOM CHARACTERISTICS

Our assessment battery has been extensive (encompassing school context and student demographic characteristics; classroom practices; classroom and school climate; teacher attitudes, beliefs, and behavior; and student attitudes, motives, behavior, and performance), and we have examined the effects of school community at multiple levels of analysis (i.e., school, classroom/teacher, student), using various statistical procedures (e.g., multivariate and univariate analysis of variance, multiple regression, covariance structure analysis).

One finding from our baseline assessment in the twenty-four schools was that sense of community was negatively correlated with school poverty level. The deleterious effects of poverty are well known and supported by our data. School experience generally is less pleasant and rewarding for both students and teachers in poor communities than it is in more affluent communities.

When analyzed at the classroom level, the baseline data showed that a number of general teacher characteristics (e.g., teacher warmth and supportiveness) and teaching practices (e.g., promotion of cooperation) were strongly related to students' sense of community, and that these relationships were independent of the school's poverty level. Moreover, students' sense of community was strongly associated with numerous measures of student attitudes, motivational orientations, and behaviors. These relationships generally were reduced in magnitude when student poverty level was controlled, but most remained statistically significant. For example, students' sense of community was consistently associated with a positive orientation toward school and learning, including enjoyment of class, liking for school, task orientation toward learning, and educational aspirations.

Most relevant here, students' sense of community was positively associated with their prosocial attitudes, motives, and behavior (i.e., concern for others, acceptance of outgroups, commitment to democratic values, altruistic behavior, and skill in conflict resolution[9]) and was negatively associated with students' use of drugs and involvement in delinquent behaviors.[10]

Given the well-known deleterious effects of poverty, and the strong negative correlation between student poverty and sense of community in the baseline data, we were particularly encouraged that many of the relationships between community and desirable student attitudes, motives, and behaviors remained statistically significant even when we controlled for poverty level. Although poverty in general was found to be negatively related to student outcomes, the positive relationships between sense of community and the student measures generally held within each level of poverty.

CAUSAL ANALYSES

Additional evidence for the importance of community comes from analyzing the effects of the CDP program on student outcomes over time. In these analyses, we combined seven of the observed classroom measures of teacher characteristics to form a coherent set of practices, consistent with what has been called "democratic"[11] and "constructivist"[12] teaching. We used structural equations modeling techniques[13] to conduct a path analysis of the effects of the seven teacher practice variables on the measure of students' sense of school community. Because we were interested in assessing *changes* in practices, behavior, and outcomes that were due to CDP, we controlled for baseline differences on the teacher and student measures. We tested the effect of program participation by estimating a path from a dichotomous indicator of program status (0 = comparison, 1 = program) to teacher practices in the third program year (with baseline scores controlled), and tested the effect on student outcome variables by estimating a path from sense of community to the measured outcome (with outcome scores at baseline controlled).

A summary of the findings from five such analyses is presented in Figure 2. For simplicity, the baseline effects are not shown, and paths to all five outcome variables are shown in the figure, although each of

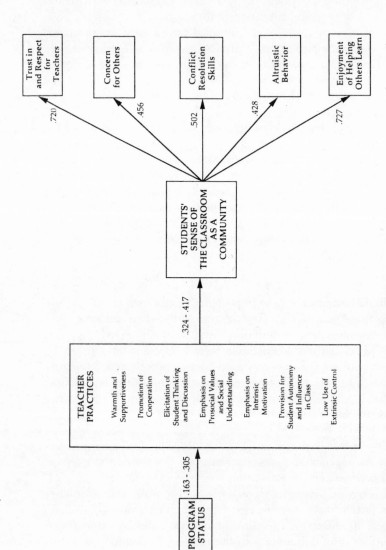

Note. All paths are statistically significant at $p < .05$. Baseline scores on teacher practices, sense of community, and outcome variables are statistically controlled.

FIGURE 2

Summary of Program Effects

these paths was actually estimated in a separate analysis. The range of values shown for the paths from program status to teacher practices, and from teacher practices to sense of community, are the range of estimated path coefficients observed in the five separate analyses.

The pattern of linkages that had first been observed in our analyses of the baseline data was essentially repeated here, with additional information on causation provided by adding program status and time changes to the mix. The findings shown in Figure 2 indicate clearly that participation in CDP had positive effects on teachers' classroom practices; that these practices, in turn, influenced students' sense of community; and that these changes in sense of community brought about changes in each of five student outcomes.

Conclusions

Overall, our research so far has shown that: (1) schools differ greatly in the extent to which their students regard them as caring communities; (2) sense of community is positively related to a large number of desirable outcomes for students, including outcomes of particular concern to character educators, such as increased prosocial behavior and reduced drug use and other problem behaviors; (3) a coherent set of teacher characteristics and practices is related to sense of community; (4) the CDP program by its third year of implementation had increased these classroom practices and behaviors, thereby producing increases in students' sense of community and in various associated outcomes. Moreover, these findings for elementary schools are generally consistent with those from other studies of community conducted in intermediate schools[14] and high schools.[15]

Many have noted that the feeling of belonging and togetherness represented by the sense of community has the potential for negative as well as positive outcomes. As our society becomes ever more diverse, we face increasing risks of polarization and social conflict. How do we develop communities that value and promote understanding of and respect for others, that are inclusive and open, with permeable rather than rigid boundaries? The development of *school* communities that promote such values may be crucial, for the school is perhaps the only remaining social institution that reaches all the diverse groups in our society. Moreover, the school traditionally has had a major responsibility for developing students' character as well as their intellect—i.e., for helping students to develop the abilities and inclinations needed by citizens in a democracy. There is still a great deal to be learned about how to accomplish this, but what we have learned so far is promising. Sense of community, as we assess it, relates positively to students' concern for others, skill in conflict resolution, altruistic behavior, and other dimensions of good citizenship in a diverse society.

Overall, we believe that the small body of research that has been conducted to date on schools as communities clearly indicates that a focus on community provides a powerful way of looking at character education, and at educational practice more generally. This focus seems to have a great deal of practical utility[16] in that it provides a clear direction for school improvements aimed at more effectively meeting the needs of both students and society. Of special interest are the indications that a caring school community may be particularly beneficial for disadvantaged students. More research certainly is needed on this issue, but caring school communities, while benefiting all students, may provide pivotal additional support, encouragement, identification, and commitment to those groups of students who traditionally have been least likely to succeed in school and are most at risk for engaging in problem behaviors.

This research was funded by grants from: The William and Flora Hewlett Foundation, The San Francisco Foundation, The Robert Wood Johnson Foundation, The Danforth Foundation, The Stuart Foundations, The Pew Charitable Trusts, The John D. and Catherine T. MacArthur Foundation, The Annenberg Foundation, The Spunk Fund, Inc., The DeWitt Wallace-Reader's Digest Fund, Inc., Louise and Claude Rosenberg, and the Center for Substance Abuse Prevention, U.S. Department of Health and Human Services. The views expressed in the paper are those of the authors, and not necessarily of the funders. A more complete and detailed description of this program of research may be found in Victor Battistich, Daniel Solomon, Marilyn Watson, and Eric Schaps, "Caring School Communities," *Educational Psychologist*, in press.

Requests for reprints or further information should be sent to Eric Schaps, Developmental Studies Center, 2000 Embarcadero, Suite 305, Oakland, Calif. 94606.

Notes

1. Anthony S. Bryk and Mary E. Driscoll, *The School as Community: Theoretical Foundations, Contextual Influences, and Consequences for Students and Teachers* (Madison, Wis.: National Center for Effective Secondary Schools, 1988); Ann Higgins, Clark Power, and Lawrence Kohlberg, "The Relationship of Moral Atmosphere to Judgments of Responsibility," in William M. Kurtines and Jacob L. Gewirtz, eds., *Morality, Moral Behavior, and Moral Development* (New York: Wiley, 1984); Philip Hallinger and Joseph F. Murphy, "The Social Context of Effective Schools," *American Journal of Education* 94 (1986): 328-355.

2. James P. Connell, "Context, Self, and Action: A Motivational Analysis of Self-system Processes across the Life Span," in Dante Cicchetti and Marjorie Beeghly, eds., *The Self in Transition: Infancy to Childhood* (Chicago: University of Chicago Press, 1990), pp. 61-97.

3. Edward Deci and Richard M. Ryan, *Intrinsic Motivation and Self-determination in Human Behavior* (New York: Plenum, 1985).

4. Daniel Solomon, Marilyn Watson, Victor Battistich, Eric Schaps, and Kevin Delucchi, "Creating a Caring Community: Educational Practices that Promote Children's Prosocial Development," in Fritz K. Oser, Andreas Dick, and Jean-Luc Patry, eds., *Effective and Responsible Teaching: The New Synthesis* (San Francisco: Jossey-Bass, 1992).

5. John Dewey, *The School and Society* (Chicago: University of Chicago Press, 1900).

6. See Daniel Solomon, Marilyn Watson, Victor Battistich, Eric Schaps, and Kevin Delucchi, "Creating Classrooms that Students Experience as Communities," unpublished manuscript (Oakland, Cal.: Developmental Studies Center, 1996).

7. Ibid.

8. Victor Battistich, Daniel Solomon, Marilyn Watson, and Eric Schaps, "Caring School Communities," *Educational Psychologist*, in press.

9. Victor Battistich, Daniel Solomon, Dong-il Kim, Marilyn Watson, and Eric Schaps, "Schools as Communities, Poverty Levels of Student Populations, and Students' Attitudes, Motives, and Performance: A Multilevel Analysis," *American Educational Research Journal* 32 (Fall 1995): 627-658.

10. Victor Battistich and Allen Hom, "Relationships between Students' Sense of School Community and Rates of Drug Use and Delinquency," unpublished manuscript (Oakland, Cal.: Developmental Studies Center, 1996).

11. Ann V. Angell, "Democratic Climates in Elementary Classrooms: A Review of Theory and Research," *Theory and Research in Social Education* 19 (1992): 241-266.

12. Rheta DeVries and Betty Zan, *Moral Classrooms, Moral Children: Creating a Constructivist Atmosphere in Early Education* (New York: Teachers College Press, 1994).

13. Peter M. Bentler, *EQS: Structural Equations Program Manual* (Los Angeles: BMDP Statistical Software, 1992).

14. Joanne M. Arhar and Jeffrey D. Kromrey, "Interdisciplinary Teaming in the Middle Level School: Creating a Sense of Belonging for At-risk Middle Level Students," Paper presented at the Annual Meeting of the American Educational Research Association, Atlanta, Ga., April, 1993; Carol Goodenow, "Classroom Belonging among Early Adolescent Students: Relationships to Motivation and Achievement," *Journal of Early Adolescence* 13 (1993): 21-43.

15. Bryk and Driscoll, *The School as Community*; Ann Higgins, "The Just Community Approach to Moral Education: Evolution of the Idea and Recent Findings," in William M. Kurtines and Jacob L. Gewirtz, eds., *Handbook of Moral Behavior and Development* (New York: Erlbaum, 1991).

16. Bryk and Driscoll, *The School as Community*.

Section Four
CRITICS OF CHARACTER EDUCATION

CHAPTER XI

The Politics of Character Education

DAVID E. PURPEL

Public discussion of moral and character education has become an overtly partisan political issue, serving as metaphor and code for those interested in pursuing the neo-conservative social and cultural agenda. Part of the strategy of neo-conservatives is to create a discourse in which the schools are blamed for not teaching values and families are blamed for teaching the wrong values. Implicit in such a discourse is the assumption that our social problems are *not* so much rooted in the failures of our social, economic, and political structures as in the attitudes and behaviors of individuals. The thrust of this approach is to move the discussion away from the extremely controversial realm of ideological dispute toward the safer and presumably more consensual realm of desirable personal traits, to convert social and political issues into educational and pedagogical ones, and to focus on stability rather than transformation.

We would all be better served by recognizing that the current so-called character education movement essentially represents an *ideological and political* movement rather than a debate about curricular and instructional matters. My basic criticisms of this approach, which are elaborated in this chapter, can be briefly stated as deploring the naivete or disingenuousness of the discourse and of the inadequacies of its political and social assumptions. I will try to show how this movement, far from being innovative and reforming, represents instead a long-standing tradition of using schools as agents of social stability, political stasis, and cultural preservation. I hope that this analysis will shed light

David E. Purpel is a Professor in the Department of Educational Leadership and Curriculum Foundations, School of Education, University of North Carolina at Greensboro.

on the more general issues of moral education and the moral nature of education.

The Politics of the Discourse:
A Historical Perspective

Deliberate intervention in the behavior and character of students is a central if not dominating theme in the history of public schooling in the United States. Indeed, our early colonial experience with formal education not only foreshadows this emphasis but much of its agenda and orientation continues to have an important influence on current views, policies, and practices. We can speculate further and posit the claim that basic to the entire colonization project were two obsessions that are fundamental to the subsequent and continuing development of American culture (and hence a critical dimension of public education): the drive to make the community morally good and the individual materially rich. The attempts to reconcile these two goals with Christianity and later with democracy have led to a social and cultural system or mythos that is highly complex, ingenious, and compelling if not contradictory, ambiguous, and controversial. This mythos represents an attempt to create a vision of America which seemingly integrates moral, religious, political, economic, social, and cultural perspectives seamlessly. The broad effort involved in creating, promoting, enforcing, and sustaining this vision has, of course, a very important *political* dimension: Who is to be involved in this process? Who is privileged by the process? Who benefits from the substance of the vision?

It is clear that public schooling has always been considered an important resource in this political task from colonial times[1] to the common school movement[2] to the present.[3] The establishment of the early Puritan schools was in response to fears that families were increasingly unable or unwilling to inculcate their children with the spiritual beliefs and moral virtues of the Puritan Commonwealth. The battle for compulsory education in the nineteenth century was led by members of the establishment who strongly believed that a system of schools with a common curriculum was the answer to the worries over national solidarity, social stability, and cultural purity. The current revival of interest in character education represents merely a revival of awareness of issues and concerns that have been a constant in discussions about education. This constancy should not be especially surprising given the essentially moral character of education. However, what is surprising about this revival is that character education is viewed as innovative and/or controversial. What is also surprising is how little the political and ideological substance of the discussion has changed over the past three hundred years.

One of the important changes in the current discourse relates to the matter of explicitness. Whereas the language of colonial and nineteenth-century education is overtly and aggressively moral in content, contemporary language tends to be circumspect and wary when it comes to moral issues. This is partly a function of a politics of legal fairness and impartiality that emerges from the constitutional separation of Church and State and a politics of accommodation that reflects the realities of a pluralistic society. Another dimension of the coyness about the moral aspects of education is intellectual; the dominant position of positivism has produced a consciousness of the primacy of objectivity and neutrality in which moral issues are seen as necessarily "subjective" and hence irrelevant and distracting. The confluence of constitutional limits, political expediency, and positivistic paradigm has produced an orientation in which education becomes a process of learning information and gaining intellectual insights that are presumed to be independent of moral and political considerations. This has allowed the phenomenon of a "new" field of moral or character education, which has transformed what used to be assumed as inevitable and inherent aspects of educational dialogue into problematic and controversial issues. The question changed over time from "What should be the moral orientation of education?" to "Should education have a moral orientation?" thereby allowing the notion of moral education to be seen as a possibility rather than an inevitability.

However, one of the anomalies of much of the recent literature in moral education is that many of the writers easily and quickly accept and postulate that moral education *is* always present, inevitably and inherently; nevertheless, they urge that the schools develop moral/character education programs! In his book, *Educating for Character*, Thomas Lickona titles a chapter "The Case for Values Education,"[4] a title that suggests that we have a choice on whether or not there needs to be values education. He lists "ten good reasons why schools should be making a clearheaded and wholehearted commitment to teaching moral values and developing good character."[5] On the very same page good reason number 6 turns out to be, "There is no such thing as value-free education." Lickona sums up this view this way: "In short, the relevant issue is never 'Should schools teach values?' but rather "Which values will they teach?' and 'How well will they teach them?'"[6]

There are troublesome issues here. If the schools are already engaged in values education, then why argue (as so much of the character education does so strongly) for the necessity for schools to do what they are already doing? Much of the discourse in both the political and educational realms has been framed in such a way that values, morality, and ethics are seen as notoriously absent from the schools and must be introduced with declarations like "Our nation needs to return to family values." If, as Lickona puts it so acutely, "the relevant issue is never 'Should schools teach values?'" then why does he begin his book with a whole chapter on "The Case for Values Education"?

The effect of such a discourse is to mischievously polarize education and other social and cultural institutions into those concerned with moral issues and those that are not. Furthermore, this absurdity has a way of giving aid and comfort to those educators and theorists who are extremely wary of concepts like "moral" and "character" and are loathe to get involved in discussions of them. It is difficult to attribute naivete to those in character education who actually affirm the inevitability of moral education; perhaps it is easier to interpret their coyness as an attempt to seize the territory as their own. The political issue at hand, then, has to do with who is to control the discussions on the moral and ethical dimensions of education. I regret that the answer to this question is that current discourse is controlled largely by those who have reified the concept of moral/character education into something distinct and separable from "curriculum" in the broadest sense and from the social-cultural context. This is especially troublesome when done by those who seem to have a particularly sophisticated understanding of how values impinge so powerfully and pervasively on all aspects of schooling.

Separating character education from the curriculum has allowed some politicians (and educators) to claim a monopoly on a concern for the moral character of society and individuals. When such people call for putting values "back" into the classroom, we might get some satisfaction from knowing that this is tautological and absurd thinking. However, such rhetoric has been used effectively in the public arena and has enhanced the political and literary ambitions of many. More important, in serving the narrow political interests of the Right it has blurred and distorted the extraordinarily important issues involved. That this reductive and misleading discourse has gone almost unchallenged only adds to the tragedy of the near impossibility of engaging the public in serious and thoughtful debate and dialogue on such complex, sensitive, and vital matters. If the question becomes "Should we or should we not have values education in the schools?", then it seems to me that the appropriate response ought to be either (politely) "Yes"; or (impertinently) "That's a silly question." How then can we account for the persistence of such silly questions?

One explanation that is persuasive to me is that there is a code operating here and that the masked issue is really not a demand for raising public awareness and moral sensitivity nor an attempt to promote the development of ethical consciousness. Rather, the call for moral/ character education coming from the character education movement and from parallel movements in the political arena turns out to be a call on behalf of a *particular and specific moral and ethical system*. It is one thing to advocate that educators and the public seriously address the moral and ethical implications of educational policies and practices and to urge us to ground our education in a moral framework; it is altogether different to urge that we buy into a distinct and particular moral orientation. Either of these discourses is to me perfectly valid; but what I find irresponsible is to blur them in such a way that to favor moral discourse on education equates to having a particular moral point of view and cultural vision.

Not only is such a discourse disingenuous but it serves to alienate further those who have always suspected that discussion of moral issues is, at best, equivalent to Sunday school and at worst to sectarian indoctrination. Furthermore, such a discourse can serve to create an artificial and destructive distinction between those who are pure of heart and those who are not, which, of course, tends to exacerbate existing suspicion, divisiveness, and distrust. Unfortunately, much of the professional discourse in this area mirrors the political rhetoric of those who seek to claim the mantle of moral righteousness exclusively for themselves as distinguished from those whose morals are of an uncertain if not dubious nature. Again, Lickona has put it trenchantly: "The relevant issue is . . . 'Which values will they [the schools] teach?' and 'How well will they teach them?'" In other words, let us end this absurdity of framing the debate over whether or not schools should be involved in moral/character issues and get on with the much more compelling question of which moral orientation(s) ought to ground our educational policies and principles.[7] It is also time that those educators who have had the courage to engage in the often thankless task of addressing these challenging and daunting issues—but who have insisted on blurring the questions with the answers—acknowledge that these are public issues requiring very wide participation by the public and the profession. Hence, they have a responsibility to frame the issues in such a way as to encourage the reluctant, the confused, the conflicted, and the squeamish to become involved in the dialogue. By the same token, those who have luxuriated in their detachment and noncommitment must not leave the struggle to those who have particular if not narrow moral orientations. They need to give up their ennui and do more than claim that dialogue on the moral dimensions of education amounts to the return of the Spanish Inquisition. We owe moral educators our gratitude for raising questions; we need to be thankful to the skeptical for their criticality; and we should respect the reluctant and uncommitted for their hesitation. Yet we must all be mindful of the insufficiency of separating criticality and affirmation from each other; criticism without affirmation can easily lead to cynicism while affirmation without criticism can just as easily lead to self-serving and bland sentimentality.

Character Education and Ideology

I turn now to the question of which values are actually being taught in the public schools. We can perhaps illumine this issue (as well as reiterate the prior point of the inevitability of moral education) by offering examples of values that are more or less uniformly imparted by way of general public and professional consensus. Schools teach that work and effort are good; that learning as well as imagination and creativity are valuable. Students are urged to be polite, respectful, and obedient to adults in general and school personnel in particular. They are taught that achievement is extremely important and that competition is inevitable if not salubrious; that those who do well in school merit certain advantages and that those who flaunt the rules and expectations deserve to be punished. Generally speaking, students are expected to talk or move around the classroom or leave it only when they are given permission. Schools teach that time is valuable; tardiness, absences, and missed deadlines are considered offenses. Students are required to do things they may not wish to do and are taught that this is a good thing.

Even though I basically agree with Herbert Kliebard's thesis that the public school curriculum represents a melange of conflicting orientations,[8] I am able to perceive some recognizable ideological shape to such moral emphases. My sense is that the values taught in the schools are very much in the line of Puritan traditions of obedience, hierarchy, and hard work, values which overlap nicely with the requirements of an economic system that values a compliant and industrious work force, and a social system that demands stability and order. There is an ideology here that puts very strong emphasis on control—adult control of children is mandated and legitimated and children's self-control of body and mind is demanded. Moreover, the state, acting as surrogate for the economic and cultural systems, exercises its power to impose this ideology by requiring children to attend institutions that the state establishes and controls and which are financed by mandatory taxation.

This cursory interpretation is meant only to indicate that it is possible (and valuable) to discern larger political and cultural meaning in school practice and to emphasize the ideological nature of moral/character education. Clearly, one can find other, sometimes conflicting, ideological forces at work in the public schools (e.g., concerns for democracy and individualism), for the point is that schools are important public arenas for ideological debate and struggle. The concerns I want to raise here have to do with the ideological nature of proposals for moral/character education and with my assumption that any such program is necessarily embedded in some larger social, political, cultural, economic vision. Moral issues are by definition socially and culturally situated, and any dialogue on proper character is based on some communal notion of propriety.

Unfortunately, one of the characteristics of the recent professional literature in this area has been the near absence of ideological analysis, never mind ideological affirmation. This again seems extraordinarily anomalous, particularly for those who are responding to a sense of cultural and moral crisis, since it would seem that a thoughtful response to crisis inevitably requires some interpretation of its etiology and nature. It is interesting that virtually all recent researchers in this field tend to provide some social and cultural perspective to their work, but their programs are largely, if not entirely, psychologically oriented. The problems are acknowledged to be largely social but the proposed solutions are largely personal! The anomaly is a discourse that seemingly recognizes the interpenetration of social, historical, cultural, economic, and personal forces but fails to acknowledge its own ideological assumptions, and therefore tends to focus only on personal intervention.

This anomaly is especially apparent in the work of those closely identified with the current character education movement.[9] These writers identify a series of serious social and cultural problems that they characterize as reflecting moral and character deterioration. They include such problems as the divorce rate, unwed parents, teen-age pregnancies, substance abuse, crime, school violence, classroom cheating, and child abuse. However, they offer little in the way of close examination of the data used to substantiate their claim that we are in the midst of moral degeneration. About the only interpretation they offer for this state of affairs is a rise in personalism and hedonism. There is no serious effort to examine the complex issues regarding teen-age pregnancies, for example, data suggesting that the rate of teen-age pregnancy tends to fluctuate and that current rates are not unprecedented.[10] Even if there has been a significant increase in teen-age pregnancies there is still a question of why it is considered a moral transgression. Is it wrong because teen-age parents will be economically or psychologically unable to provide appropriate child care? If the problems are economic in origin, then we have to ask why we have an economy that makes it so difficult to raise children at a time when parents are at an optimal age for rearing their young. Or is the problem one of morality? That is, do the writers believe that teen-agers simply should not be sexually active. What is the basis for such a morality? Community convention? Part of a larger religious framework? Personal opinion? Moreover, why is this issue lumped together with certain other issues like substance abuse and school violence and not with issues of social inequality and multinational capitalism? Surely, these writers ought to have some reasonably comprehensive framework that gives order and meaning to their critique and program. The framework they offer is skimpy and thin.

The reluctance or inability of the character education movement to elaborate and clarify its larger world view is unfortunate for at least two reasons. First, it represents a truncated dialogue that deprives us of a chance to recognize the way in which educational and social, cultural, and political issues are interrelated, thus significantly weakening the opportunity for a more thorough and comprehensive public discussion. Second, it allows others (like me) to attempt to fill in the missing links, and we may not do justice to their orientation. This vacuum will be filled by others as long as those in the movement fail to fully own up to their prior political, spiritual, and theoretical assumptions.

As it stands, the character education movement seems to have an uncanny resemblance to certain historical traditions as well as to particular strains of contemporary political ideology. Historically, the emphasis on the maintenance of the *status quo*, order, hard work, obedience, sexual restraint, stability, and hierarchy represents the continuation of the Puritan tradition, minus the explicit affirmation of Christianity. Its rhetoric of fear and trembling, of rapid moral and social deterioration, and its insistence on a return to an ethic of communal responsibility, sobriety, delay of gratification, respect for authority, industriousness, and conventional morality can hardly be differentiated from the pietistic language of nineteenth-century advocates of the common school.

In his book *Pillars of the Republic*, Carl Kaestle has interpreted the common school movement as a triumph of an "ideology centered on republicanism, Protestantism, and capitalism, three sources of social belief that were intertwined and mutually supporting."[11] He delineates several of what he terms "major propositions" of native Protestant ideology.[12] The presence of some of these themes, as well as the absence of others, in the current character education movement is revealing and instructive. Among these themes are: a concern for the "fragility of the republican polity"; the "importance of individual character in fostering social morality"; the critical importance of "personal industry" as a determinant of merit; a respected but "limited domestic role for women"; the critical importance for character building of a strong and appropriate "familial and social environment" (in contrast to those of certain ethnic and racial groups); the "superiority of American Protestant culture"; the equality and abundance of economic opportunity"; the "grandeur of American destiny"; and the "necessity of a determined public effort to unify America's polyglot population, chiefly through education."[13]

This nineteenth-century ideology clearly bears striking resemblance to the rhetoric and program of the neoconservative movement of the past two decades as exemplified currently in the political arena by the likes of Newt Gingrich and Patrick Buchanan and in the cultural arena by people like William Bennett and Pat Robertson. It is surely not the same, for the conditions are very different and the language does not resonate well with present historical circumstances. However, it is also clear (and reasonable to expect) that the culture continues to engage passionately in issues that confronted the nation in its early history. It is also apparent that the orientation toward the issues that Kaestle describes as the native Protestant ideology of the mid-nineteenth century overlaps substantially with the perhaps dominant political ideology of the 1990s and, more to the point, has significant resonance with the character education movement.

I want to make it clear that I am not suggesting that there is collusion and conspiracy between the professional and political figures of the character education movement or even that the professional movement is totally congruent with the agenda of the political Right. I am saying, however, that at the very least there is an implicit, fairly consistent, and coherent political orientation embedded within the message of character education and that this message has strong and vital resonance with neoconservative political and cultural programs. Edward Wynne, for example, urges schools to promote "traditional values," which he defines as "the panoply of virtues connoted by phrases such as the work ethic and obedience to legitimate authority and by the important nonreligious themes articulated in the Ten Commandments."[14] Note the attempt to define "traditional values" as unproblematic and to focus on work and obedience. Wynne makes a case for the close connection between character development and academic performance, claiming that "academics and character are coincident, since persons with character are by definition industrious."[15] In a discussion of teacher-student relations, he asserts that "adults who routinely deal with children and adolescents are gradually driven to recognize that adult-child relationships in schools cannot and should not be governed by so-called democratic theories."[16] This is hardly an affirmation of the traditional values of democracy and autonomy.

Another major figure in character education, Thomas Lickona, lists ten current "signs of a moral decline": violence and vandalism, stealing, cheating, disrespect for authority, peer cruelty, bigotry, bad language, sexual precocity and abuse, increasing self-centeredness and declining civic responsibility, and self-destructive behavior.[17] In its focus on individual behavior and the absence of structural criticism, this is hardly distinguishable from what might be heard in a political speech by a neo-conservative.

We can gain further insight into the ideology of character education by reflection on what is not considered, that is, by what is presumably not a "sign of moral decline." For example, and in sharp contrast to the nineteenth-century ideology, there is only token mention of the importance of sustaining a democratic consciousness. The references seem to be mostly concerned with procedural issues like voting rather than notions of social democracy; there certainly is no intimation that the vitality of democratic institutions is in jeopardy. Clearly there is not even an implied affirmation of the American tradition of revolutionary democracy as an expression of resistance to authoritarianism, nor of the spiritual traditions that command us to afford human dignity to all as an expression of divine will.

Nor is there a concern for the harshness and cruelty of an increasingly unbridled free market economy, of growing economic inequality, of the systemic nature of poverty, of the enormous disparity in the quality of medical care, of ecological devastation, of the ever-increasing desperation of have-not nations, or of the continuing dangers of international conflicts. The basic explanation that the character education movement offers for moral decline is a psychological one, that the problems are rooted in an inflated sense of personalism and self-centeredness rather than in social, economic, and cultural institutions. Therefore, it takes on, at least implicitly, the ideology of the struggle to preserve the social and political *status quo*: there are serious problems out there and what we have to do is not make structural changes in the economic system, the social class structure, or the political hierarchy but instead insist that individuals change. According to this ideology, society is being victimized by unvirtuous (lazy, selfish, indulgent, and indolent) individuals rather than seeing individuals as victims of an unvirtuous (rapacious, callous, competitive, and heartless) society.

The politics of the preservation of the *status quo* involves the privileging of those already in positions of power, influence, and advantage and maintaining the barriers against those who are relatively powerless and disadvantaged. In our present social reality we find ourselves in a particularly divisive situation in which virtually all the major social, political, and cultural institutions and traditions have been seriously challenged if not threatened by dramatic changes in consciousness. The most visible of these changes can be seen not only in such phenomena as the movements for civil rights, peace, multiculturalism, women's liberation, and gay rights, but also in the pervasive mood of alienation, disenchantment, and frustration. Much of the energy behind the conservative movement is in counterreaction to the challenge to and disaffection with the *status quo*, and it is in this context that the character education movement can best be understood. The context is like the one in which an army that is winning but has not yet won the war calls for peace. The conservative call for an increase in such admirable qualities as civility, deference to the community, stability, and orderliness serves to consolidate the gains and authority of those already in power. It also serves to distract attention from a potentially disruptive substantive critique of established social institutions and focus on the more emotionally charged issues of personal morality and conduct. Better to discuss poverty in terms of personal laziness and moral flabbiness than as an inevitable consequence of our economic system; better to discuss the alienation of youth in terms of school violence than as an aspect of a culture drowning in dispiriting materialism and consumerism. This is not to say that we should ignore the real dangers inherent in a doctrine of social and cultural determinism or forget that individuals have important responsibilities and opportunities to be agents for change. It strikes me, however, that we would be better served by an analysis that accepts a dynamic dialectic between the social and the individual, between the forces of social realities and the possibilities of individual responsiveness, and between individual rights and social responsibility.

It is also extremely important to point out that the current character education movement does not exhaust by any means the literature on moral/character education and by the same token to note that all other such orientations also require political and ideological examination, analysis, and interpretation. For example, my work has focused on the necessity to ground education in a commitment to pursue a vision of a just and loving community within a consciousness of moral outrage and personal responsibility.[18] In addition, there are other major orientations such as the program for democratic schools reflected in the work of Ralph Mosher[19] and the idea of teaching for compassion, nurturance, and caring as developed in the work of Nel Noddings and of Jane Roland Martin.[20] The orientations of these authors are based on quite different but equally strong ideological, political, and cultural assumptions in varying degrees of explicitness. We simply cannot allow those in the character education movement to monopolize and control the moral discourse of education. Conservatives like any other political group have not only the right but the responsibility to lay out the educational implications of their ideology, and like other groups, they have a corresponding responsibility to engage in good-faith dialogue on the realities of divergent viewpoints.

It is also vital to remember that this realm is not exhausted by those who write explicitly about moral/character education for we must also examine work that impinges directly and indirectly on efforts to develop particular moral values and behaviors such as material on school discipline, instructional theory, school counseling, attendance policies, and curriculum development. In a word, to talk of education is inevitably to talk of personal character and a moral community, and to talk of personal character and a moral community is inevitably to speak of political, social, cultural, and economic structures.

Problematics of the Field

I believe very strongly that the most important aspects of education are moral and that the term "moral education" is largely redundant. Because of this, I have argued that we would be better off without a "field" of moral/character education[21] because discourse in such a "field" is distracting and misleading. As I have maintained above, this discourse tends toward reification as it ignores and separates itself from the moral aspects of the larger school and social settings. A major anomaly in much of this field is the tendency to base its program on broad diagnosis and narrow treatment, on locating the problems in the society and culture and the responses in schools and classrooms. Those who work in this field have made a very important contribution by drawing our attention to these problems and issues, for the reality is that mainstream educators have allowed moral discourse to atrophy, perhaps out of a naive faith in the possibility of so-called value-free education. In addition, by stressing the importance and possibilities of individual responsibility they have provided a much needed balance to the theories of social and economic determinists. Leaders in moral/character education also provide much needed energy and hope. Perhaps most important, they remind us of our responsibility to honor our moral commitments. Our quest for the morally good society and our efforts to become good persons cannot be limited to compiling lists of attractive characteristics but must be extended to a serious examination of the conditions under which the contradictions between our aspirations and our deeds continue to persist. Our task as educators is not limited to striving for morally sound schools and to improving the character of the students; it also involves participation in the broader task of creating a just and loving society and a culture of joy and fulfillment for all. This task requires that we embrace a politics that does not privilege some and exclude or demean others but rather one that includes, affirms, and empowers everyone. Whatever advances that vision is sound moral/character education.

NOTES

1. Bernard Bailyn, *Education in the Forming of American Society: Needs and Opportunities for Study* (New York: Norton, 1962).

2. Carl Kaestle, *Pillars of the Republic: Common Schools and American Society* (New York: Hill and Wang, 1983).

3. David E. Purpel, "Goals 2000, The Triumph of Vulgarity and the Legitimation of Social Justice," in Ron Miller, ed., *Educational Freedom for a Democratic Society: A Critique of National Goals, Standards, and Curriculum* (Brandon, Vt.: Resource Center for Redesigning Education, 1995).

4. Thomas Lickona, *Educating for Character: How Our Schools Can Teach Respect and Responsibility* (New York: Bantam, 1991).

5. Ibid., p. 20.

6. Ibid., p. 21.

7. David Purpel, "Moral Education: An Idea Whose Time Has Gone," *Clearing House* 64 (May/June, 1991): 309-312.

8. Herbert Kliebard, *The Struggle for the American Curriculum, 1893-1958* (Boston: Routledge and Kegan Paul, 1986).

9. For example, Lickona, *Educating for Character*; Edward A. Wynne and Kevin Ryan, *Reclaiming Our Schools: A Handbook on Teaching Character, Academics, and Discipline* (New York: Merrill, 1993).

10. Deborah Rhode and Annette Lawson, *The Politics of Pregnancy: Adolescent Sexuality and Public Policy* (New Haven, Conn.: Yale University Press, 1993).

11. Kaestle, *Pillars of the Republic*.

12. Ibid., p. 76.

13. Ibid., pp. 76-77.,

14. Edward A. Wynne, "Transmitting Traditional Values in Contemporary Schools," in Larry B. Nucci, ed., *Moral Development and Character Education* (Berkeley, Calif.: McCutchan, 1989), p. 19.

15. Ibid., p. 31.

16. Ibid., p. 34.

17. Lickona, *Educating for Character*, pp. 12-18.

18. David E. Purpel, *The Moral and Spiritual Crisis in Education* (Granby, Mass.: Bergin and Garvey, 1989).

19. Ralph Mosher and Robert A. Kenny, *Preparing for Citizenship: Teaching Youth to Live Democratically* (Westport, Conn.: Praeger, 1994).

20. Nel Noddings, *The Challenge to Care in Schools: An Alternative to Education* (New York: Teachers College Press, 1992); Jane Roland Martin, *The Schoolhome: Rethinking Schools for Changing Families* (Cambridge: Harvard University Press, 1992).

21. Purpel, "Moral Education: An Idea Whose Time Is Gone."

CHAPTER XII

The Trouble with Character Education

ALFIE KOHN

If recent discussions about character education sometimes seem confused, with critics and proponents appearing to talk past each other, it may be because the very term "character education" has acquired two distinct meanings. In the broad sense, it refers to almost anything that schools might try to provide outside of academics, particularly when the purpose is to help children grow into good people. In the narrow sense, the term denotes a particular style of moral training, one that reflects particular values as well as particular assumptions about the nature of children and about how people learn. Unfortunately, the two meanings of the term have become blurred, with the narrow version of character education dominating the field to the point that it is frequently mistaken for the broader concept. Thus, educators who are keen to support children's social and moral development may turn, by default, to a program with a certain set of methods and a specific agenda that, upon reflection, they might very well find objectionable.

Consider three strategies currently being promoted. When President Clinton mentioned the importance of character education in his 1996 State of the Union address, the only specific practice he recommended was requiring students to wear uniforms. The premise here is that children's character can be improved by forcing them to dress alike, and further, that if adults object to students' clothing, the best solution is not to invite them to reflect together about how this problem might be solved, but instead to compel them to wear the same thing. A second strategy, also consistent with the dominant philosophy of character education, consists of emphasizing one value after another, with each assigned its own day, week, or month. Common sense suggests that this seriatim approach, which might be called "If It's Tuesday, This Must Be Honesty," is unlikely to result in a lasting commitment to any of these values, much less a feeling for how they may be related.

Yet another practice popular in character education programs is to offer rewards to students who are "caught" being good. Unfortunately,

---

Alfie Kohn, author of several books and articles on human behavior and education, lives in Belmont, Massachusetts.

a considerable body of evidence suggests that individuals who have been rewarded for prosocial or otherwise admirable actions become less likely to think of themselves as caring or helpful people—and more likely to attribute their behavior to the reward. Moreover, recent research has found that children who are frequently rewarded—or, in another study, children who receive positive reinforcement for caring, sharing, and helping—are *less* likely than other children to keep doing those things.[1] The prospects for achieving anything of value decline even further when competition is introduced, that is, when students are set against each other in a race for tokens of recognition whose numbers have been artificially limited. The likely result of making students beat out their peers for the distinction of being the most virtuous is not only less intrinsic commitment to virtue but also a disruption of relationships, and ironically, of the experience of community that is so vital to the development of children's character.

Unhappily, the problems with character education (in the narrow sense, which is how the term will henceforth be used unless otherwise indicated) are not restricted to these discrete strategies. More troubling are the fundamental assumptions, both explicit and implicit, that inform character education programs. Let us consider four basic questions that might be asked of any such program: At what level are problems addressed? What is the underlying theory of human nature? Which values are to be promoted? And finally, How is learning thought to take place?

At What Level Are Problems Addressed?

Defenses of character education typically begin with a recitation of dire social problems, the assumption being that all are attributable to the erosion of traditional virtues. The reader is encouraged to believe that people steal or rape or kill solely because they possess bad values—that is, because of their personal characteristics—and, by extension, that political and economic realities are irrelevant and need not be addressed. A key tenet of the "Character Counts!" Coalition, a project of the Josephson Institute of Ethics that bills itself as a nonpartisan umbrella group devoid of any political agenda, is the highly debatable proposition that "negative social influences can and usually are overcome by the exercise of free will and character." What is presented as common sense is, in fact, conservative ideology.

Politics aside, when character education programs proceed by attempting to "fix the kids," they ignore the accumulated evidence from the field of social psychology demonstrating that much of how we act, and who we are, reflects the situations in which we find ourselves. Virtually all the landmark studies in this discipline have been variations on this theme. Set up children in an extended team competition at summer camp and you will elicit unprecedented levels of aggression. Assign adults to the roles of prisoners or guards in a mock jail and they will start to become their roles. Move people to a small town and they will be more likely to rescue a stranger in need. In fact, so common is the tendency to attribute to an individual's personality or character what is actually a function of the social environment that social psychologists have dubbed this the "fundamental attribution error." Presumably, then, most social psychologists would recommend transforming the structure of the classroom rather than trying to remake the students themselves—precisely the opposite of the character education approach.

What Is the View of Human Nature?

Character education's "fix the kid" orientation follows logically from the premise that kids need fixing. Indeed, the movement seems to be driven by a stunningly dark view of children—and, for that matter, of people in general. A "comprehensive approach [to character education] is based on a somewhat dim view of human nature," acknowledges William Kilpatrick, whose book *Why Johnny Can't Tell Right from Wrong* contains such assertions as: "Most behavior problems are the result of sheer 'willfulness' on the part of children."[2] Even when proponents of character education refrain from expressing such sentiments explicitly, they often frame their mission as a campaign for teaching children self-control. This is noteworthy because the virtue of restraining one's impulses has historically been preached by those, from St. Augustine up to the present day, who see people as basically selfish or aggressive. Considerable evidence exists to support a more benign view of human nature,[3] and any educator who is persuaded by that evidence might hesitate before joining an educational movement that is finally inseparable from the doctrine of original sin.

Which Values?

By the mid-1990s, it had already become a cliché to reply that the question "Whose (or which) values should we teach?" need not trouble us because, while there may be disagreement on certain issues, all of us can agree upon a list of basic values that children ought to have. In fact, though, character education programs often emphasize values that are distinctly conservative and, to that extent, potentially controversial. The famous Protestant work ethic is prominent: Children should learn to "work hard and complete their tasks well and promptly, even when they do not want to," according to Kevin Ryan, a leading figure in the character education movement.[4] His colleague, Edward Wynne, defines the moral individual as someone who is not only honest but also "diligent, obedient, and patriotic,"[5] leading readers to wonder whether these traits really qualify as *moral*—and perhaps to reflect on the virtues that are missing from this list. Character education curricula also stress the importance of things like "respect," "responsibility," and "citizenship." But these are slippery terms, frequently used as euphemisms for uncritical deference to authority. Following a recent article about character education in the *New York Times Magazine*, a reader mused, "Do you suppose that if Germany had had character education at the time, it would have encouraged children to fight Nazism or to support it?"[6] To spend time in schools that are enthusiastically implementing character education programs is to be haunted by that question.

Even with values that are widely shared, a superficial consensus may dissolve upon closer inspection. Educators across the spectrum are concerned about excessive attention to self-interest and are committed to helping students transcend a preoccupation with their own needs. But how does this concern play out in practice? For some, it may take the form of an emphasis on *compassion*; for the dominant character education approach, the value to be stressed is *loyalty*, which is, of course, altogether different. Similarly, while any number of educators may profess to endorse the idea of cooperation, we may want to know their views on the practice of setting groups against each other in a quest for triumph, such that cooperation becomes the means and victory is the end. While some might see this as even more objectionable than individual competition, others have endorsed "school-to-school, class-to-class, or row-to-row academic competitions" as part of a character education program,[7] along with contests that lead to awards for things like good citizenship. The point, once again, is that it is entirely appropriate to ask which values a character education program is attempting to foster. It is quite different to promote loyalty and obedience as opposed to, say, "empathy and skepticism."[8]

What Is the Theory of Learning?

We come finally to what may be the most significant, and yet the least remarked on, feature of character education: the way that values are taught—and, more generally, the way learning itself is thought to take place. The great majority of character education programs consist largely of exhortation and directed recitation. The leading providers of curriculum materials walk teachers through highly structured lessons in which character-related concepts are described and then students are drilled until they can produce the right answers. Teachers are encouraged to praise children who respond correctly, and some programs actually include multiple-choice tests to ensure that students have learned their values. The Character Education Institute recommends "engaging the students in discussions," but only discussions of a particular sort:

Since the lessons have been designed to logically guide the students to the right answers, the teacher should allow the students to draw their own conclusions. However, if the students draw the wrong conclusion, the teacher is instructed to tell them why their conclusion is *wrong*.[9]

Students are told what to think and do, not only by their teachers but by highly didactic stories, such as those in the Character Education Institute's "Happy Life" series, which end with characters saying things like, "I am glad that I did not cheat" or "Next time I will be helpful." Most character education programs also deliver homilies by way of posters, banners, and murals throughout the school. Children who do as they are told are presented with all manner of rewards, typically in front of their peers.

Does all of this amount to indoctrination? Absolutely, says Wynne, who declares that "school is and should and must be inherently indoctrinative."[10] Even when character education proponents refrain from using that word, their model of instruction is clear: good character or values are *instilled in* or *transmitted to* students. We are "planting the ideas of virtue, of good traits in the young," writes William Bennett.[11] The virtues or values in question are fully formed, and, in the minds of many character education proponents, divinely ordained. The children are passive receptacles to be filled—objects to be manipulated rather than learners to be engaged.

Ironically, some people who readily accept character education are quite articulate about the bankruptcy of this model when it comes to teaching academic subjects. Many teachers have abandoned the use of worksheets, textbooks, and lectures to fill children full of disconnected facts and skills. Many administrators are working to create schools where students can actively construct meaning around scientific and historical and literary concepts. Many educators realize that memorizing right answers and algorithms does not promote a deep understanding of ideas.

The mystery, then, is why those who know that the "transmission" model fails to facilitate intellectual development would uncritically accept the same model to promote ethical development. In the case of individual educators, the answer may simply be that they failed to recognize that "a classroom cannot foster the development of autonomy in the intellectual realm while suppressing it in the social and moral realms," as Constance Kamii and her colleagues put it not long ago.[12] In the case of the proponents of character education, the reason for supporting techniques that seem strikingly ineffective at fostering autonomy or ethical development is that they generally are not *trying* to foster autonomy or ethical development. The goal is not to support or facilitate children's social and moral growth, but simply to "demand good behavior from students," in Ryan's words.[13] The idea is to get compliance, to *make* children act the way we want, to inculcate habits (that is, unreflective actions).

To be sure, the character education movement is internally consistent in that its process matches its product. The transmission model, along with the use of rewards and punishments to secure compliance, seems entirely appropriate if the values one is trying to transmit are things like obedience and loyalty and respect for authority. Moreover, the techniques of character education may succeed in temporarily buying a particular behavior. But they are unlikely to leave children with a *commitment* to that behavior, a reason to continue acting that way in the future. We can turn out automatons who utter the desired words or perhaps even engage in the desired actions. But the words and actions are unlikely to continue—much less transfer to different environments—because the child has not been invited to integrate them into his or her value structure. As Dewey observed, "The required beliefs cannot be hammered in; the needed attitudes cannot be plastered on."[14] Yet character education programs today amount to a strenuous exercise in hammering and plastering.

The traditionalists dismiss a constructivist model as a waste of time. "Must each generation try to completely reinvent society?" asks Wynne, rhetorically.[15] The answer is no—and yes. It is not as though everything that now exists must be discarded and entirely new values fashioned from scratch. But the process of learning does indeed require that meaning, ethical or otherwise, be actively invented and reinvented, from the inside out. It requires that children be given the opportunity to construct meaning around concepts such as fairness or courage, regardless of how long the concepts themselves have been around. Children must be invited to reflect on complex issues, to recast them in light of their own experiences and questions, to figure out for themselves—and with each other—what kind of person one ought to be, which traditions are worth keeping, and how to proceed when two basic values seem to conflict. In this sense, reinvention is necessary if we want to help children become moral people, as opposed to people who merely do what they are told—or reflexively rebel against what they are told.

Traditionalists are even more likely to offer another objection to the constructivist approach, one that boils down to a single epithet: relativism! If we do anything other than insert moral absolutes in students, if we let them construct their own meanings, then we are saying that anything goes, that morality collapses into personal preferences. Without character education, our schools will just offer more Values Clarification, where adults are allegedly prohibited from taking a stand. The reality is that Values Clarification, arguably popular in some circles a generation ago, survives today mostly in the polemics of conservatives anxious to justify an indoctrinative approach. Some of these polemics also attempt to connect constructivism to relativism, lumping together the work of the late Lawrence Kohlberg with programs like Values Clarification. In fact, Kohlberg, while opposed to what he called the "bag of virtues" approach to moral education, was not much enamored of Values Clarification either, nor of relativism in general.[16]

If Kohlberg can fairly be criticized, it is for emphasizing moral reasoning, a cognitive process, to the extent that he slighted the affective components of morality, such as caring. However, the traditionalists' objection to constructivism is not that empathy is eclipsed by justice, but that children—or even adults—should not have an active role to play in making decisions and reflecting on how to live. What they want is uncritical acceptance of ready-made truths. Any deviation from this approach is regarded as indistinguishable from full-blown relativism; we must "plant" traditional values in each child and demand their unconditional acceptance, or else morality is nothing more than a matter of individual taste. Such dichotomous thinking, long since discarded by serious moral philosophers,[17] continues to drive character education and to perpetuate the confusion of education with indoctrination.

To say that students must construct meaning around moral concepts is not to deny that adults have a crucial role to play: educators, parents, and other adults are desperately needed to offer guidance, to act as models, to pose challenges that promote moral growth, and to help children understand the effects of their actions on other people, thereby tapping and nurturing a basic concern for others that is present in children from a very young age.

Happily, programs do exist whose promotion of children's sociomoral development is grounded in a constructivist vision of learning as well as a commitment to transform the culture of schools in order to meet students' basic needs. The Child Development Project, designed by the staff of the Developmental Studies Center in northern California, is a notable example.[18] But, as a rule, the idea of character education has been appropriated by people who would sooner remake children than change educational structures, who begin with an unduly pessimistic assessment of human nature, whose agenda consists largely of getting students to work harder and do what they are told, and whose idea of teaching values is to drill students in specific behaviors rather than engaging them in deep, critical reflection about certain ways of being. Educators troubled by any of these premises will be inclined to challenge character education in its current form in order to reclaim the broader vision of helping children to become decent human beings.

NOTES

1. Among the relevant studies: C. Daniel Batson, Jay S. Coke, M. L. Jasnoski, and Michael Hanson, "Buying Kindness: Effect of an Extrinsic Incentive for Helping on Perceived Altruism," *Personality and Social Psychology Bulletin* 4 (1978): 86-91; Richard A. Fabes, Jim Fultz, Nancy Eisenberg, Traci May-Plumlee, and F. Scott Christopher, "Effects of Rewards on Children's Prosocial Motivation: A Socialization Study," *Developmental Psychology* 25 (1989): 509-15; and Joan Grusec, "Socializing Concern for Others in the Home," *Developmental Psychology* 27 (1991): 338-42. Also see Alfie Kohn, *Punished by Rewards* (Boston: Houghton Mifflin, 1993).

2. See William Kilpatrick, *Why Johnny Can't Tell Right from Wrong* (New York: Simon and Schuster, 1992), pp. 96, 249.

3. For example, see the research reviewed in Alfie Kohn, *The Brighter Side of Human Nature: Altruism and Empathy in Everyday Life* (New York: Basic Books, 1990).

4. See Kevin Ryan, "Mining the Values in the Curriculum," *Educational Leadership* 51 (November 1993): 16.

5. See Edward A. Wynne, "The Great Tradition in Education: Transmitting Moral Values," *Educational Leadership* 43 (December 1985/January 1986): 6.

6. Marc Desmond's letter appeared in the *New York Times Magazine*, 21 May 1995, p. 14.

7. Edward A. Wynne and Herbert J. Walberg, "The Complementary Goals of Character Development and Academic Excellence," *Educational Leadership* 43 (December 1985/January 1986): 17.

8. These two core values—"the ability to see a situation from the eyes of another and the tendency to wonder about the validity of what we encountered"—have been

suggested by Deborah Meier and Paul Schwarz of the Central Park East Secondary School in New York. See their chapter, "Central Park East Secondary School," in Michael W. Apple and James A. Beane, eds., *Democratic Schools* (Alexandria, Va.: Association for Supervision and Curriculum Development, 1995), pp. 29-30.

9. This passage is taken from page 21 of an undated 28-page "Character Education Curriculum" produced by the Character Education Institute in San Antonio, Texas. Emphasis in original.

10. See Wynne, "The Great Tradition in Education."

11. This is from William Bennett's introduction to his *The Book of Virtues* (New York: Simon & Schuster, 1993), pp. 12-13.

12. See Constance Kamii, Faye B. Clark, and Ann Dominick, "The Six National Goals: A Road to Disappointment," *Phi Delta Kappan* 75 (May 1994): 677.

13. See Kevin Ryan, "Character and Coffee Mugs," *Education Week*, 17 May 1995, p. 48.

14. See John Dewey, *Democracy and Education* (New York: Free Press, 1916/1966), p. 11.

15. See Wynne, "Character and Academics in the Elementary School," in Jacques S. Benninga, ed., *Moral, Character, and Civic Education in the Elementary School* (New York: Teachers College Press, 1991), p. 142.

16. Kohlberg's model, which holds that people across cultures progress predictably through six stages of successively more sophisticated styles of moral reasoning, is based on the decidedly nonrelativistic premise that the last stages are superior to the first ones. See his *Essays on Moral Development, vol. I: The Philosophy of Moral Development* (San Francisco: Harper & Row, 1981), especially the essays entitled "Indoctrination Versus Relativity in Value Education" and "From *Is* to *Ought*."

17. For example, see James S. Fishkin, *Beyond Subjective Morality* (New Haven, Conn.: Yale University Press, 1984); and David B. Wong, *Moral Relativity* (Berkeley: University of California Press, 1984).

18. For example, see Daniel Solomon, Marilyn Watson, Victor Battistich, Eric Schaps, and Kevin Delucchi, "Creating a Caring Community: Educational Practices that Promote Children's Prosocial Development," in Fritz K. Oser, Andreas Dick, and Jean-Luc Patry, eds., *Effective and Responsible Teaching: The New Synthesis* (San Francisco: Jossey-Bass, 1992). For more information about the Child Development Project, write to Developmental Studies Center, 2000 Embarcadero, Suite 305, Oakland, California, 94606.

CHAPTER XIII

Commercial Culture and the Assault on Children's Character

ALEX MOLNAR

Americans live what author Leslie Savan has referred to as sponsored lives.[1] Virtually every facet of life in the United States now comes with sponsorship of some sort. From the radio programs we listen to and the television programs we watch to the clothes we wear and the leisure activities we pursue, we are surrounded by commercials. According to Savan, television-watching Americans see about one hundred commercials a day.[2] Add other commercial venues such as billboards, shopping carts, clothing labels, and city buses, and the number of ads that clamor for attention from each American reaches 16,000 a day.[3]

In American commercial culture anything can be turned into a product and put up for sale—and everything has a price, from dog food to automobiles, from hair spray to time-share condos, from companionship to political action. Increasingly, people are defined by what they purchase and valued for what they possess.

It would be impossible for a cultural impulse as strong as the commercialism that now lies at the heart of American life not to affect the character of children. Anyone who has seen the highly stylized ads for children's clothing in the relentlessly upscale *New York Times Magazine*, or watched a soft drink commercial on television, or listened to an athletic shoe ad on the radio knows that Madison Avenue has designs on America's children.[4] Indeed, Madison Avenue probably sends more messages to children about who they are and who they should strive to be than all of the character educators in all of America's schools combined. Yet, surprisingly, the literature on character education, despite its focus on morals, values, and social dissolution is largely mute on the subject of commercialism, which is a corrosive

Alex Molnar is a Professor of Education in the Department of Curriculum and Instruction at the University of Wisconsin-Milwaukee. Parts of the material used in this chapter have been previously published either in his book, *Giving Kids the Business: The Commercialization of America's Schools* (Boulder, Colorado: Westview/HarperCollins, 1996) or in *Education Week*, 16 September 1996.

phenomenon that comes between parents and children, threatens nonmaterial human relationships, and undermines democratic values.

Modern character education is driven by a broadly based consensus that the United States is in a period of moral decline. Unlike character education advocates in the 1960s and 1970s, who attempted to help students "clarify" their values[5] or to progress toward a higher level of moral reasoning,[6] contemporary character educators such as Thomas Lickona, Jacques Benninga, and Edward Wynne[7] advocate instruction in "core" ethical values. They also link the development of children's character to civic renewal.

The ascendant view links character education in its most fundamental aspects to a vision of society that assumes that the independent value-based behavior of individuals is the best explanation for social virtue or moral decay. This popular view helps explain the success of William Bennett's *Book of Virtues*.[8] Although character educators discuss the need to promote civic renewal and promote collaborative endeavor,[9] the implicit conception of character advanced by the modern character education movement assumes that each individual is able to choose to do good regardless of context or circumstance. This is a view that resonates with Americans' attachment to the ideal of the rugged individualist as master of her or his own destiny--a person willing and able to stand against the tide in defense of personal conviction and enduring values. In America's mercantile culture the ideal of the rugged individualist has been transformed into the ideal of the savvy consumer who controls the marketplace by making well-informed, independent decisions about what sort of mouth wash, candy bar, or stereo to buy.

Since context and circumstance are left unaccounted for in the epistemology of contemporary character education, it is hardly surprising that character education can offer only a rudimentary and simplistic understanding of how powerful cultural phenomena influence the social boundary markers that shape and define the moral understanding and ethical behavior of children. In practical terms, this deficiency no doubt often results in children regarding the well-intentioned exhortations built into character education programs as out of touch with the real world that they inhabit.

This probably explains, at least in part, why it is so difficult to document any lasting impact of character education on children's ethical behavior.[10] To be sure, children seem to have no trouble learning to *identify* what proper behavior (as defined by the character educator) is or in swearing allegiance to it. However, identifying and giving verbal

endorsement to behavior preferred by character education programs is
not the same as actually behaving that way.

If children are able to tell character educators what they want to
hear while they go on behaving in ways defined as sensible by their
economic, social, and cultural milieu, they are also happy to tell anyone who asks that advertisements have no effect on their behavior at
all.[11] They do this despite the fact that children as a group tend to
demand the same products from jeans and sneakers to soft drinks and
hair gel.

American children have learned the meta-message of commercial
culture very well, i.e., that consuming is the best way to express one's
individuality and celebrate one's uniqueness. As Savan has noted, advertisers ". . . have learned that to break through . . . they have to be as
cool, hip, and ironic as the target audience likes to think of itself as
being."[12] Small wonder that children (and adults) in America are often
part of what David Riesman called a "lonely crowd"[13]—a crowd that
represents the negation of both the individual and genuine community. Members of the Riesman's lonely crowd define themselves by
their possessions and express their individuality by looking, smelling,
and thinking like everyone else. In this world, people are asked to
believe that fads, for example, emerge from a magical confluence of
independent judgments rather than being the result of deliberate promotion by advertisers.[14]

If character educators were to take seriously their rhetoric about
promoting enduring values and democratic civic engagement, they
would devote a good deal of time to the analysis of commercial culture
and to what Vance Packard labeled "the hidden persuaders."[15] The
underlying emotional content of advertising deployed for the express
purpose of manipulating behavior is inherently and profoundly anti-
democratic. If the strength of a democracy rests on a foundation of
reasoned judgments made by people capable of genuine human attach-
ments, then anyone who has observed the extent to which commercialism has infiltrated and corrupted the American political process cannot
help but be alarmed. Candidates are now "packaged" and marketed to
the public like any other product, political programs are built on illu-
sory rather than real differences, and political debate is a lexicon of
corrupted meanings.

The father of modern mass advertising, Edward Bernays (Sigmund
Freud's nephew) pointed the way. After he had been hired by the American Tobacco Company, Bernays drew on the psychological research
of A. A. Brill that suggested that, for women, smoking represented

emancipation. Using that knowledge, Bernays transformed cigarettes into "torches of liberty," and arranged for ten young women to march in the 1929 Easter parade on Fifth Avenue in New York smoking their "torches of liberty" to protest against women's inequality.[16] Orwell's vision of a world in which good is bad, love is hate, and peace is war, arrived long before 1984 for America's marketers.

While character educators busy themselves decrying the "apathy, distrust, cynicism, and dishonesty"[17] of America's young people the commercial tide rising in American schools promotes precisely these qualities and debases the humanity of everyone it touches. Every school day children all over the United States are subjected to dishonest propaganda supplied by a variety of corporate interests. There is no altruistic impulse in commercialism—marketing to children is big business.

When Michael Milken, the junk bond king, was let out of prison, he said that he wanted to be involved in education because he considered it to be one of the biggest moneymakers for American business.[18] He is right. According to Consumers Union, elementary school children spend around $15 billion a year, and also influence the spending of another $160 billion. Teenagers spend an estimated $57 billion of their own money and another $36 billion of their families' cash.[19]

The attempt to mine childhood for commercial advantage is nothing new. As early as 1929, concern about the influence of corporations on school curriculum was strong enough for the National Education Association to impanel a "Committee on Propaganda in the Schools."[20] However, the subsequent NEA report and other mild efforts by professional educators to set boundaries around commercial activities in the schools, have been ineffectual in the face of the commercial onslaught.

In 1959, Saatchi & Saatchi, the New York advertising agency, created the first television ad aimed exclusively at children. The only problem was that there was nowhere on television to show it. Not willing to let the star of their commercial, the Trix rabbit, go homeless, Saatchi & Saatchi invented Saturday morning children's television so that their ad would have programming to interrupt.[21] Thirty years later, when Channel One was brought to life with millions of high-voltage advertising dollars, the "vast wasteland" of American commercial television spread to the classroom.

Sheila Harty's 1979 book, *Hucksters in the Classroom*,[22] documented the extent to which corporate propaganda was being used in the nation's schools in the areas of nutrition, nuclear power, the environment, and economics. Yet, as alarming as they were, the practices Harty detailed were only a prelude to the unparalleled commercial onslaught that was to come.

In the 1980s, a Rubicon of sorts was crossed. Not only did the volume of advertising reach new levels of intrusiveness—often under the guise of helping cash-strapped schools fill in the gap left by missing tax dollars—but marketing efforts were unashamedly characterized as legitimate contributions to curriculum content, as helpful teaching aids, and as a good way of promoting school-business cooperation.

It was not long before a commercial wave broke over the schools. In homes across America, parents may have discovered that their daughters and sons had been given a "Gushers" fruit snack, told to burst it between their teeth, and asked by their teacher to compare the sensation to a geothermic eruption (compliments of General Mills). Children were taught the history of the potato chip (compliments of The Potato Board and the Snack Food Association). Adolescent girls learned about self-esteem by discussing "good hair days" and "bad hair days" in class (compliments of Revlon). Tootsie Roll provided a lesson on "The Sweet Taste of Success." Exxon sent out a videotape, "Scientists and the Alaska Oil Spill," to help teachers reassure students that the Valdez disaster was not so bad after all. And Prego spaghetti sauce offered to help students learn science by comparing the thickness of Prego sauce to that of Ragu.

One or two examples of dishonest, self-serving, corporate material might be laughed off as aberrations. But it is hardly a laughing matter when, by their sheer volume, sponsored materials threaten to turn the school curriculum into a booming, buzzing confusion; when the energy and focus of a school are diverted from the education of children to the promotion of commercial interests; when the trust parents have that what their children are being taught is important information, honestly presented, is routinely violated; and when children are encouraged to associate a particular product with personal worth and success.

By 1990, the situation was bad enough for Consumers Union to call for schools to be made ad-free zones.[23] In 1995, a Consumers Union report, *Captive Kids*, documented a commercial assault that was continuing unabated.[24]

School-related debates over sex education, religious values, censorship, drug use, and yes, *character* regularly find their way into the media. However, the ethical problems created by using corporate-sponsored materials in the schools rarely rise to the surface. In part, this is because of the extent to which commercial values have now assumed the status of common sense. And, in part, it is because, as right wing radio personality Rush Limbaugh discovered, it is about power.

The "BOOK IT!" program sponsored by Pizza Hut awards a free pizza to children who meet their reading goals. Limbaugh had criticized the offer (justifiably) as little more than "bribes for books." During his May 25, 1995 radio show, he learned that the "BOOK IT!" program was sponsored by Pizza Hut, a company for which he did commercials. In response he proclaimed: "I'm demonstrating my independence. Just because I do a Pizza Hut commercial does not mean that I have been purchased hook, line, and sinker."[25]

It took only one day for Limbaugh to adjust his attitude: "Since the program ended yesterday, I have been in, and my staff have been in, almost hourly contact with the officials at Pizza Hut. . . . Now, I've got my mind right, ladies and gentlemen. I've had it 'splained to me by a number of different people and I'm prepared here to do a mea culpa because I didn't understand what the whole thing was about yesterday."[26]

What it was about was power. And Limbaugh was taught that the people paying the piper call the tune. As comical or inconsequential as the programs they purchase may sometimes seem, sponsorship dollars come from powerful special interests that are very serious about pressing for advantage, whether on our airwaves or in our schools.

The pervasiveness of commercial activities now carried out in the school has helped to blur the distinction between promoting special privilege and advancing the general welfare in education and has transformed children into commodities along the way. There is now little talk of valuing children for their own right—just because we love them. Quite the contrary. At a time when poor children have killed each other for a pair of over-priced, over-hyped sports shoes, they are forced to watch advertising messages for high-priced sneakers in school. At a time when American children are increasingly overweight and at risk of coronary disease, they have been taught how the heart functions by a poster advertising junk food and they have been served high-fat meals by the fast-food concessionaires that run their school cafeterias. And at a time when many children are literally made sick by the air they breathe they are told that some of the country's biggest polluters are their friends. At a time when young people hunger for real connections and genuine relationships, they are fed illusions.

The promotional materials distributed by one company, Scholastic, illustrate the ethical bankruptcy of America's commercial culture. Scholastic promotes itself as ". . . the *only* publishing pipeline covering the entire pre-K to 12th grade marketplace."[27] For the right price,

Scholastic will develop marketing vehicles such as single-sponsor magazines, inserts, and special sections, contests, posters, teaching guides, videos, software, research, and books. When it promotes itself to potential clients, Scholastic gives examples of past school-based ad campaigns such as: "*Discover Card* and Scholastic Give Teens Extra Credit," "*Minute Maid* Puts the Squeeze on the Competition with a Summer Reading Program," and "To Billy Joel, *CBS Records* and Scholastic History Is Hot."[28]

Mother Jones magazine contacted Modern Talking Pictures, another firm that specializes in helping corporations put messages into schools and classrooms, and pretended to be representing a potential client concerned about the bad publicity that nuclear power had been getting.

> *Mother Jones:* This is the company's pet project. They're very concerned about putting out material that will help correct the antinuclear bias in most educational materials. So we don't want much tampering with the material. Is that a problem?
>
> *Modern Talking Pictures:* I understand exactly what you're saying. We wouldn't want to write anything our client didn't want us to. It would have to be factual, of course.
>
> *MJ:* Of course.
>
> *MTP:* But we try to be sensitive to our clients aims. . . . We wouldn't want to write anything that makes the sponsor unhappy.
>
> *MJ:* Now, we're talking national—we want to get this into every school in the country. Can you handle that?
>
> *MTP:* We've done that for a lot of our corporate clients—Proctor & Gamble, IBM. . . . We know how to get materials into the hands of educators.
>
> *MJ:* I understand there's quite a demand for these kinds of materials now.
>
> *MTP:* Educators just eat them up.[29]

Even more insidious is the saga of Old Joe Camel, the corporate dromedary that pitches Camel cigarettes, and *Weekly Reader*, a venerable children's newspaper that has been a staple in American classrooms for decades. Since 1991, *Weekly Reader* has been owned by K-III Communications, a subsidiary of Kohlberg, Kravis, Roberts & Company, a major shareholder in RJR Nabisco whose R.J. Reynolds division is the corporate home of Old Joe.[30]

Old Joe is a bad actor, but children love him. Introduced in 1988, the Old Joe ad campaign puts the cartoon camel on billboards, phone booths, baseball caps, and T-shirts. Often he is pictured on a motorcycle or in a pool hall, surrounded by girl camels. Like Ronald McDonald, he also hangs out at promotional events. It did not take long for observers to begin wondering who the intended target of the Old Joe cartoon campaign was. Research has suggested an answer. Between 1988 and 1991, Camel sales to children rose from $6 million to $476 million a year.[31]

Either Old Joe is an unguided marketing missile or he is doing exactly what he is supposed to do. Critics point out that people rarely start smoking after the age of eighteen and charge that with the shrinking of more health-conscious adult market for their product, R.J. Reynolds is trying to build an early customer base.

Research published in the *Journal of the American Medical Association* revealed, among other things, that 91 percent of six-year-olds could match Old Joe with a cigarette (about the same number that could pair Mickey Mouse with the Disney Channel); that teenagers were more likely to respond favorably to Old Joe than adults; and that, although only 9 percent of adult smokers identified Camel as their brand, 33 percent of school-age smokers did.[32]

When Old Joe was featured on the cover of an issue of *Weekly Reader* with the headline "Are Camel Ads Attracting Kids to Smoking?", some people saw a double message and wondered about *Weekly Reader's* motives. They had reason to be concerned. In 1995, *Education Week* reported that researchers evaluating tobacco-related articles in *Weekly Reader* and another weekly children's magazine between 1989 and 1994 found that 68 percent of the *Weekly Reader* stories included the tobacco industry's views as compared to 32 percent in the other magazine. More significantly, the researchers found that after *Weekly Reader* was purchased by K-III, the number of articles on tobacco-related topics that contained an anti-smoking message declined dramatically. Before K-III owned *Weekly Reader*, 65 percent of its tobacco-related stories contained an anti-smoking message; after K-III took over, only 24 percent of the stories did.[33]

While all of this is going on, character educators tut tut and cluck cluck about the moral crisis that has overtaken our *young*. As adults wring their hands and decry youthful cynicism, school children are routinely treated as resources to be exploited for adult advantage. Wendell Berry exposes the underlying moral rot:

It seems that we have been reduced almost to a state of absolute economics, in which people and all other creatures and things may be considered purely as economic "units," or integers of production, and in which a human being may be dealt with, as John Ruskin put it, "merely as a covetous machine." And the voices bitterest to hear are those saying that all this destructive work of mindless genius, money, and power is regrettable but cannot be helped.[34]

Despite the obvious ethical problems with using schools to make sales pitches to children and their families, it is rare to hear education, business, or community leaders voice either ethical or educational objections to school-based commercialism. Instead, they are apt to support the idea that commercial activities in the school are legitimate "partnerships" between the public schools and the business community.

The danger to our democracy and our children posed by commercialism is great. As Ralph Nader argues,

Any culture that surrenders its vision and its self-sustaining human values to the narrow judgment of commerce will be neither free nor just. . . . The commercialistic cocoon enveloping children with the "entertainment" of violence, addiction, and low-grade sensuality reflects the displacement of more nurturing values by a "marketing madness."[35]

A character education movement that genuinely valued children would, at the very least, demand an end to commercial activities in the schools and an end to the dubious co-marketing plans that educational organizations have entered into with any number of businesses. Even these basic steps are unlikely, however, so long as character education remains so philosophically muddled, so conceptually empty, so attached to lists of "good" behaviors, and so silent in the face of the corrupting influence of entrenched corporate power. How much easier it is to simply tell children to "do the right thing."

NOTES

1. Leslie Savan, *The Sponsored Life: Ads, TV, and American Culture* (Philadelphia: Temple University Press, 1994).

2. Ibid., p. 1.

3. Ibid.

4. See, for example, James U. McNeal, *Kids as Customers: A Handbook of Marketing to Children* (New York: Lexington Books, 1992).

5. See, for example, Louis E. Raths, Merrill Harmin, and Sidney B. Simon, *Values and Teaching* (Columbus, Ohio: Charles E. Merrill, 1966).

6. See, for example, F. Clark Power, Ann Higgins, and Lawrence Kohlberg, *Lawrence Kohlberg's Approach to Moral Education* (New York: Columbia University Press, 1989).

7. See Thomas Lickona, *Educating for Character: How Our Schools Can Teach Respect and Responsibility* (New York: Bantam Books, 1991); Jacques Benninga, "Schools, Character Development, and Citizenship," this volume, and Edward A. Wynne, "The Moral Character of Teaching," in Allan Ornstein, ed., *Teaching: Theory into Practice* (Boston: Allyn and Bacon, 1995), pp. 190-202.

8. William J. Bennett, ed., *The Book of Virtues: A Treasury of Great Moral Stories* (New York: Simon and Schuster, 1993).

9. A good window on the conventional wisdom of the modern character education movement is provided by materials made available by the Character Education Partnership, an organization based in Alexandria, Virginia, that describes itself in its brochure as "A nonpartisan coalition of organizations and individuals who are concerned about the moral crisis confronting America's youth and dedicated to developing moral character and civic virtue in our young people as one way of promoting a more compassionate and responsible society." The brochure goes on to assert, among other things, that "We are a compassionate society if we demonstrate in our life together an active concern for the welfare of others," and "We are a responsible society if we guard the fundamental rights of all citizens to carry out the obligations of citizenship by working toward a common vision of the common good." Character Education Partnership, *Character Education: Questions & Answers* (Alexandria, Va.: Character Education Partnership, n.d.).

10. James S. Leming, "In Search of Effective Character Education," *Educational Leadership* 51 (November 1993): 63-71.

11. Hugh Rank, *The Pitch* (Park Forest, Ill.: Counter Propaganda Press, 1991).

12. Savan, *The Sponsored Life*, p. 6.

13. David Riesman, Nathan Glazer, and Reuel Denney, *The Lonely Crowd: A Study of the Changing American Character* (Garden City, N.Y.: Doubleday, 1955).

14. See Vance Packard, "The Psycho-Seduction of Children," in Vance Packard, *The Hidden Persuaders* (New York: Pocket Books, 1963).

15. Packard, *The Hidden Persuaders*.

16. Russell Jacoby, *The Last Intellectuals: American Culture in the Age of Academe* (New York: Noonday Press, 1987), p. 38.

17. Character Education Partnership, *Character Education: Questions & Answers*, p. 1.

18. Alex Molnar, *Giving Kids the Business: The Commercialization of America's Schools* (Boulder, Colo.: Westview Press, 1996).

19. Ibid., p. 21.

20. Edwin C. Broome, "Report of the Committee on Propaganda in the Schools," presented at the meeting of the National Education Association in Atlanta, Ga., July 1929.

21. WBZ-TV, Boston, Mass. A broadcast interview with a spokeswoman for Saatchi & Saatchi, November 13 1995).

22. Sheila Harty, *Hucksters in the Classroom: A Review of Industry Propaganda in Schools* (Washington, D.C.: Center for the Study of Responsive Law, 1979).

23. Consumers Union, *Selling America's Kids: Commercial Pressures on Kids of the 90s* (Yonkers, N.Y.: Consumers Union, 1990).

24. Consumers Union, *Captive Kids* (Yonkers, N.Y.: Consumers Union, 1995).

25. Fairness and Accuracy in Reporting, "A Word from the Sponsor," *EXTRA! Update* (October 1995), p. 3.

26. Ibid.

27. Scholastic, Inc., *Experience the Power of Trust with Scholastic*, promotional brochure (New York: Scholastic, Inc., n.d.).

28. Ibid.

29. "Kiddie Corps," *Mother Jones* (July-August 1992): 14.

30. Jessica Porter, "Study Chides *Weekly Reader's* Tobacco Coverage," *Education Week*, 15 November 1995.

31. Geoffrey Cowley, "I'd Toddle a Mile for a Camel," *Newsweek*, 23 December 1991, p. 70.

32. Ibid.

33. Porter, "Study Chides *Weekly Reader's* Tobacco Coverage."

34. Wendell Berry, "Economy and Pleasure," in Charles I. Schuster and William V. Van Pelt, eds., *Speculations: Readings in Culture, Identity, and Values* (Englewood Cliffs, N.J.: Prentice-Hall, 1993).

35. Ralph Nader, "Foreword," in Michael F. Jacobson and Laurie Ann Mazur, *Marketing Madness: A Survival Guide for a Consumer Society* (Boulder, Colo.: Westview Press, 1995).

Section Five
CHARACTER EDUCATION: SEARCHING FOR A DEFINITION

CHAPTER XIV

What Is Character Education?

ALAN L. LOCKWOOD

In a recent *New Yorker* cartoon, two young toughs slouching along a city street are talking. One indicates to the other that he has been "screwed up for years."[1] He ends his comment by wondering when someone is going to step forward and take responsibility for his deviant behavior. This cartoon suggests a number of questions. Who does have responsibility for his behavior? Who *should* have responsibility for his behavior? What responsibility does schooling have in all of this? In a broad sense, our answer to these and related questions defines our position in the current debate on character education. The chapters in this volume offer a variety of perspectives on this issue.

Schooling should do more than prepare students who are reasonably well-versed in the skills and knowledge associated with academic pursuits. Since its inception, schooling in America has been expected to help develop the capacities necessary for a strong democratic citizenry. Although this nonacademic purpose of schooling has not always been clearly defined or realized, some version of a democratic character-building role has historically held a place in public discussion of the aims of education.[2]

In 1980, R. Freeman Butts urged schools to refocus on their historical role in promoting citizenship education. Identifying social phenomena, particularly pluralism and privatism, which threatened public interest in community and the common good, Butts called for a revival of civic learning to combat forces destructive of democracy.[3]

Alan L. Lockwood is Professor in the Department of Curriculum and Instruction, University of Wisconsin at Madison.

Butts and other advocates of citizenship education perceived social conditions as requiring a resurgence in schooling for what some came to identify as civic literacy. Similarly, contemporary advocates for character education see their educational agenda as a response to perceived fraying of the social fabric. Their proposals, however, do not focus primarily on the political. Instead, they want education to address a broad array of urgent social problems.

Character education advocates long for an orderly society in which individuals pursue their lives with courtesy and respect for others, themselves, and the environment. The good are praised and rewarded. The bad are condemned and punished. Workers do their jobs efficiently and responsibly. Employers manage their businesses with integrity and social concern. Students study hard and prepare themselves for further education and careers. Legitimate authority is obeyed. Grievances are pursued politely through proper channels. Crime is rare. The arts inspire and edify. Streets are clean. Neighbors are neighborly. Justice prevails.

Certainly not all would endorse this caricature of an ideal society. Nonetheless, we all could paint some portrait of a desirable society drawn without the scars that deface our current picture. Like many others, advocates of character education bemoan the burgeoning dysfunctions that disfigure the social landscape. Like many others, they yearn for a healthy society free from the woes that currently beset us. Like many others, they are especially distressed by the widely reported prurient destructiveness of youth and by the deep irresponsibility and criminality believed to afflict a growing proportion of young people. Like many others, they believe that egregious behavior by the young is a consequence of a failure to instill proper values. For advocates of character education, the quest for civic decency demands a determined effort from social institutions, particularly schools, to address the alleged moral emptiness of youth.

In addressing some of the central questions raised by the current character education movement, I intend to show that a clearer definition and conceptualization of character education is needed if the movement is to develop productively.

The Need for a Definition

Anyone who has written about character education in recent years has doubtless received calls from journalists eager to prepare features on this burgeoning movement in schooling. Of character education they invariably ask questions like How widespread is it? Is it a good idea? Is there evidence that it is effective? What are local schools doing about it? Such questions and our responses presume some clarity as to what "it" is. Although we may be easily tempted to facilely present our views on various aspects of character education, I remain troubled by the need for a sharper working definition of "it."

We need a clearer, or at least an agreed-upon, definition of character education, not merely to satisfy the transient inquiries of fad-following journalists but for more significant and enduring reasons. There are at least three such reasons, one of which relates to *implementation*. Curriculum developers attracted to the general rationale for character education may wish to pursue some such initiative in their schools. A clear definition provides guidance for these efforts. A second reason relates to *evaluation*. For a variety of reasons, schools have an obligation to assess the effectiveness of their programs, including programs for character education. At minimum, clarity as to aims and practices is necessary for such evaluation to proceed. A third reason pertains to *critical analysis*. Responsible advocates of school reform recognize the need for constructive and critical analysis of their efforts. The dialogues promoted by such analyses help us reformulate, clarify, and hone our rationales and recommendations. Without an established definition, critical examination can become unfocused, disparate, and pointlessly divisive.

Drawing on the writings of character educators, I will consider and assess some candidates for a definition. Finally, a definition will be proposed which may prove useful for curriculum developers, evaluators, and critical analysts.

In Search of a Definition

In the writings of leading character education advocates it is difficult to find a clear, agreed-upon definition. What these writers have in common is a perception of the social ills for which character education is seen as a cure. Virtually all character education advocates recite a litany of criminal and other irresponsible behaviors among the young. In one early (1983) call for character education, Goble and Brooks concluded that "the explosive increase in crime, violence, vandalism, drug abuse, youthful suicide, and other costly human problems clearly indicates that our society is failing in the crucial area of character education."[4] Thomas Lickona cites increases in the following grim trends among youth: violence and vandalism, dishonesty, disrespect for authority, peer

cruelty, bigotry, bad language, sexual precocity and abuse, self-centeredness and civic irresponsibility, and self-destructive behavior.[5]

For character education advocates these troubling trends reflect a
paucity of good character among young people—the absence of
proper morality and values. Kevin Ryan is quite clear on this. Citing
James Q. Wilson, he emphasizes that these social problems stem from
defects in character formation.[6] Similarly, Edward Wynne contends
that "we should note that the 'acts' that reveal character are usually
tied to very simple values."[7]

Character educators emphasize that schooling must play a role in
promoting good character and behavior through instruction in values:
"The emphasis on pupil's right conduct, that is, the moral elements of
education, has been undervalued by many observers of contemporary
education."[8]

One question which emerges in the search for a definition arises
from the ultimate focus on youth behavior. As we have seen, calls for
character education cite the distressing incidence of poor behavior
among young people. Would character education advocates then say
that any effort to combat this destructive behavior is character education?

If character education is construed as any effort to combat undesirable behavior, the definition becomes so diffuse that the concept becomes pointless and discourse about it futile. Virtually all programs and
policies directed at the young hope to promote desirable behavior and to
eliminate undesirable behavior. Casting out the character education
rubric as a net to cover all such practices adds nothing distinctive to our
consideration of them. To some extent, Jacques Benninga understands
character education in this all-encompassing sense.[9] When he writes of
the "long reach" of character education, his illustrations range from one
school system's strict discipline policy, to dress codes in other systems, to
the Million Man March, to Wisconsin's welfare reform program.[10] If
character education is defined so expansively, its focus becomes blurred.
At times, Wynne adopts this enlarged view: "The for-character approach
to education is older than written history."[11] That there are various historical manifestations of a broad cultural commitment to promoting
good behavior among members of a society is a truism. Identifying such
a commitment as character education is a superfluous denotation.

In addition to the behavioral focus, the focus on values is also clear
throughout the writings of contemporary advocates for character education. Any satisfactory definition of character education would also
need to capture their explication of this dimension. As with behavior,

however, a definition which focuses exclusively or even primarily on values takes in too much of the educational landscape.

In their essays in this volume, David Purpel and William Schubert clearly see character education as representing this broad historical and curricular sense. For Purpel, "the current revival of interest in character education represents merely a revival of awareness of issues and concerns that have been a constant in discussions about education. This constancy should not be especially surprising given the essentially moral character of education."[12] For Schubert, "every curriculum shapes character."[13] While these macro-level analyses and critiques direct us to important questions about schooling, they apply to perennial issues of values and schooling in general. Alex Molnar criticizes character educators for failing to speak to "the ethical problems created by using corporate-sponsored materials in the schools."[14] Unless character education is defined in a more delimited way, its position on values and schooling will remain excessively broad, inviting wide-ranging discourse directed at morality and education rather than at character education as a particular set of policy recommendations.

While advocates of character education stress the importance of teaching values, they lean toward a particular conception of such instruction. Most wish to distance their advocacy from the "values clarification" and moral development movements of recent decades. For example, "the focus of values clarification is to exalt process, and its effect on moral education and character education has been, by and large, to undermine to the point of making insignificant any notion of the school's passing on society's core values."[15] Proponents of the moral development approach also undermine these efforts and are characterized by hostility to the concept of direct moral education.[16]

Character education advocates persistently disavow ethical relativism. They contend that there are traditional moral truths which educators should pass on to the young. Lickona is quite clear on this: "There *are* rationally grounded, nonrelative, objectively worthwhile moral values."[17] As we work toward a definition, then, this nonrelativistic stance toward moral values must be incorporated.

An examination of specific curricular preferences of the character education advocates might aid the pursuit of definition. Clues to a definition may lurk in the array of programs they endorse. If there are stable commonalities across these practices, some definitional characteristics could be induced. As I dig through their recommended practices, however, I cannot unearth distinctive similarities which provide specific guidance for building a definition. While I understand that postmodern eyes may behold phenomena in strikingly different ways, my perception is that suggested practices lack thematic unity and, in some cases, may conflict with one another.[18] Simply put, currently recommended practices do not yield a clear, overarching definition of character education.

A Tentative Definition

What, then, is character education? Based on my observations so far, let me offer the following tentative and general definition: *Character education is defined as any school-initiated program, designed in cooperation with other community institutions, to shape directly and systematically the behavior of young people by influencing explicitly the nonrelativistic values believed directly to bring about that behavior*. I do not know if character education advocates would accept this definition, but it is consistent with my reading of their general position.

I believe this definition captures three linchpin propositions of those who advocate character education.

1. They want their goals of moral education to be deliberately pursued, not left as an unsystematic, uncontrolled consequence of the hidden curriculum. They also recognize that while educators may initiate these efforts, there must be community support and consensus for the enterprise.[19] The proposed definition emphasizes the explicit nature of their recommendations pertaining to values.
2. They want the aims of values education to address directly connections to student behavior. The proposed definition emphasizes the behavioral goals of their recommendations.
3. They believe that the destructive, antisocial behavior of young people stems from the failure of character—the absence of correct moral, behavior-determining values. The proposed definition emphasizes this presumed relationship between values and behavior.

Employing the Definition

I have argued here that it is time for the contemporary character education movement to sharpen the definition of what it is advocating. I believe that such a definition would provide a service to curriculum developers, program evaluators, and critical analysts. Drawing on my understanding of the positions of character education advocates, I have proposed a definition intended to incorporate key tenets of their work. My assumption is that useful discourse over a critical educational issue requires a relatively clear understanding of what is being debated. This raises the question of whether or to what extent the proposed definition can productively focus discussion and debate over character education.

The definition delimits for us what character education is and, conversely tells us what it is not. This suggests that some programs claiming to be character education may or may not be, that some research claiming to assess character education may be relevant or irrelevant, and that some critical analysis of character education may be on target or off the mark. In what follows I will consider where this definition leads us as we attempt to better understand and evaluate the complexity of current arguments for character education.

From a *curriculum development* perspective, the definition points to programs that pursue behavioral outcomes by directly influencing the values of young people. Consequently, curriculum planners wishing to establish programs in character education should state clearly the behavioral outcomes at which they are aiming, and design methods of instruction that explicitly address the values believed to be responsible for bringing about the desired behavioral goals.

Curricular uncertainty about what constitutes character education is illustrated in Geneva Gay's questions about the relationship between multicultural education and character education.[20] For example, she wonders if the two approaches are compatible in their treatment of the value of honesty. She contends that honesty in multicultural education entails telling the truth about the history of minority oppression: "This process involves dispelling cultural hegemony, debunking ethnic and racial stereotypes, and resurrecting the stories of ethnic groups and individuals that have been 'lost' or ignored in mainstream historical records and cultural priorities. Essential to the latter is accessing the insider's perspective, the internal voice of ethnic group members."[21] More generally, the value of honesty requires multiple perspectives "because no single truth about such issues is absolute or universal."[22] On the other hand, "if character education is conceived as teaching a single standard of normative behavior based only on cultural values derived from Greco-Roman origins, and assumed to be universally applicable, then it is highly contestable from a multicultural education perspective."[23]

The definition of character education proposed here initially answers Gay's question of whether her conception of multicultural education is compatible with character education. On the surface the answer would appear to be that it is not. Gay's apparent relativism would appear to conflict with character educators' moral universalism.[24]

This example shows how a clearer definition of the meaning of character education can further constructive discussion. Here the definition leads to a focus on the treatment of moral values in the two curricular positions. If multicultural education is to be understood as a form of character education, this issue of moral universalism needs to be resolved.

Educators have a general obligation to determine the effectiveness of their programs and those recommending new practices have a special obligation to provide such information. When an extraordinary array of school programs claims to be "doing" character education, we need to determine which best exemplify it so that main effects can intelligently be assessed. From the perspective of *program evaluation*, then, the definition should help focus assessment on programs that most clearly embody the key features of character education.

James Leming's review of research illustrates, in part, why a definition of character education is needed.[25] In seeking research to help inform the current character education movement he ranged across assessments of values clarification, moral development, drug education, sex education, and school atmosphere. Among the multitude of dependent variables considered in these studies were supportive and friendly behavior, higher-order reading comprehension, feelings of loneliness, alcohol usage, and absentee rates. Leming was frustrated by how "atheoretical thinking and research on character education hampers the effort to develop effective programs."[26] He called for "a more coherent view that can integrate the available research, provide focus to the movement, and guide the curriculum planning and research in a way that yields cumulative knowledge regarding the schools' role in fostering character."[27]

A tighter conceptualization of character education would also provide focus for *constructive analysis* of the movement. Promising educational reforms require critical analysis if they are to fully develop and shape their rationale and mission. To be useful, such analysis must be directed at central tenets of reform efforts. Otherwise, both friendly and unfriendly critics may seize upon features of the reform that its advocates do not see as central to their aims, and thus unworthy of serious consideration. Alfie Kohn acknowledges this and shows how his analysis speaks to a particular conception of character education.[28]

The proposed definition, for example, suggests to me that Purpel's and Schubert's reminders that all education is tinged with morality, while analytically correct, do not speak directly enough to character education. On the other hand, this definition highlights the assumption that destructive behavior is a consequence of an individual's failed character development. This emphasis on personal responsibility requires that Purpel's concern for the connections of social and economic conditions to behavior be taken seriously. He reads the current character education movement as one whose ideology excessively blames individuals for social moral decline. In this ideology, "society is being victimized by unvirtuous (lazy, indulgent, and indolent) individuals rather than seeing individuals as victims of an unvirtuous (rapacious, callous, competitive, and heartless) society."[29] Character education advocates may or may not endorse the ideology attributed to them by Purpel. Nonetheless, the definition makes this a relevant issue and asks that their ideological stance be further explicated.

The definition suggests as irrelevant or marginal a consideration raised by Hugh Sockett.[30] In the course of discussing the moral significance of volition in behavior, he questions whether pharmaceuticals with the potential for behavior control should be employed. Character educators wish schooling to shape or transform the behavior of young people. Would they advocate or promote the use of drugs or perhaps extreme versions of aversive conditioning portrayed in such works as *Brave New World*[31] or *A Clockwork Orange*?[32] These works and others envisage a world in which social order is maintained through the use of behavior controlling technologies which bypass human choice. Given their emphasis on value-related individual responsibility, I suspect character education advocates, although their writing has not been definitive on this, would not support such real or imaginary practices.

The connection of values with character and behavior discussed by character education advocates and identified in the definition does point to the relevance of Beverly Cross's preliminary research findings.[33] Character educators frequently claim that misbehavior of youth is, in part, a consequence of their failure to hold appropriate values. One central aim of character education is to see that children are taught these values. Cross's work suggests that, *at least at the level of verbal endorsement*, inner-city youth already hold the values that appear on character educators' lists of virtues. If her findings are replicated, they have important implications for character education. For example, large investments in time and teaching aimed at gaining children's verbal assent to listed moral virtues may not be required. Such energies may best be spent elsewhere.

The definition also captures the acknowledgment of character education advocates that their aims cannot be realized without substantial community support. Because of that, the questions raised by

Nel Noddings[34] should be addressed. She helps us see that communities are not repositories of virtue simply because they are communities. Communities may support enlightened or repressive practices—democratic or fascistic policies. As Noddings cautions, we must consider both "the bright side and the dark side of community."[35]

Summary and Conclusions

In this final chapter I have argued that contemporary advocates for character education should clarify and sharpen the meaning of the character education they advocate. This call for a definition should not be understood as reflecting some perversely cramped need of an order-obsessed taxonomist. There is much more at stake here. The legitimate work of curriculum developers, program evaluators, researchers, and critical analysts requires more coherence and focus from the leaders of the character education movement. For example, the proposed definition highlights the emphasis of character educators on value-related behavior and the need to teach moral values directly to children. These oft-asserted features of character education demand further explication on at least two points: (1) the problematic connection between values and behavior, and (2) the dilemma of conflicting values. In my judgment neither of these issues has been treated with the depth it deserves. Research on the relationship of values to behavior shows no clear or direct connection between the two. Character educators should acknowledge this and set out a more complex, research-based psychology of moral behavior than what they currently offer. Similarly, while we might generate a list of abstract moral values to which all, or most, would subscribe, there are many situations in which desirable values conflict or general values do not provide clear guidance.[36] A richer development of these philosophical matters would serve well the intellectual credibility of the current movement. As Leming concluded: "the current character education movement lacks either a theoretical perspective on character education or a common core of practice. The movement is eclectic both in terms of its psychological premises and its pedagogical practices."[37]

It is my wish that the proposed definition will aid in directing attention to the major premises of character education and that its advocates will respond to relevant issues raised here and elsewhere. Leming has argued that the demise of values clarification was hastened by its advocates' failure to take careful critical analysis seriously in refining their program.[38] We may hope the current character education movement not suffer the same fate. The quest for civic decency is a worthy one for us all. Responsible educators must decide how they wish to pursue their journeys. Character education advocates urge us to join them. However, if they wish us to travel with them, they should define for us more clearly the routes they are proposing and the destination they have in mind.

NOTES

1. *The New Yorker*, 23 October 1995, p. 78.

2. See, for example, Carl F. Kaestle, *Pillars of the Republic: Common Schools and American Society* (New York: Hill and Wang, 1983), pp. 75-104.

3. See, for example, R. Freeman Butts, *The Revival of Civic Learning: A Rationale for Citizenship in American Schools* (Bloomington, Ind.: Phi Delta Kappa Educational Foundation, 1980), pp. 51-89.

4. Frank G. Goble and B. David Brooks, *The Case for Character Education* (Ottawa, Illinois: Green Hill Publishers, 1983).

5. Thomas Lickona, *Educating for Character: How Our Schools Can Teach Respect and Responsibility* (New York: Bantam Books, 1991).

6. Kevin Ryan, "In Defense of Character Education," in *Moral Development and Character Education*, ed. Larry P. Nucci (Berkeley: McCutchan Publishing Corporation, 1989), p. 24.

7. Edward A. Wynne, "Transmitting Traditional Values in Contemporary Schools," in *Moral Development and Character Education*, ed. Larry P. Nucci (Berkeley: McCutchan Publishing Corporation, 1989), p. 3.

8. Edward A. Wynne and Kevin Ryan, *Reclaiming our Schools: A Handbook on Teaching Character, Academics, and Discipline* (New York: Macmillan Publishing Company, 1993), p. 34.

9. Jacques S. Benninga, "Schools, Character Development, and Citizenship," this volume.

10. Ibid., p. 88.

11. Edward A. Wynne, "For-Character Education," this volume, p. 65.

12. Purpel, "The Politics of Character Education," this volume, p. 141.

13. William H. Schubert, "Character Education from Four Curriculum Perspectives," this volume, p. 17.

14. Alex Molnar, "Commercial Culture and the Assault on Children's Character," this volume, p. 167.

15. Ryan, "In Defense of Character Education," p. 6.

16. Wynne and Ryan, *Reclaiming Our Schools*, p. 121.

17. Lickona, *Educating for Character*, p. 230.

18. Alan L. Lockwood, "A Letter to Character Educators," *Educational Leadership* 51 (November 1993): 72-75.

19. Lickona is especially clear on this. See "Educating For Character: A Comprehensive Approach," this volume.

20. Geneva Gay, "Connections between Character Education and Multicultural Education," this volume.

21. Ibid., p. 100.

22. Ibid., p. 101.

23. Ibid., p. 97.

24. See William Kilpatrick, *Why Johnny Can't Tell Right from Wrong: Moral Illiteracy and the Case for Character Education* (New York: Simon and Schuster, 1992), especially chapter 6.

25. James S. Leming, "In Search of Effective Character Education," *Educational Leadership* 51 (November 1993): 63-71.

26. Ibid., p. 70.

27. Ibid.

28. Alfie Kohn, "The Trouble with Character Education," this volume.

29. Purpel, "The Politics of Character Education," p. 150.

30. Hugh Sockett, "Chemistry or Character?," this volume.

31. Aldous Huxley, *Brave New World: A Novel* (New York and London: Harper & Brothers, 1946).

32. Anthony Burgess, *A Clockwork Orange* (New York: Norton, 1986).

33. Beverly Cross, "What Inner-City Children Say about Character," this volume.

34. Nel Noddings, "Character Education and Community," this volume.

35. Ibid., p. 6.

36. Lockwood, "A Letter to Character Educators."

37. James S. Leming, "Research and Educational Practice in Character Education: A Historical Perspective," this volume, p. 41.

38. Ibid., pp. 37-38.

Name Index

Subject Index

Academic achievement, search for explanations for, 78

American Association of Colleges for Teacher Education (AACTE), statement of, to promote cultural pluralism, 100-1

Aspen Summit Conference on Character Education (1990), 87

Attention Deficit/Hyperactivity Disorder (ADHD), 110; social consequences of diagnosis of, 118

Caring community of learners, essential features of, 128-29

Center for the 4th and 5th Rs, at State University of New York (Cortland), 46-47

Character: concept of, 64-65; formation of, 65; "for-character" factors affecting development of, 65; impact of all curricula on, 17-18; influence of four curricular perspectives on, 18-19, 28-29; keys to, in four curricular perspectives, 21-22, 22-23, 24-25, 26-27; role of communities in development of, 63-64; role of public schools in development of, 141

Character-based sex education, principles and guidelines for, 60

"Character Counts!" Coalition, key tenets of, 155

Character education: as central feature of all curricula, 107-8; centrality of stories in, 2; changes in, after World War II, 35-42; complementary relationship of, with multicultural education, 97-98; commercial activities in schools ignored by, 171; community as the foundation of, 1; concerns of, shared with multicultural education, 99-104; current status of research on, 40-41; definition of, 46; examples of strategies for, 154; need for clear definition of, 175-76; proposed definition of, 179; reasons for schools to engage in, 45; skills to be fostered by, for functioning in a multicultural setting, 104-7; two meanings of, 154

Character education, comprehensive approach to, 46, fig., 47: classroom strategies for, 47-57; schoolwide strategies for, 57-60

Character education, current movement for: advocacy of instruction in core values by, 164; advocacy of specific moral and ethical system by, 144; assumed relationship of, to a larger vision of society, 146; assumptions of, regarding individual behavior, 164; change in nature of discourse about moral education in, 142-43; "fix the kid" orientation of, 155-57; indoctrination as a feature of, 158-59; insights into ideology of, 149-50; lack of attention in, to cultural phenomena shaping children's ethical behavior, 164; lack of framework in, to explain moral degeneration, 146-47; lack of theoretical perspectives or common core of practices in, 41; nature of, 41; perception of, as an ideological and political movement, 140; problem of agreement in, on values to be taught, 157; reluctance of, to elaborate its larger world view, 147; resonance of, with neoconservative ideology of 1990s, 148-49, 157; role of adults in, 160-61; separation of character education in, from broader curriculum, 143

Character education, traditionalist approach to: current examples of, 87-89; deep roots of, 1, 86-87; districtwide programs of, 89-90; objections to constructivist model of learning by advocates of, 159-61; rewards for efforts to implement, 91-92

Character education advocates: emphasis of, on undesirable behaviors of youth as reason for character education, 176-77; particular conception of instruction favored by, 178; rejection of values clarification and ethical relativism by, 178; teaching of values stressed by, 177-78

Character Education Institute (San Antonio), 158

Character Education League, curriculum of, 3

Character Education Partnership, 60

Child Development Program (CDP) of the Developmental Studies Center, 127, 161: effects of, on student outcomes over time, 135-37, fig., 136; essential features of, 131-32; implications of, for

INFORMATION ABOUT MEMBERSHIP IN THE SOCIETY

Membership in the National Society for the Study of Education is open to all individuals who desire to receive its publications. Membership dues for 1997 are $30. All members receive both volumes of the current Yearbook.

For calendar year 1997 reduced dues are available for retired NSSE members and for full-time graduate students *in their first year of membership*. These reduced dues are $25.

Membership in the Society is for the calendar year. Dues are payable on or before January 1 of each year.

New members are required to pay an entrance fee of $1 in addition to the annual dues for the year in which they join.

Members of the Society include professors, researchers, graduate students, and administrators in colleges and universities; teachers, supervisors, curriculum specialists, and administrators in elementary and secondary schools; and a considerable number of persons not formally connected with educational institutions.

All members participate in the election of the Society's six-member Board of Directors, which is responsible for managing the affairs of the Society, including the authorization of volumes to appear in the series of Yearbooks. All members whose dues are paid for the current year are eligible for election to the Board of Directors.

Each year the Society arranges for meetings to be held in conjunction with the annual conferences of one or more of the major national educational organizations. All members are urged to attend these sessions at which the volumes of the current Yearbook are presented and critiqued. Members are also encouraged to submit proposals for future Yearbooks.

Members receive a 33 percent discount when purchasing past Yearbooks that are still in print from the Society's distributor, the University of Chicago Press.

Further information about the Society may be secured by writing to the Secretary-Treasurer, NSSE, 5835 Kimbark Avenue, Chicago, Illinois 60637.

RECENT PUBLICATIONS OF THE NATIONAL SOCIETY FOR THE STUDY OF EDUCATION

1. The Yearbooks

Ninety-fifth Yearbook (1996)

Part 1. *Performance-Based Student Assessment: Challenges and Possibilities.* Joan B. Baron and Dennie P. Wolf, editors. Cloth.

Part 2. *Technology and the Future of Schooling.* Stephen T. Kerr, editor. Cloth.

Ninety-fourth Yearbook (1995)

Part 1. *Creating New Educational Communities.* Jeannie Oakes and Karen Hunter Quartz, editors. Cloth.

Part 2. *Changing Populations/Changing Schools.* Erwin Flaxman and A. Harry Passow, editors. Cloth.

Ninety-third Yearbook (1994)

Part 1. *Teacher Research and Educational Reform.* Sandra Hollingsworth and Hugh Sockett, editors. Cloth.

Part 2. *Bloom's Taxonomy: A Forty-year Retrospective.* Lorin W. Anderson and Lauren A. Sosniak, editors. Cloth.

Ninety-second Yearbook (1993)

Part 1. *Gender and Education.* Sari Knopp Biklen and Diane Pollard, editors. Cloth.

Part 2. *Bilingual Education: Politics, Practice, and Research.* M. Beatriz Arias and Ursula Casanova, editors. Cloth.

Ninety-first Yearbook (1992)

Part 1. *The Changing Contexts of Teaching.* Ann Lieberman, editor. Cloth.

Part 2. *The Arts, Education, and Aesthetic Knowing.* Bennett Reimer and Ralph A. Smith, editors. Cloth.

Ninetieth Yearbook (1991)

Part 1. *The Care and Education of America's Young Children: Obstacles and Opportunities.* Sharon L. Kagan, editor. Cloth.

Part 2. *Evaluation and Education: At Quarter Century.* Milbrey W. McLaughlin and D. C. Phillips, editors. Paper.

Eighty-ninth Yearbook (1990)

Part 1. *Textbooks and Schooling in the United States.* David L. Elliott and Arthur Woodward, editors. Cloth.

Part 2. *Educational Leadership and Changing Contexts of Families, Communities, and Schools.* Brad Mitchell and Luvern L. Cunningham, editors. Paper.

Eighty-eighth Yearbook (1989)

Part 1. *From Socrates to Software: The Teacher as Text and the Text as Teacher.* Philip W. Jackson and Sophie Haroutunian-Gordon, editors. Cloth.

Part 2. *Schooling and Disability.* Douglas Biklen, Dianne Ferguson, and Alison Ford, editors. Cloth.